# Leadership For Dummies®

## Embracing Responsibility

Embracing responsibility is an attitude:

- Drop the word "no" from your vocabulary.
- Learn to volunteer.
- Take an interest in people around you and learn to like people.
- Promise little — deliver a lot.

## Eliciting Cooperation

Your goal is to have your followers trust you:

- Find out what people want — and why they want it.
- Figure out ways of trading what you have — the power of a leader — for what you need — the cooperation of your group.
- Smile at people and look them in the eye. It's the start of trust, and trust is the beginning of cooperation.
- Share information with your team and keep them informed.

## Visions

Leading starts with developing a vision:

- Visions are more than ideas. They are doable dreams.
- Visions link the present to the future.
- Use visions to inspire your followers to achieve more than they thought possible.
- Make your visions positive. Everyone wants to make the world a better place.

## Planning

Planning is necessary if your team is to attain its goals. Keep these things in mind:

- Plan for every contingency — and remember that you can't plan for every contingency.
- Leave a lot of wiggle room in your plans. When things go wrong, you can adjust.
- Make certain you have adequate resources. If you get into the lifeboat without food and water, be sure there's someone on board who has the skill to get both.
- Plan for change. Be happy when it arrives.

## Listening

Strive to take in as much information as you can:

- Pay attention to the nuances of what people say and how they say it.
- Pay attention to the needs of your group.
- Focus and concentrate — listen to only one person at a time.
- Learn to develop your own inner voice — and then learn to listen to it.
- Pay attention to the world around you. Seeing is a form of listening and visual impressions are often the most powerful.
- Learn to hear the voices of the downtrodden. Their needs can become your cause.

P9-CEH-725

*For Dummies: Bestselling Book Series for Beginners*

## Developing Missions

The mission you create is the path to your team attaining its goals:

- Don't take an untakeable hill. The cost is too high.

- Approach your mission incrementally. Do many small things well, and you'll have a big success.

- Bring your group into mission development and planning at an early stage. Listen to what they have to say, and make the modifications you need at the start.

- Work to get ownership of the mission from everyone in the group. Your followers are going to do the heavy lifting, so they have to know what they're in for.

- Make certain that you have a "point of no return." If the mission is not going well, know how far you can go and still regroup. You're not General Custer and leading shouldn't be the Battle of the Little Bighorn.

- Lead people; manage events. Keep your troops motivated.

## SWOT Chart

| X = Team X O = Team O | Opportunities | Threats |
|---|---|---|
| **Strengths** | X = Excellent defensive team | X = Three best pitchers in league<br>O = Powerful cleanup hitter<br>O = Good shortstop<br>O = Good pitcher |
| **Weaknesses** | O = Lack of range of outfielders<br>O = First baseman can't catch | X = No consistency in hitting<br>X = Team demoralizes easily |

Copyright © 1999 Wiley Publishing, Inc.
All rights reserved.

Item 5176-0.

For more information about Wiley Publishing, call 1-800-762-2974.

## For Dummies: Bestselling Book Series for Beginners

# Leadership
## FOR
## DUMMIES®

by Marshall Loeb
and
Stephen Kindel

Wiley Publishing, Inc.

**Leadership For Dummies®**

Published by
**Wiley Publishing, Inc.**
909 Third Avenue
New York, NY 10022
www.wiley.com

Copyright © 1999 by Wiley Publishing, Inc., Indianapolis, Indiana

Published simultaneously in Canada

For general information on our other products and services or to obtain technical support, please contact our Customer Care Department within the U.S. at 800-762-2974, outside the U.S. at 317-572-3993, or fax 317-572-4002.

Wiley also publishes its books in a variety of electronic formats. Some content that appears in print may not be available in electronic books.

*Library of Congress Cataloging-in-Publication Data:*

Library of Congress Catalog Card No.:99-64598

ISBN: 0-7645-5176-0

Manufactured in the United States of America

10 9 8 7 6

1B/SX/QY/QS/IN

# About the Authors

**Marshall Loeb** is the former managing editor of *Fortune* and *Money* magazines, as well as the former editor of the Columbia Journalism Review. His program "Your Dollars" is broadcast daily on the CBS Radio Network and his "Your Money" column is published in newspapers across the country. Marshall has won every major award for excellence in business journalism and is currently an online columnist for CBSmarketwatch.com and Quicken.com.

**Stephen Kindel** has served as a senior editor at *Financial World* magazine and *Forbes,* as well as associate editor at *Newsweek International.* Stephen has held several executive-level positions for various companies in marketing and strategy. He is currently consulting for a number of companies migrating their businesses to the World Wide Web.

# Dedication

For Peggy, Michael, Margaret, Marjorie, Michael II, Katie, Caroline, Jeremy, and Marc.

# Acknowledgements

We want to pay tribute to Mark Reiter, agent extraordinary and a genuine leader, who made possible the publication of this book. Also, let us each take a deep bow to those great talents at Hungry Minds, notably Senior Acquisitions Editor Mark Butler and Senior Project Editor Kyle Looper, who smoothly edited the work. For copy editing so gracefully, let us thank Elizabeth Kuball, Patricia Yuu Pan, Donna Love, Kathleen Dobie, Rowena Rappaport, Barry Childs-Helton, and Kim Darosett. Production Coordinator E. Shawn Aylesworth brought the book to press promptly.

Finally, our thanks to Vice President and Publisher Kathleen Welton, Editorial Director Kristin Cocks, and Project Editor Tere Drenth.

—Marshall Loeb and Steve Kindel

## Publisher's Acknowledgments

We're proud of this book; please send us your comments through our online registration form located at www.dummies.com/register.

Some of the people who helped bring this book to market include the following:

*Acquisitions and Editorial*

**Project Editors:** Kyle Looper, Tere Drenth

**Senior Acquisitions Editor:** Mark Butler

**Copy Editors:** Elizabeth Netedu Kuball, Patricia Yuu Pan, Donna Love, Rowena Rappaport, Kathleen Dobie, Barry Childs-Helton

**Technical Editor:** Sandra Martinez

**Associate Permissions Editor:** Carmen Krikorian

**Editorial Manager:** Leah P. Cameron

**Media Development Manager:** Heather Heath Dismore

**Editorial Assistant:** Beth Parlon

*Production*

**Project Coordinator:** E. Shawn Aylsworth

**Layout and Graphics:** Angela F. Hunckler, Dave McKelvey, Brent Savage, Janet Seib, Michael A. Sullivan, Brian Torwelle, Mary Jo Weis, Dan Whetstine

**Proofreaders:** Henry Lazarek, Marianne Santy, Rebecca Senninger

**Indexer:** Sharon Hilgenberg

*Special Help*
Valery Bourke

---

*Publishing and Editorial for Consumer Dummies*
**Diane Graves Steele,** Vice President and Publisher, Consumer Dummies
**Joyce Pepple,** Acquisitions Director, Consumer Dummies
**Kristin A. Cocks,** Product Development Director, Consumer Dummies
**Michael Spring,** Vice President and Publisher, Travel
**Brice Gosnell,** Publishing Director, Travel
**Suzanne Jannetta,** Editorial Director, Travel

*Publishing for Technology Dummies*
**Richard Swadley,** Vice President and Executive Group Publisher
**Andy Cummings,** Vice President and Publisher

*Composition Services*
**Gerry Fahey,** Vice President of Production Services
**Debbie Stailey,** Director of Composition Services

# Contents at a Glance

# Cartoons at a Glance

## By Rich Tennant

The 5th Wave — By Rich Tennant

"Excuse me, Hannibal, but would crossing the Alps on, ohh let's say—MOUNTAIN GOATS severely compromise your vision?"

page 253

The 5th Wave — By Rich Tennant

SQUARE DANCE PICNIC

"...pretty soon we realized we were lost. That's when Frank, the band's Caller, took charge, and before you knew it, he dosey-doed our way through the woods and back to civilization."

page 101

The 5th Wave — By Rich Tennant

"Great! The Scarecrow and I get coffee makers, the Lion gets an Instamatic camera and Tin Man gets RayBan sun glasses. Next time we get in there, let me do the talking!"

page 71

The 5th Wave — By Rich Tennant

"Remember when Bruce wanted to 'rally the troops', we all just got a memo in email?"

page 317

The 5th Wave — By Rich Tennant

FREE BEER

"...and what makes you think you're a leader of men all of a sudden?"

page 7

The 5th Wave — By Rich Tennant

"I think Dick Foster should head up that new project. He's got the vision, the drive, and let's face it, that big white hat doesn't hurt either."

page 227

The 5th Wave — By Rich Tennant

"The first thing you need to know about coaching Little League is that it takes patience, understanding their limitations, and allowing them to feel like they're participating. And that's just the parents..."

page 163

Cartoon Information:
Fax: 978-546-7747
E-Mail: richtennant@the5thwave.com
World Wide Web: www.the5thwave.com

# Table of Contents

# Introduction

*L*eadership For Dummies is a book not only for would-be chief executive offi-cers or five-star generals, but for *anyone* with the desire to take the lead. Leadership is a people-centered skill that's critical in almost every situation in which two or more people come together in pursuit of a common goal. Knowing how to lead is a vital skill that we all should learn as early in life as possible.

Hundreds of books have been written on the subject of leadership, and many gifted thinkers have tried to define what it takes to be a leader. Many of the people who write about leadership see a leadership crisis, a shortage of lead-ers in a world that desperately needs them. Others see not crisis but opportunity; if you can identify leaders early or become a leader yourself, then your future is assured.

We tend to fall in the opportunity group, because we believe that many potential leaders are out there, just waiting for a chance. We also believe that becoming a leader is not as complex a process as people make it. Although many books have wrestled with the problems of leadership, few have both-ered to define the skills you need to become a leader: We believe that successful leadership really requires that you do only three things: elicit the cooperation of others, listen, and put others before yourself. The purpose of these three practices should be to achieve a goal.

This book focuses mainly on how to develop these three key leadership skills, but it also tells you much more. This book shows you how to add leadership skills to your arsenal of personal traits and explains how doing so helps you to achieve more happiness and contentment in all areas of your life. *Leadership For Dummies* can help you get more out of your life right now by helping you gain

- ✔ **Greater respect.**
- ✔ **Greater success.**
- ✔ **Greater recognition for the job you do.**
- ✔ **Greater cooperation from your friends and family.**
- ✔ **Greater and more effective direction in your life and the ability to make a greater contribution to the world around you!**

Although we want to tackle some of the pitfalls of leadership in this book, *Leadership For Dummies* is not about the negative qualities of leadership. Leadership should be a positive force, and true leaders — the kind we look up to, admire, and wish we could emulate — all demonstrate the ability to put the needs of the group far above their own needs. If a group is looking to you for leadership, it means the group can't reach their goal without someone — you — taking them there, and if you can't or won't do that, you can't lead.

Leaders are trained by experience, by their successes, and most often, by their failures. Every great leader has had to overcome significant obstacles: Franklin Roosevelt had infantile paralysis and braces to beat. Abraham Lincoln repeatedly lost elections until he won the race for President in 1860. Joe Torre, manager of the New York Yankees, had a lifetime losing record as a manager until his record-shattering 1998 season was nearly over.

This all goes to show you that your expertise in leadership doesn't matter when you start. Leadership and the people skills associated with leading can all be gained through practice.

# Who Needs to Read This Book?

Even though we have spent a good part of our careers writing about success-ful business executives, we didn't write *Leadership For Dummies* solely for managers who want to advance their careers. We believe that learning leader-ship skills can add new dimensions to anyone's life, and make their time more exciting, more rewarding, and more satisfying. Becoming an effective leader can be a life-changing experience.

- ✔ **It's for you** — whether you're already a leader at some level or have never been asked to lead anything in your life.
- ✔ **It's for you** — whether you're unemployed and want a job or you're employed and want a promotion.
- ✔ **It's for you** — whether you're a young person who wants to attract the attention of an adult or an adult who is ready to take on more responsibility.
- ✔ **It's for you** — whether you're a teacher searching for better ways to get through to your students or a parent wanting to communicate more effectively with your children.
- ✔ **It's for you** — whether you have an idea that could help others or you want to improve your personal relationships.
- ✔ **It's for you** — whether you're assuming a leadership position in a com-pany or you want to improve the quality of your daily life.

# How to Use This Book

We've laid out the basics of leadership in a series of steps. You can go through the steps in sequence or you can skim the Table of Contents and locate a title or heading that strikes you as interesting. Read that section first. Then go on to another area that you think will benefit you the most.

If you're new to the idea of being a leader, or if you think the experience may soon be thrust upon you, you may want to stay up late a couple of nights and read this book from cover to cover.

If you want to use these skills in one particular area of your life, find an appropriate topic to develop the particular skill and use the tips we've included.

If you want to use these skills for a special project or a particular leadership situation, you can go through the book with a highlighter in hand and highlight what you find to be helpful.

Instead of relying solely on our own experiences, we have assembled a vast collection of anecdotes and stories that will illuminate the wisdom of leaders from the worlds of business, politics, religion, and sports as well as leaders from everyday life for the readers of *Leadership For Dummies*. We tell you the good stories and the bad ones; that way, you'll remember them when you get into similar situations. We hope that you'll use this book to develop the tools you need to become more dynamic in your everyday life. And should someone overthrow a government and be photographed waving this book or be elected president of a Fortune 500 company, that won't be so bad, either.

If you're truly going to benefit by becoming a leader, why not pull out all the stops and learn the strategies and tactics that have been proven to work for others?

# How This Book Is Organized

*Leadership For Dummies* is organized into seven parts. The chapters within each part cover specific topic areas in detail.

## Part I: What It Takes to Be a Leader

In this part you find out that anyone can be a leader. We also show you that leadership is temporary and explain what is and what isn't leadership. Because learning about misconceptions is the beginning of understanding, in the chapters that make up "What It Takes to Be a Leader," we explore the realities of how leadership affects your everyday life. We take you through the characteristics of a leader's personality, the different types of leadership, and the different roles that leaders take on to get the job done.

# Part II: Leadership Is a Process

Preparation is the key to leadership, and before you can begin to lead, you have to ask yourself a couple of critical questions. Do you have the skills necessary to be a successful leader? Do you know what you're expected to do? Do you really know the people you're supposed to be leading, and what they want? Is their mission different from the people who put you in charge? In this part, we cover the steps to preparation that will set you apart from average leaders and help you become more effective at accepting a leadership role.

# Part III: The Art of Leadership

Welcome to the reality of leadership. Now that you know more about yourself, you need to know what skills you need in order to become a dynamic leader. You have to figure out how to harness your strengths and your weaknesses, and you have to know how to differentiate leading from merely managing. Perhaps the most important thing you discover in this part is that often, you don't have to wait for a title in order to become a leader.

# Part IV: Leadership in Everyday Life

Leadership is about accepting responsibility, and not just when it suits you. Some of the toughest leadership challenges are right in your own backyard: in your home as well as in the institutions that support your personal life, such as your community, your schools, your children's teams, and your religious life. This part shows you how to recognize the needs of leadership in personal situations and gives you the tools to lead in "real life."

# Part V: Leadership and Vision

Think of leadership as the point of an arrow and you'll understand that vision is the target to be hit! This part explains what vision is, why vision is necessary, how to develop a vision, and how to implement it after you develop one.

## Part VI: Team Building

This part is about one of the most important skills of leadership: cooperation. In this section, we explain why teams are more effective than leadership from on high, how to create a winning team, how to ensure that whatever a team learns is spread among all of the team's members, and how to lead when your followers suddenly won't follow you. Teams, you'll find, require more work and self-discipline than old-fashioned command leadership. But properly motivated, they can produce great things.

## Part VII: The Part of Tens

These short chapters are packed with quick ideas about leadership and the art of persuading that you can read anytime you have a few minutes. They're a great way to get yourself psyched up for a presentation or for a meeting. They're also good for pumping up your attitude and getting you excited about jobs you're about to do. And remember: No one will want you to lead if you're not excited about the responsibility you've been given.

# Icons Used in This Book

Important information is flagged here and there throughout this book. Look for these icons to help you understand the purpose of the information next to them.

This icon highlights the crucial pieces of information and skills needed for leading anyone. It's a red flag because it is a warning as much as an icon: Forget these hints at your peril.

This icon highlights advanced strategies and tips that go beyond the basics of becoming a Champion at leadership.

This icon highlights edifying stories about leadership from our own experience and the experiences of well-known leaders.

This icon highlights words of wisdom to use for all kinds of leadership situations.

This icon is a friendly reminder of information discussed elsewhere in the book or stuff you definitely want to remember.

This icon marks things to avoid and common mistakes people make.

# Where to Go from Here

Look through the book and find which part, chapter, or section you're most interested in. That's the best place to begin.

Most people won't choose to start in an area in which they need the most help, primarily because they don't know that they don't know the material. Instead, they'll probably choose their favorite area, the one they're already pretty good at. That's okay. If you do that, you'll see some increases in your successes after you start to apply this book's strategies in such areas. But to benefit the most from this material, you need to do a little self-analysis to see where you're the weakest. We know that admitting your faults, even to yourself, is tough; but doing so and learning the material in your weaker areas will bring you the greatest amount of success.

The most important point to consider right now is that you're already probably on your way to becoming a leader. We've long thought that the most successful people in life are those who continue to learn. The fact that you're reading these words right now is an indication that you agree with us and that you believe that you have farther to go in your life than your present station.

In that case, we applaud you for believing in yourself, in your ability to change for the better, in your ability to improve your lifestyle, and in your ability to improve the lives of the people you help with this book's many tips on the art of leadership. We wish you nothing but success and greatness. And if you use this book's suggestions, we're sure that's what you'll see.

# Part I
# What It Takes to Be a Leader

The 5th Wave    By Rich Tennant

"...and what makes you think you're a leader of men all of a sudden?"

## In this part . . .

Anyone can be a leader, but all leadership is temporary. In this part, you find out what is and what isn't
leadership and how to judge your leadership potential
and work on the skills that leaders share. We clue you in
to the common misconceptions about leadership and
explore the realities leadership and how it affects your
everyday life. We take you through the characteristics
of a leader's personality, the different types of leadership,
and the different roles that leaders take on to get the
job done.

# Chapter 1

# A Marshal's Baton in Every Soldier's Knapsack

*Every French soldier carries a marshal's baton in his knapsack.*
—Napoleon Bonaparte

**N**apoleon believed that, under the right circumstances, every soldier in his army had the potential to be a general and lead the army in his absence. Whether you hold that belief or not, the plain fact is that "natural" leaders don't just happen, nor does anyone have a divine right to lead or rule.

In this chapter, we dispel the most common misconceptions about leaders and leadership. You do indeed have a marshal's baton in your own knapsack. Recognizing your leadership potential is the first step toward leading others.

## What Is Leadership?

*Leadership* is the set of qualities that causes people to follow. Although this definition may be circular, it does demonstrate that leadership requires at least two parties, a leader and a follower. Many experts have argued over what exactly causes a group to follow one person and not another, but the decision to follow a leader seems to come down to just a few things.

Leaders have the ability to inspire people to go beyond what they think they are capable of doing, making it possible for a group to attain a goal that was previously thought unattainable. Leaders carry their followers along by

- ✔ Inspiring their trust.
- ✔ Acting consistently.
- ✔ Motivating them by words and deeds.

Although these actions explain what a leader *does*, it doesn't really answer the question of what leadership *is*. In reality, leadership boils down to a willingness to accept responsibility and the ability to develop three skills that can be acquired through practice. When you properly put these skills together, people begin to turn to you when they need direction. The following sections explain what these skills are and how you can use them to lead effectively.

## Responsibility and accountability

Leadership begins with the willingness to embrace responsibility. Accepting the responsibilities that you are given is not enough. You have to be the one who steps forward and says, "I want to do that!"

You can't be a leader if you're afraid of responsibility and accountability.

Harry Truman had a sign on his desk that said, "The buck stops here." With the idea of accepting responsibility goes the concept of accountability. You are saying to people, "If things go wrong, I'm ultimately the reason why. The failure is mine and no one else's." Do you have enough confidence in yourself to accept responsibility for failure? If not, you'll have a hard time becoming a leader. One of the realities about placing the needs of others above your own is that you cannot blame other people. If you're the type of person who looks outward for an excuse instead of inward for a reason, you'll have a hard time earning the trust of others. An absence of trust makes eliciting their cooperation more difficult, which, in turn, makes it more difficult for you to lead, even if you've been given the title of leader.

On the other hand, the leader gets most of the accolades and rewards when things go well. No matter how hard your followers worked, no matter how modest you are, no matter how much you attempt to deflect credit to your entire team, yours is the name that people will remember. That's the great benefit of being the leader.

In the early 1970s, two housewives, one Protestant and one Catholic, were appalled by the sectarian violence in Northern Ireland. The pair, Betty Williams and Mairead Corrigan, formed an organization, Peace People, to begin a dialogue between women and children of the warring factions, reasoning that if hatred could be overcome in the home, it could also be overcome in the streets. The pair's success led them to be recognized in 1976 with the Nobel Peace Prize.

Jody Williams did volunteer work for the Vietnam Veterans of America, an organization that raised money for veterans' programs. After talking to a large number of veterans who were victims of land mines, and after reading about the large number of children whose hands and feet were being blown off by land mines planted years before, Williams decided to learn more about the subject. She found dispirited support for a treaty banning mines, and took it upon herself to create something called the International Campaign to Ban Landmines, and became the coordinator of an effort that spanned hundreds of organizations in more than 100 countries. Her leadership resulted in an international treaty banning such mines, which has been signed by more than 120 nations. She, too, received the Nobel Peace Prize for her efforts, in 1997.

In both cases, and in hundreds of others, change took place because people who were not leaders in any accepted sense embraced the responsibility for bringing about change.

# Three key leadership abilities

After you decide that you can embrace responsibility, leadership requires that you be able to do three things well:

- ✔ **Elicit the cooperation of others.** You must be able to get others to buy into your vision of the future and the right way to get there.

- ✔ **Listen well.** You have to be able to gather many kinds of information from others in order to lead; doing so requires that you hone your listening skills.

- ✔ **Place the needs of others above your own needs.** Leadership requires that you be willing to sacrifice for a greater goal.

The trick to becoming a leader is to be able to elicit cooperation, to listen to the needs of others, and to put other people's needs ahead of your own *with great consistency.* The smallest child can elicit cooperation from his parents when he wants or needs something. Only a complete egomaniac does not occasionally listen to the needs of others. Putting someone else's needs ahead of your own for a little while isn't difficult, especially if it's going to eventually get you something that you want. The skill is to be able to harness these abilities on a regular basis so that you can become a *consistent practitioner* of leadership skills.

## Leading means leading consistently

Charlie Lau and Harvey Penick are probably the best proponents of the idea that leading requires consistency. Charlie Lau was probably the greatest baseball hitting coach who ever lived. He was the man who was responsible for bringing George Brett, a good hitter, closer to Ted Williams' immortal .401 single-season batting average than any hitter since.

Lau argued that almost anyone with reasonable eyesight and reflexes can hit a major league pitch once in a while, but that it was consistency of behavior that made some people into major league ball players, and inconsistency that made the rest of us into mere spectators.

Absolute mastery of the strike zone and the discipline to maintain that mastery, said Lau, turned a hitter into an All-Star and a potential Hall-of-Famer. According to Lau, success was less about mechanics than about consistency.

Golf legend Harvey Penick, like Lau, was never a great practitioner of his sport. He never won a major tournament, but he knew exactly what went into the mechanics of a golf swing, and he could take any golfer with the willingness to work and teach those mechanics better than anyone. Penick strongly believed that golfers were defeated not by their inability to hit the ball, but their inability to hit it well, with consistency.

# Leadership Myths

Understanding what leadership *isn't* is as important as understanding what leadership *is*, because much of the information circulating about leadership is false. Because leadership and power are inextricably linked, many misconceptions and untruths have arisen around the topic. Some of these mythologies have come about as a way to validate an existing power structure or to serve as a justification of one group's domination over another. Other myths arise from misunderstandings about leadership. In the following sections, we expose some of the myths that still shape beliefs about leadership today.

## The myth of the natural leader

Just as most people used to believe that leaders ruled by divine right, another myth exists — that of the natural leader. Call it the "sword in the stone" doctrine, which contends that only a single person, pure of heart and purpose, can draw a sword embedded in a stone and be acclaimed the new king. T.H. White, who wrote *The Once and Future King* about King Arthur, took the myth of the natural leader from all the mythology that supports Western civilization.

## Remember Rudy

Although sports are important — athletic skills can create temporary schoolyard leaders — the idea that physical prowess predetermines leadership at an early age is nonsense. A kid with no apparent physical skills can still become a leader.

If you don't believe me, watch the movie *Rudy*. The true story is about a poor, undersized, tagalong teenager whose only aspiration is to follow his father and brother into a steel mill job. After a friend is killed in a mill accident, Rudy, a big Notre Dame football fan, starts to think that he should go to Notre Dame and play football instead. He's too small, has no football skills, and isn't academically prepared, but through perseverance and the help of one of the school's professors, Rudy is admitted to the school and is

allowed to practice with the team. The coach, however, won't let him play. On the last play of the last day of his last season of football eligibility, the entire team refuses to take the field unless the coach sends Rudy in for a play. With the entire stadium cheering, he makes a critical play, after which his teammates carry him off the field on their shoulders.

Rudy was never the captain of the team, never became an All-American, never had his picture on the cover of *Sports Illustrated*. However, every member of the Notre Dame football team during the Rudy years acknowledges Rudy as their leader. His unyielding determination to make the team became an example to athletes who were far more gifted, making it possible for them to achieve their own goals.

This myth — for it is indeed a myth — has been used for generations to foreclose entire groups of people from leadership roles. For years, the "sword in the stone" doctrine prevented a black man from playing quarterback in the National Football League, until Doug Williams won Superbowl XXII for the Washington Redskins. For decades, the doctrine blocked any Catholic from being President of the United States, until John F. Kennedy was elected in 1960.

The myth of the natural leader has been used to excuse a host of social ills — nearly all of which have prejudice at their root — and have helped create the very leadership crisis that stirs media pundits to print.

## The myth that the biggest or fastest will lead

Because children begin to exhibit leadership qualities at an early age, many people wrongly believe that victorious leadership begins in the schoolyard. As author and historian Sir William Fraser once described it, "The battle of

Waterloo was won on the playing fields of Eton." People tend to believe that the fastest, strongest child — the one who can throw the ball the farthest — automatically becomes the group leader. They further suppose that the child who lacks those skills becomes a follower, putting him or her on a lifelong path of supporting roles. Today's support for women's athletics comes from the strongly held belief that leadership skills begin with physical dominance and are determined — possibly set — at a very early age.

## The misconception that command is leadership

The biggest single mistake that people make about *leadership* is that they think leadership means *command. Command is the authority to lead. It is not leadership.* Leadership is often tied up with the problems of command, but the two things are completely different. Most organizations are structured much like the military. You see a defined chain of command, an organization chart, a track of authority, if you will, that all decisions have to follow, as do all potential decision-makers. If you want to be a leader in such an organization, by definition, you must already be in a leadership position. You cannot lead from the lower ranks. You must start within a leadership track and become part of the command structure.

### Commanders may be unfit

The difficulty with command structures is that such structures place people in positions of leadership based on non-leadership criteria. In the military and in most corporations, for example, a college education is one prerequisite for a position of command, even though the correlation between education and intelligence is unknown. The presumption is that if you've been through college, then you are reasonably smart and sufficiently disciplined to have completed schoolwork voluntarily.

Another requirement for command is that you have been properly indoctrinated with the values of the organization. Both the military and numerous companies spend endless amounts of training time attempting to instill a "company way" of doing things in their potential leaders and then wonder why those people fail in critical leadership situations that require ingenuity and resourcefulness.

During the Vietnam War, countless college-educated second lieutenants with little or no previous leadership training were sent into combat and put in charge of platoons. The smart ones deferred to their more experienced, combat-seasoned sergeants and depended on their sergeants to see them through the horrors of jungle warfare. Others made the mistake of thinking that command authority conferred upon them the wisdom of leadership, and so *they did not listen.* These second lieutenants made errors that imperiled their own lives and the lives of the men under their command.

### Business depends on leaders

Many of the positive changes that have taken place in business over the past two decades have been with the recognition that a shift has taken place away from command and toward leadership. One of the reasons that entrepreneurial companies tend to grow faster than traditional companies is that they are less structured and, because they are often short of key people, have to allow leadership to arise from beyond the normal chain of command.

### Command focuses on managing tasks, not people

Most people within a command structure receive well-defined tasks to accomplish, and they are then graded on how well they do those tasks. The structure helps to identify leaders, by giving the most senior executives of the enterprise a handle on who is doing what, and how well they are doing it. At the same time, a command structure hinders the development of leaders, because so much of how a person does a job depends on the support he or she receives.

Companies such as Xerox have attempted to take negative performance factors out of the evaluation process by requiring that a supervisory employee share some responsibility for the failure of a person performing a given task, but that solution does not really address the problems of a command structure.

Too much of the command structure is not about leading at all, but about managing, keeping the enterprise moving in the direction it is already moving, rather than finding out whether a new direction is needed.

# Understanding Your Leadership Potential

Leadership is an integral component of human interaction. Even in a world where work is done by consensus, the qualities of leadership — listening to others, eliciting cooperation from others, and the ability to place the needs of others or the group above your personal needs — are essential to human progress. Few things get done if people don't pull together, and little is accomplished without the motivation that leadership supplies. Thus, you must have a very clear picture of who leaders are and how they emerge.

Remember these basic premises about how leaders emerge:

✔ **Every person has the potential to be a leader.** Eliciting the cooperation of others, listening well, and placing the needs of others above your own needs are qualities that any person can choose to make their own. That is what we mean when we say that every person has the potential to be a leader. But you have to *choose* to be a leader. After choosing to make these traits central to your character and conditioning your responses to others with those traits, it is only a matter of time and circumstance before you are recognized as a leader in some way.

✔ **Leaders are made by circumstance, not by birth or genetics.** Sometimes, the pathway to leadership can be blocked by circumstances. Women, in the era before women's rights, as well as blacks and Hispanics, before the era of civil rights, often found their pathways to leadership were blocked by prejudice. In spite of this, people such as Ralph Bunche, Jesse Owens, Jim Thorpe, Marian Anderson, Eleanor Roosevelt, Amelia Earhart, Clara Barton, Marie Curie, and scores of others managed to achieve respect as leaders in their fields despite the obstacles placed in their paths.

✔ **Leadership begins with the willingness to embrace responsibility.** The reason that leaders emerge out of circumstance is that leaders embrace the idea of accepting responsibility. Helen Keller could have remained nothing but sightless and deaf, if Annie Sullivan hadn't embraced the responsibility of finding a way to break through to the brilliant child entombed in her own world, and Keller could have remained a curiosity, if she hadn't decided to become a spokesperson for handicapped people. When we read the stories of such people, we tend to read about them as gifted writers, artists, musicians, diplomats, or athletes, but we must remember that they were leaders as well.

Although we wouldn't consider it a trait of leadership, good leadership generally improves the level of human dignity of the group being led. All the people named in the above list greatly increased the store of human dignity by their actions and their leadership and have to be viewed in the larger context of leadership, instead of the narrow contexts of their professional successes.

Almost everyone has been a leader, at least for a little while at some time, although they may not realize it. For example, almost every parent becomes a leader. Taking on the role of parent means accepting a leadership role in ensuring the well-being and survival of a baby. If you've ever volunteered to serve on a committee, even in a subordinate role, the very act of volunteering — of putting yourself out for the good of the group — makes you a leader.

Most people hold leadership roles in their personal lives before parenting, as well. If you're married and you proposed to your spouse, you took on a leadership role. You *took the lead* in making a commitment. If you planned your wedding, you *took the lead* in making the decisions that would ensure the happiness of your guests and that everything went smoothly. If you've volunteered to coach a kid's soccer team, you *took the lead* in helping those kids develop their skills.

Long before your adult life, you were taking the lead as a child all the time. As you learned how to study, you *took the lead* for learning how to manage your time, how to make the decisions to defer fun in favor of work. You may only have been leading yourself, but you were still leading.

# What Leaders Need

Perhaps you aren't convinced that anyone can be a leader. Your natural reaction is, "If it's so easy, why aren't I leading something?" In the section entitled "Leadership Myths" earlier in this chapter, we point out that leaders aren't born, they're made. Leadership doesn't happen naturally, and it doesn't occur overnight. Leadership is a happy joining of someone who has the desire, training, and circumstances to lead, with a group of people that requires leadership. The following sections explain these necessities in detail.

## Leaders must be trained

Leaders are out there; they just need to be encouraged and taught. And leaders *do* have to be taught. Even the Dalai Lama, recognized at age 2 as the leader of Tibetan Buddhists in what is considered a divine event, received a thorough education in the roles and responsibilities expected of him by the monks who searched among the villages and farms of Tibet for the next living incarnation of Buddha.

Napoleon underwent a long education at St. Cyr (France's equivalent of West Point) before he started on his way to field marshal. Winston Churchill was a newspaper reporter, an adventurer, a member of Britain's Parliament, and a junior Cabinet minister before he emerged as a leader on the eve of World War II.

All leaders go through a period of training, of taking on increased responsibilities and increased learning; and no leader rises to the top without the assistance and, sometimes, the patronage of people who will give a potential leader the encouragement and opportunities needed for him or her to hone leadership skills.

## Leaders require a goal

Another way to look at the problem of why emerging as a leader is so tough is this: Leadership requires a goal that can't be attained without a leader's help. If a group of people is capable of dealing with its own problems on a day-to-day basis, it does not need leadership.

When Bill Clinton's campaign advisors told him and the nation, "It's the economy, stupid," what they were saying, in effect, was, "It's not leadership, stupid." As students of history, Clinton's advisors rightly observed that the best thing to do in boom times is to get out of the way, and to help the economy along with loosened regulation and lower interest rates. These are not leadership decisions, but rather, calculated thinking that recognized that the economy has a life force of its own. By being smart enough to stay out of the path of the great engine of market capitalism, Clinton could ride a wave of good feeling all the way to the White House.

Conversely, after a person is in the White House, he or she is expected to lead, even when few leadership tasks are available. What is perhaps Bill Clinton's greatest undoing is that he could not find a leadership role for himself, and, like Queen Elizabeth's children, allowed his life to become embroiled in scandal.

## Leaders need followers

The idea that leadership depends on reaction isn't hard to understand. Leadership requires that you listen to the needs of others. But if people tell you they don't need anything from you, then you have no leadership opportunity. If you persist in trying to lead when leadership isn't required, you come to be regarded as a pest or a bore, or worse. Moreover, you are likely to marginalize yourself; the few people who do recognize that a problem (that needs a leader) exists will bother to listen to you.

Sometimes, as in Churchill's case, a marginalized leader moves to the center because of circumstances. This movement characterizes *reactive leadership*. Churchill was given a chance to lead as a result of a reaction to events, not because he was necessarily a great leader. The fact that he turned out to be a great leader was Britain's — and the world's — great fortune, but he could just as easily have proven himself incompetent or indecisive in the midst of crisis.

Perhaps the best way to help you understand the idea of the reactive leader is to look at the enigma of the worst leader of all time, Adolf Hitler. As Ron Rosenbaum writes in his excellent book, *Explaining Hitler:*

> *Is it possible to find in the thinly distributed, heatedly disputed facts of Hitler's life before he came to power one single transformative moment, some dramatic trauma, or some life-changing encounter with a Svengali-like figure — a moment of metamorphosis that made Hitler Hitler? It is a search impelled by the absence of a coherent and convincing evolutionary account of Hitler's psychological development, one that would explain his transformation from a shy, artistically minded youth, the dispirited denizen of a Viennese homeless shelter, from the dutiful but determinedly obscure army corporal, to the figure who, not long after his return to Munich from the war, suddenly leapt onto the stage of history as a terrifyingly incendiary, spellbinding street orator. One who proceeded to take a party whose members numbered in the dozens and used it to seize power over a nation of millions; made that nation an instrument of his will, a will that convulsed the world and left forty million corpses in its wake.*

Hitler's early background reveals nothing that indicates the makings of a leader: no training, no situations that called for him to respond as a leader and be recognized, and no group that especially needed his leadership. Nevertheless, a set of circumstances arose that called forth the worst in the German nation and gave rise to Hitler, just as the worst in British circumstances called forth the best of Britain and gave rise to Churchill. Hitler and Churchill were both reacting to something; hence the name *reactive leaders*.

# Making the Emotional Connection

In order to elicit cooperation, listen well, and place the needs of others above your own, you have to have some emotional maturity, wisdom, and humility. Psychologist Daniel Goleman describes the ability to embrace responsibility as *emotional intelligence,* the measure of a person's self-awareness, self-regulation, motivation, empathy, and social skill. According to Goleman, the higher up in an organization you go, the more critical the leadership skills of people become and the higher the level of emotional intelligence that successful people exhibit.

Each of the components that make up Goleman's idea of emotional intelligence depends on at least one of the critical skills necessary for good leaders. Here's how they tie in:

✔ **The ability to elicit cooperation:** Motivation depends upon the ability to elicit cooperation: first from yourself, and then from others.

The idea of cooperating with yourself may seem funny, but taking on an unpleasant or unpopular task and then excelling at its execution often requires an act of conscious will. Bob Christopher, long-time editor of *Newsweek* and *Newsweek International,* used to tell young writers, "Anybody can do a great job when there's nothing at stake. It's when you don't want to do the assignment but you write a great story anyway that you know you're a professional."

✔ **The ability to listen:** Self-awareness, self-regulation, and empathy all begin with the ability to listen, both to your own inner voice (to understand your own motivations) and then to the voices of others (to find out what drives them).

✔ **The ability to place the needs of others above your own:** Self-regulation depends largely on your ability to place the needs of others above your own needs, so that you don't automatically rise to anger when things don't go your way.

Social skills require all of these elements — the ability to elicit cooperation, the ability to listen, and most definitely, the need to put others above yourself.

## Keeping your cool

Have you ever walked the floor at night trying to calm a newborn baby, but refusing to lose your cool when you couldn't? That kind of behavior is self-regulation at an almost exquisite level.

What about when you're stuck in traffic and you absolutely have to be someplace at a certain time? Do you fly into a rage, accept the fact that the moment is beyond your control, or listen to the radio and use your cell phone to call in case of emergencies?

Self-regulation is all about maintaining your calm in any situation, or, as Kipling said, "Keeping your head when all around you are losing theirs."

A high degree of emotional intelligence accounted for 90 percent of the difference between average leaders and star performers, according to studies by Goleman.

## *Self-awareness*

Self-awareness is the ability to recognize and understand your moods, emotions, and drives, as well as their effect on others. When you are about to take the lead, about to accept responsibility, how you project your decision has a big effect on the outcome. Think about when you proposed marriage. Did you think about it, and about its effects on your spouse-to-be? Did you propose confidently or timidly? Did you have an honest expectation that your proposal would be accepted, an unrealistic hope that it would, or the fear you would be rejected? If your proposal was accepted, chances are you were realistic and self-confident. It's what women mean when they say, "He swept me off my feet." The romantic proposer of marriage didn't do it literally, like Rhett Butler carrying Scarlett O'Hara up the stairs, but figuratively, by communicating the infinite possibilities of a better life joined as husband and wife.

On the job, the way you accept your responsibilities and your assigned role is a critical measure of self-awareness. Do you just do the task you've been given, or do you embrace the task and try to look for the real value in your work? Do you allow trivial events to derail you, or can you push through to a goal? Can you deal with failure, which is always a possibility?

Self-aware people demand more of themselves than they do of others, so they can focus their energy on the task at hand. Watch any great athlete under adversity, such as Michael Jordan or John Elway. After they've missed a shot or a pass, they are likely to smile. They've admitted their mistake to themselves and shrugged it off, because they know that the task of scoring and winning the game still lies ahead.

# Self-regulation

Self-regulation is the ability to control or redirect disruptive impulses — anger, prejudice, stubborness, for instance — and moods. Self-regulation involves the abilities to suspend judgment and to think before acting. Often, in critical situations, a person with good self-regulation skills slows the action down, instead of speeding it up. He or she buys time to assess a situation, trying to figure out exactly the right thing to say or do to bring agreement or movement toward a goal.

David Halberstam, a journalist who has made a career out of writing about the behavior of the powerful, wrote this of Michael Jordan late in his career: "In 1995, after Jordan returned to basketball from his year-and-a-half long baseball sabbatical, he spent the summer in Hollywood, making the movie *Space Jam,* but he demanded that the producers build a basketball court where he could work out every day. Old friends dropping by the Warner lot noticed that he was working particularly hard on a shot that was already a minor part of his repertoire but which he was now making a signature shot — a jumper where he held the ball, faked a move to the basket, and then, at the last minute, when he finally jumped, fell back slightly, giving himself almost perfect separation from the defensive player. Because of his jumping ability and his threat to drive, that shot was virtually unguardable. . . . What professional basketball players were now seeing was something that had been partly masked earlier in his career by his singular physical ability and the artistry of what he did, and that something was a consuming passion not just to excel but to dominate."

Jordan later used that shot to put away the Utah Jazz in the pivotal fifth game of the 1998 NBA championships. It was a moment, Jordan would describe later, when he knew exactly what to do and how to do it, as if he had already lived through it. "I never doubted myself," Jordan said after the game.

# Motivation

Motivation is the passion for what you're doing that goes beyond money, power, or status. It is marked by a tendency to pursue goals with energy and persistence. Unfortunately, too many people work solely for money, without ever really having their heart in a task. The need to earn a living often distorts personal values to the point where people will work at jobs at which they are terribly bored, or stay in relationships that have lost their meaning. Motivated people drive themselves to achieve beyond their own or anyone else's expectations.

Motivation also involves your ability to communicate your passion to others. Approaching your work with dedication and gusto is not enough. You have to radiate your commitment so that your enthusiasm is contagious to the people around you. **Remember:** One of the key components of leadership is the ability to elicit cooperation from others. That's what motivation is all about. By your willingness to do a task, you serve as an example to others to take on that task as well.

# Empathy

*Empathy* is the ability to understand other people's emotional makeup, and the skill of treating people according to their emotional reactions. Empathy is not some kind of touchy-feely experience. It hinges on both the ability to listen and the ability to put someone else's needs above your own.

In recent years, many companies have become aware that they have as many *stakeholders* as stockholders. Besides the shareholders or partners who own the company, many others — suppliers, customers, workers, the communities in which the company operates, and larger "communities" of people with a stake in the company — can determine whether people view a company favorably. For example, how a company treats its personnel may be more important to community perception than where a company situates a factory.

Treating all these stakeholders fairly while still working diligently to make a profit requires a high degree of empathy. Would-be leaders bear the burden of finding innovative solutions that satisfy legitimate needs, while ensuring that the company remains competitive. People who are highly empathic look for solutions that head off problems before they ever emerge.

## Empathy loves company

Imagine this situation: You are a manager whose company has just decided to outsource all its manufacturing. As a result, you have to close down an entire plant. You have a number of choices. You can call in guards, announce the layoffs via a notice on the plant gate, and give every employee a couple of hours to get personal possessions out of the factory. You can apologize for the layoff, but let people know that these things just happen.

Or, you can explain the company's decision and commit yourself to trying to help every employee find a new position. Leaders with a high degree of empathy choose this option because they understand the people's pain.

## Empathy pays off

A number of years ago, a public interest group called the Council on Economic Priorities published a guide titled *Shopping for a Better World*. The book's premise was simple: Consumers, by their buying choices, can influence company policy in a wide variety of areas. *Shopping for a Better World* rated companies on a group of social indicators, such as how well a company protects the environment, whether it does any defense contracting, whether it subjected animals to inhumane treatment when testing its products, and how easily women and minorities can find opportunities to rise within the company.

Most of the companies rated — consumer giants such as Procter & Gamble and Phillip-Morris — ignored the book, thinking it was nothing more than a leftist critique of capitalism.

But Reuben Mark, the CEO of Colgate-Palmolive, decided to take the book seriously. He looked at all the issues that *Shopping for a Better World* addressed and issued instructions that changes be made in all areas to make Colgate-Palmolive a better company. When the next edition of the book was published, Colgate began to rise in the guide's rankings.

As Colgate's rankings began to rise, its sales — and profitability — began to rise as well. Colgate began to outrank much larger consumer products companies in terms of gross margins. Although Reuben Mark is cautious in drawing a one-to-one relationship between Colgate's rise in its *Shopping for a Better World* rankings and increased sales, he believes that consumers are willing to make distinctions among companies on an empathic basis. If a company exhibits empathy to the community around it, the community returns that empathy.

## *Social skill*

*Social skill* is a proficiency in managing relationships and building networks, and the ability to find common ground and build rapport. Chrysler CEO Robert Eaton once said that the first thing he learned when he became a chief executive was that nobody can know everything and nobody can do everything. So he had a choice: Either he could limit Chrysler to what he knew and what he could do, or he could depend upon other people to know and do for him. As a strong leader, Eaton chose the smarter course of action, allowing Chrysler to grow and expand around him as his managers formed strong, multidisciplinary teams to rebuild the company.

## Your opinion counts

In work situations, motivation is often the factor that gets one project off the ground over another. Michael Eisner, Disney's CEO, says, "What amazes me is that it's always the person with the strong point of view who influences the group, who wins the day. Around here, a powerful point of view is worth at least 80 IQ points." You don't have to be smarter than the next person, just more motivated to get your ideas put into practice.

In order to manage relationships successfully, you need the ability to find common ground quickly with people, in order to move them to agreement on what problems need to be solved. To do so, you need to be open and friendly in your demeanor, and optimistic in your outlook. People have to trust you without your asking for their trust.

# Where Have All the Leaders Gone?

If leading is simple, why do some people go around bemoaning the shortage of leaders? Pick up any business publication, from *Fortune* to the *Harvard Business Review,* and you can read articles that contend that there is a critical shortage of leaders at every level. Where are the eloquent, inspirational Churchills and Roosevelts, writers ask, and the rough-hewn, plain-spoken but ultimately charismatic Harry Trumans and Abe Lincolns, now that we really need them?

Leadership is a set of skills and traits that can be learned and worked on, yet the general perception is that good leaders are scarce. Take a look at the following sections to see why.

## Leaders come in all guises

You become a leader through social skill by finding kindred spirits in a company who will meet, often informally, to approach a problem. In 1987, just such a group of dispirited junior engineers and managers got together at Chrysler to talk about the company's then ongoing problems: the lack of quality in the cars Chrysler was manufacturing, a steadily eroding market share, and Japanese competitors, especially Honda, who were eating Chrysler's lunch. Given an ear by top management, the group, which called itself the Youth Advisory Committee, attacked the problem with gusto.

Interestingly, the Youth Advisory Committee was composed mostly of people who would've been considered outsiders in Chrysler's ultraconservative management system.

One of the group's leaders, a Japanese-American woman named Reiko McKendry, was effective in questioning Honda executives because she understood Japanese social skills. Jim Finck, another group member, was the complete antithesis of the stereotypical pocket-protectored, white short-sleeve shirt, buzz-cut engineer. Says Finck, "It was amazing. After starting the study, we quickly discovered that nobody at Chrysler was talking to anybody else."

By employing the most basic social skills — talking about things — the Youth Advisory Committee launched the rebirth of a company. The group's final report, presented to an often startled Chrysler senior management, was wholeheartedly adopted, setting in motion a chain of events that sent the company from the bottom of the automotive scrap heap to the top of the profits pyramid.

# Leaders may rise only in response to a situation

Leaders may already be all around us, working at lower levels, awaiting the circumstances that will thrust them into the spotlight. If leadership potential exists in almost everyone, then rather than having a shortage of leaders, we may have a shortage of the *circumstances* for leadership.

Pick almost any of the great leaders and examine their ascent to leadership closely, and, with rare exceptions, you can see that the events created the leader, not the other way around. Had the Great Depression not taken deep root in 1931, we could be remembering Herbert Hoover as a great humanitarian and Franklin Roosevelt as a weak-willed patrician who was a pale imitation of his cousin Teddy Roosevelt. But Hoover did not respond adequately to the Depression, and Roosevelt scrapped his existing economic policies, which were even more poorly designed than Hoover's. Instead, Roosevelt focused his attention on listening to the misery of the common man and creating plans to ease it. That's what made Roosevelt a great leader.

Harry Truman was a haberdasher from Missouri, a hireling of the St. Louis Pendergast political machine, who was foisted on a weakened and reluctant Roosevelt in the waning days of World War II. When Roosevelt died unexpectedly, shortly after winning a fourth term, it fell to Truman to pick up the mantle of leadership and do something with it. To his credit, he rose to the occasion, bringing the war to a swift and decisive conclusion and extending the benefits of Roosevelt's economic reforms to much of rural America.

The simple fact is that any of these people probably wouldn't have emerged as leaders if circumstances hadn't demanded more from them in times of crisis. But it is also true that Churchill, Roosevelt, and Truman had the qualities needed to respond in such ample measure that they far exceeded what was expected of them.

# Leaders may be unwanted until needed

A cynical, but pragmatic, explanation of why many feel that leaders are in short supply is that we really don't want leaders until we need them. Possibly, the very qualities that allow people to meet the most difficult challenges make them unwelcome during times when those challenges don't exist.

Winston Churchill is a case in point: His was a shrill, unwanted voice in the wilderness during the 1930s, as Hitler's evil power grew almost daily. Great Britain had been decimated by World War I, left dispirited by internal strife and economic depression for two decades afterward. The British didn't want to sacrifice still more lives, honor, or scant fortune on Europe's seemingly petty quarrels. When British Prime Minister Neville Chamberlain returned from Munich in 1938, hailing as "peace in our time" his surrender of the Sudetenland area of Czechoslovakia to the Germans, he received cheers in the streets of London. Barely two years later, with Hitler still on the march and English troops on the defensive at Dunkirk, the British people rallied to Churchill's call to fight. After the end of the war, however, the British quickly grew tired of Churchill's leadership.

# Leaders may be mistaken for managers

Sometimes, leaders are mistaken for managers. In this idea, leaders are leading well all the time, but the success of their leadership is attributed to a good management model.

In the time since World War II, many corporations have adopted the concept of *management science*. Management science is the idea that mathematical models can be applied to any component of an organization, from production to consumer behavior, allowing managers to make reasonable predictions about the outcomes of various actions.

Most management models are based on the idea of *feedback*, which is the ability to modify behavior based on the information you receive. Good leadership is based on feedback, as well. In order to elicit cooperation, you have to listen, and in order to move people forward toward their chosen goal, you have to defer your needs to their needs, which means modifying your behavior in response to the needs of the group you are leading. So the best management models automatically incorporate, at least to some extent, the qualities of leadership into each of their components. Thus, in a well-managed organization, the qualities of leadership often pass unnoticed.

## Flattening the pyramid

In the past two decades, some business models have called for highly dispersed leadership and responsibility, called *flattening the pyramid*. Flattening the pyramid is the process of distributing leadership roles broadly across a company, rather than concentrating responsibility among a few people at the top. When every person in a company is held responsible for the company's success, the leader's role is more narrowly defined. In this case, all workers assume responsibility, and the leader provides the long-range goal and vision for the company.

Take companies such as Federal Express or United Parcel Service (UPS). Every employee is a shareholder, and every employee is indoctrinated from the first day on the job with the idea that every time the employee picks up or delivers a package, his or her behavior will affect the entire future of the company. Moreover, employees have a fair degree of latitude in how they get their jobs done, so they are forced to take responsibility — to lead themselves, in effect — at ground level. The sole roles of both companies' senior management teams are to provide the vision to determine where to go next, and to create plans for moving the companies to that next step.

### Understanding the difference between leadership and management

Many people think that management and leadership are the same thing, but they're not. Leaders ask the what and why questions, not the how questions. Leaders think about *empowerment,* not control. Empowerment means that you don't steal responsibility from people. Good companies such as Federal Express and UPS empower their people, allowing them to take responsibility for doing things right.

Two important distinctions separate leadership and management:

- ✔ **You manage things, but you lead people.** Grace Hopper, a late management expert who later became the first woman admiral in the U.S. Navy, observed that a difference between management and leadership was the object of the actions. Managers work with processes, models, and systems — things. But leaders must work with people and their emotions.

- ✔ **Managers do things right, but leaders do the right things.** Warren Bennis, the University of Southern California professor who has made a career of studying leaders (particularly corporate executives) pointed out that when you think about doing things right, you think about control mechanisms and the how-to of accomplishing things. This process is management. When you think about doing the right things, on the other hand, your mind immediately goes toward thinking about the future, thinking about dreams, missions, strategic intent, and purpose. This approach is leadership.

# Chapter 2

# Remember, They're Not Electing You Dictator for Life

*The Moving Finger writes; and having writ, Moves on.*
—Omar Khayyam, *The Rubaiyat*

*The people who get on in this world are the people who get up and look for the circumstances they want, and, if they can't find them, make them.*
—George Bernard Shaw

*J*ust because you take the lead, don't think that you'll always be in the lead, because all leadership is temporary. Leadership takes place because of an intersection of a need, a goal, and a person willing to assume responsibility. Leadership often depends on being in the right place at the right time.

Different combinations of time and circumstance call forth different kinds of leadership. Sometimes, the circumstances require leadership, and the right person to lead is available. This set of circumstances brings about the optimal type of leadership, *situational leadership*. Other times, the stars don't align perfectly, and either the leader doesn't match the situation or the leader is right but the timing is wrong. When leadership takes place in these out-of-whack situations, either *transitional leadership* or *hierarchical leadership* ensues. In this chapter, you sample the various flavors of leadership and find out how to tell the differences among them.

# The Transient Nature of Leadership

Leadership is temporary, and a leader gets just so many chances to succeed before followers look somewhere else for a new leader. The following story illustrates this concept.

After Joseph Stalin died, a struggle ensued for leadership within the Russian Communist Party. Nikita Khrushchev came to power, but his hold was shaky. While he was rummaging through Stalin's old desk in the Kremlin, he came across a locked box, which he pried open. Inside were three letters wrapped in a red ribbon with a note attached that read, "To My Successor." On the first envelope were printed the words, "To be opened during your first crisis." Since Khrushchev was still in the midst of a power struggle, he opened the envelope. The note inside had two words written on it: "Blame Me!" Khrushchev promptly called what became the Third Party Congress, denounced Stalin, won widespread support, and averted the crisis.

Several years later, when Russia's satellite states were in revolt and another crisis loomed, Khrushchev again opened the lock box, and took out the second letter. It read, "Do as I did." Khrushchev did just that, brutally crushing opposition in Hungary, Poland, and East Germany. Again he prevailed, for a while. By the mid-1960s, with the economy in turmoil and his policies failing, Khrushchev opened Stalin's last letter. It read: "Choose a new leader and write him three letters." The vacuum that Stalin left made the time ripe for someone to take the lead, but Khrushchev's leadership didn't last forever.

Leadership is a transient condition for a couple of good reasons:

- ✔ **The situation that requires leadership may come to an end.** If leading is about helping groups reach their goals, what happens when the goal is reached? Or, as Shelly Zelaznick, the former managing editor of *Forbes*, used to say, "What does the dog who's chasing a car do with it once he catches it?"

- ✔ **Times change and circumstances change.** Today's respected leader may be out of touch with the realities of tomorrow. The goals that called forth all of a leader's skill and energies may have changed. Tomorrow's struggle may, in fact, be diametrically opposed to everything a leader stood for yesterday.

To picture how time and circumstance work together to create an atmosphere conducive to leadership, take a look at Figure 2-1, which shows what happens when the right and wrong circumstances and times coincide.

|  | Time | |
|---|---|---|
|  | Right | Wrong |
| Right | Situational Leadership | Hierarchical Leadership |
| Circumstances | | |
| Wrong | Transitional Leadership | Chaos |

**Figure 2-1:** Time and circumstances must be right for leadership.

# Situational Leadership

The best place to find out about situational leadership — the right person in the right place at the right time — is to read a daily newspaper. The news reports are full of people who responded to circumstances at exactly the right time to fulfill a leadership role.

To prove to you just how common situational leadership is, take a look at this experiment we did. We took a local paper — not *The New York Times, The Washington Post,* or *The Wall Street Journal* — and carefully went through its stories, searching for examples of leadership of word or deed. *The Morning Call* (Allentown, Pennsylvania) is a typical medium-circulation newspaper. For Dec. 30, 1998, the main news sections carried 81 stories, not counting obituaries. We didn't count sports stories, because many of them are automatically about leadership — or the lack of it — due to a particular athlete's performance or some decision that a coach made. You can do the same experiment with your own newspaper. In fact, reading the paper to look for examples of leadership in action is a good way to understand just what situational leadership is and how often it pops up in real life.

In situational leadership, a chain of events creates a need for a leader to emerge from the crowd. The examples of the news accounts we include in this chapter illustrate a circumstance or set of circumstances that call for a stand or a decision to be made, right at that time, before the moment could be lost. Each of the people or institutions making the decisions became leaders at that moment, rising to the needs of the situation.

Each of the situations we highlight is different, often dramatically so, from the examples surrounding it. We've done this because leadership situations aren't always obvious. Sometimes, leadership emerges in moments of great crisis. Other times, it emerges out of an argument or disagreement that needs to be settled. Yet other times, a leader has to stand up for a principle or defend the defenseless. The circumstances may vary from situation to situation, but in every case, the situation represents an opportunity that requires someone to step forward and advance a cause or a goal, or merely take charge of the situation to ensure a better outcome.

Situational leadership is all around you. To become a situational leader, you need to

✔ Recognize when the time and circumstances combine to require leadership.

✔ Be willing and able to assume the responsibility of leading. To do this, you must

- Listen.

- Take responsibility for helping the group achieve its goal.

- Draw out the group's cooperation so that the goal can actually be reached.

## *No-cost decisions*

The first news story deals with an ill-timed yacht race that culminated in deadly tragedy, as high winds and fierce waves swamped or sank many of the boats in the race. Despite the best efforts of rescuers, several sailors drowned. Larry Ellison, who is both the captain of the *Sayonara* and the chief executive of a large corporation, faced a critical decision as the rescue operation began: Should he abandon ship and allow all of his crew to be taken aboard helicopters, or should he attempt to bring the yacht in, with its crew? The decision is an interesting one.

## Yachtsmen reluctant to sail after fatalities

Larry Ellison, chief executive officer and founder of software giant Oracle Corp., and his 80-foot yacht *Sayonara* crossed the finish line Tuesday to win the famed [Sidney, Australia, to Hobart, Tasmania] race a second time. "It wasn't a race," he said. "We were focused on getting the boat here in one piece and every one of the crew here."

As a billionaire, Ellison could have afforded either decision. Losing his multi-million-dollar yacht would not have resulted in any economic loss to him. And paying the costs of having helicopters come out and pluck Ellison and his crew from the decks of *Sayonara* would not have been much of a financial hardship. Ellison was therefore unencumbered by anything except the needs of the situation. As a leader, he consulted his crew, assessed his circumstances, and made the decision to sail on, knowing that he could always call for help later if circumstances changed. (If, for example, the storm had become even more violent.)

## Moral decision

This second story deals with the personal decision of a Chinese dissident leader to go on fighting for what he believes in, even though it will cost him another 13 years in jail. Xu Wenli could easily renounce his beliefs and live a normal life, but by sacrificing himself for a cause — freedom and democracy — Xu Wenli hopes to inspire millions of ordinary Chinese who may not otherwise have the courage to fight for political change. In addition to leadership, Xu Wenli exhibits heroism.

Xu had to exercise a completely different kind of situational leadership. Leadership is about helping a group of people move toward a goal, but often the goal is distant and abstract. Xu, who was one of the leaders of the Tiananmen Square uprising in China more than a decade ago, has had many opportunities to abandon the abstract defense of the Chinese people's rights to self-determination, and he has refused to do so every time.

# Chinese dissidents get hard labor without trial

Another dissident, Xu Wenli, said in an open letter from prison, dated Monday, that he will not appeal his 13-year sentence, out of contempt for the Chinese legal system. The letter ended with the words, "penned in handcuffs."

By refusing to make an appeal, Xu is questioning the very legitimacy of the government that has imprisoned him on behalf of all the Chinese people, at great personal sacrifice to himself. He has used the situation to assert his leadership and to bring the issue of democracy into sharper focus.

## Solomonic decisions

One of the discoveries that you make as a leader is that you are never going to make everybody happy. Often, the people who will appeal to you to make a decision will have diametrically opposed viewpoints. How do you handle these situations? Like the story of King Solomon, you look for a solution that is so polarized that it causes one side to give way out of common sense, lest a decision be reached that causes harm. In one story told about Solomon, two women lay claim to the same baby, and each "proves" that she is the mother. Solomon draws his sword and says that because he cannot tell who is lying, he will cut the baby in half and give a part to each mother. The woman who is the real mother gives up her claim, because she doesn't want to see her baby die. King Solomon gives her the baby because she has demonstrated a genuine concern for its welfare.

Rabbi Moshe Shaul Klein was exercising a more narrowly defined version of leadership in his ruling. He knows that Orthodox Jews have had trouble reconciling what they know to be their religious laws regarding the writing of God's name with a new technology. Rabbi Klein had to listen to his people's entreaties for a resolution to this problem, lest Orthodox Jews be precluded from using computers and benefiting from the most advanced technology, as any other people would.

## Find infernal computers godless? Okay, rabbi says

A leading Orthodox rabbi ruled this week that the word *God* may be erased from a computer screen or disk, because the pixels do not constitute real letters. Rabbi Moshe Shaul Klein published his ruling this week in a computer magazine aimed at Orthodox Jews. According to Jewish law, printed matter with the word God — *elohim* in Hebrew — and its manifestations in any other language must be stored or ritually buried.

By ruling as he did, Rabbi Klein is following in the footsteps of King Solomon, looking for a middle ground that both sharply defines the issue and at the same time leaves room for a little vagueness. The situation requiring Rabbi Klein's ruling could not have come about before the advent of computers, nor will it re-emerge unless a segment of the group refuses to accept Rabbi Klein's ruling.

## Decisions for the greater good

Call this the "Joan of Arc" style of leadership. Joan was a peasant girl who grew up during a period of civil war in France. One day she had a vision and raised an army to support a young man who was a prince, arguing that he was the rightful heir to the French throne. Her army carried the day, and the prince became a king. Likewise, today, people are aroused by situations that they may not be directly a part of but that nevertheless cause them to start a crusade on behalf of a cause. It's one of the most important ways in which the world changes for the better.

# Do siblings have a constitutional right to stay together?

"The time has come to examine how much we value children and their interests," said Madelyn Freundlich, executive director of the Adoption Institute, a New York think tank.

Madelyn Freundlich, executive director of the Adoption Institute, the think tank that has taken a position on a case involving the separation of a brother and sister in a proposed adoption, is exercising leadership in the abstract. She has no legal standing in the case, but she has an interest borne out of research and a concern for what she sees as a serious potential psychological harm that may be done to children who are pulled apart from each other's love. The timing of this particular case happens to coincide with the raised profile of adoption issues, which used to be solely the province of the courts and adoption agencies.

The precedent for Freundlich's position goes back to the late 1960s. At that time, the Sierra Club filed an *amicus curiae* (friend of the court — a group with no legal standing in a lawsuit) brief on behalf of a group of old-growth redwoods in California. The Sierra Club filed suit on the grounds that the trees could not sue to protect their rights on their own. Likewise, although the court has appointed legal representatives for the two children affected by the separation, Ms. Freundlich is attempting to exercise a leadership role by asking the courts to consider larger issues than the narrow issues of custody.

## *Mediative decisions*

Leadership mostly involves getting other people to move toward a goal, but sometimes, it means getting people to wait if there is an unresolved conflict. In this case, Riverside, California, police chief Jerry Carroll's primary aim is to keep part of his community from erupting into riot and protest, while not giving in to the temptations of another segment of his community to become defensive and angry. Leadership is often about stepping into situations and imposing yourself between warring factions until you can cool both sides down and get them to talk to each other. This kind of leadership is the most difficult, because you have to be able to win the trust of groups that may be deeply suspicious of your motives.

> # Family: Deadly police shooting of teenager was unprovoked
>
> Police chief Jerry Carroll met with black community leaders Monday after relatives who saw Tyisha Shenee Miller die said she was unconscious and couldn't have raised a gun at officers, as police claimed.

In the case of the shooting death of Tyisha Shenee Miller in Riverside, California, police chief Jerry Carroll has witnessed the rioting that has taken place in nearby Los Angeles when police officers have been accused of unprovoked attacks on minority citizens.

Chief Carroll has encountered a situation that requires multiple leadership responsibilities: He has to maintain order in the community at large; conduct an impartial investigation on behalf of Ms. Miller's family and the larger black community of Riverside; and maintain the trust and morale of his officers while he is conducting his investigation.

The fact that Chief Carroll previously has won the trust and cooperation of Riverside's minority communities in past incidents involving community problems and the police, as the article indicates, tells us that chief Carroll is a very strong leader. He listens carefully to all groups, is highly successful in eliciting cooperation, and can successfully place the needs of different groups above his own, all in the interest of maintaining peace and harmony in Riverside.

## *Princely decisions*

*Princely decisions* is a variety of the moral leadership shown by Xu Wenli. Few kings or queens nowadays have much power. In most countries, the hereditary leaders who continue to rule have had their powers severely limited by constitutions and courts. But countries that maintain royalty do so for a reason: The king or queen is considered to be the living embodiment of the national will. So when an opportunity to represent that will comes along, a wise ruler will take it.

## Cambodian chiefs differ on Khmer Rouge fate

"Taking into account the very wide and undeniable discontent of the majority of the Khmer people, I announce to this majority that I respect them and will not renew my power of amnesty for major Khmer Rouge criminals," said King Norodom Sihanouk.

Norodom Sihanouk had been an ineffectual prince and prime minister whose weakness as a leader helped bring about the atrocities of the Khmer Rouge. So Sihanouk's statement would be easy to dismiss as just one more instance of Sihanouk's blowing with the wind. As king, though, Sihanouk shouldn't be simply the emblem of the state. He should be the living embodiment of the will of his people.

Sihanouk's decision not to extend amnesty to two Khmer Rouge chieftains is recognition by Sihanouk that the present situation calls for strong leadership. The Cambodian people want to be led away, finally, from the horrors of the killing fields. Only Sihanouk can lead them, and he has chosen to do so.

## Community decisions

One of the criteria for leadership is the ability to elicit cooperation from others. In a community, cooperation may begin with a committee that decides on a goal that will benefit the community at large. If that goal is worthwhile, and if the committee members take their job seriously, they can often win the cooperation of the community at large, which recognizes the value of the proposed goal. Community decisions are, thus, for and by the community, and leadership is spread among all the participants who help to realize a larger vision.

## Hotel buyers get more time

Christmas City Hotel Corporation wants more time to close its $1.9 million deal to buy Hotel Bethlehem now that it has become clear that the investment partnership may not get approval for a $1.5 million loan in local money by Thursday's deadline. The request for the extension to January 15 has received the blessing of U.S. Bankruptcy Court Trustee John Carroll and First Community Bank.

The story about the Hotel Bethlehem is only the latest episode in an ongoing saga. The tale began when the hotel — which has been a fixture of downtown Bethlehem, Pennsylvania, for nearly a century — suddenly closed in 1997. Christmas City Hotel Corporation is a community-based partnership that has put in funds to reopen and renovate the hotel, in the belief that it is the anchor to the downtown.

Because this group has invested its own leadership on behalf of the community, U.S. Bankruptcy Court Trustee John Carroll and First Community Bank, from whom additional renovation funds are going to be borrowed, felt that it was incumbent to allow the partnership more time to play out the situation. Good leadership — by the Christmas City Hotel Corporation partners — begets the cooperation of others, in this case the bankruptcy trustee and the bank.

## Philanthropic decisions

One of the factors that can make leadership inspiring is the desire to improve the lot of the people. You can decide to help one person at a time, a group, or an entire community, but the decision to form a group whose sole purpose is philanthropic is not only noble, but also often practical. (*Philanthropic* means "for the love of mankind.") Often, people don't have the time to get involved in helping, but they do have the money. Fund-raising for worthy causes thus becomes an avenue for participation, and for leadership.

## Christmas spacesuit helps boy, 9, fulfill his dream to play outside

A new NASA suit fulfilled 9-year-old Jonathan Pierce's Christmas wish to play outside like other children. Jonathan suffers from erythropoietic protoporphyria (EPP), a rare skin disorder that causes skin to swell, blister, and redden when exposed to the sun's ultraviolet radiation. Kiwanis International Foundation bought Jonathan the $2,500 pants, jacket, gloves, mask, goggles, and a gel-filled "cool suit," which he wears underneath to keep from overheating.

The leadership of the Kiwanis International Foundation in providing a special garment for Jonathan Pierce is obvious. One of the roles that Kiwanis, and other groups such as the Lions Club and Rotary International, have long played is that of cooperative leadership. By banding groups of like-minded citizens together to achieve a common goal, each of these organizations magnifies the efforts of the individual, and provides opportunities for ordinary citizens to excel in a leadership situation.

## Institutional decisions

We often believe that our institutions don't do a very good job of helping us. We look at the rules that a government agency makes, and all we see is more bureaucratic red tape. But sometimes, an institution or a government rule-making body will find a way to get to the heart of the matter — and turn civic concerns into a path for action.

Can an institution lead? Often, individual leaders are invisible, because of the requirements of an organization. For years, nobody knew who "M" was in the British intelligence organization MI 5, but everybody knew that MI 5 was an effective organization. In a complex world, it is often difficult to know from what direction leadership is coming, but we know it when it arrives.

## Elder abuse hot line launched by state

The state Department of Aging is launching television and radio ads to promote a new, confidential, toll-free, elder abuse hot line, 1-800-490-8505.

The elder abuse hot line launched by Pennsylvania's Department of Aging is an example of institutional leadership, of an organization listening to the needs of a group and then working with the governor and the legislature to provide a solution. Leadership in this case is indirect, to be sure, and the leadership that brought about the hot line may be a group effort, but the leadership provided by the Department of Aging is there for anyone to see.

## Leaders, heroes, and *ER*

The dictionary describes a *hero* as a person of great courage. Situational leadership also often requires great courage, so consider whether heroes and leaders are the same thing. Sometimes they are, but often they are not. A hero is always a situational leader, but a situational leader is not always a hero.

Situational leadership requires that you take responsibility at the moment action is required; otherwise, the critical moment may be lost. Heroism requires only that you sacrifice your needs to the needs of another. It does not require that you listen. Often, the only voice a hero hears is her own, pushing her to deal with a critical situation. Sometimes, the hero mobilizes others, at which point she becomes a leader.

An episode of the popular television drama, *ER*, features the character John Carter, the young emergency room intern and resident heartthrob. He takes command of the emergency room when the attending physician, Kerry Weaver, suddenly becomes ill from benzene poisoning brought on

when an injured chemical plant worker enters the emergency room for treatment. Other, more senior, doctors are present but they're too busy taking care of their own patients to realize that no one is taking charge of the entire situation. Carter mobilizes all the doctors, nurses, orderlies, and physicians' assistants to stage an orderly evacuation, while continuing the treatment of those most in need.

After the situation is brought under control, the fire chief who has supervised the decontamination of the emergency room congratulates Carter on the job he has done, and asks him to serve on an emergency task force. Carter demurs, saying he is only an intern. The fire chief looks at him, gives him a wink, and says, "Yeah, but we really know who took charge."

That episode was good television, but it also illustrates the similarities and differences between leaders and heroes. Carter kept the needs of the group in mind, providing leadership, so that each of the doctors could do their own thing.

# Transitional Leadership

Transitional leadership exists when the time is right but the circumstances are wrong. In some instances, leadership is required at a certain moment, but the person who is the "leader" may not be capable of delivering leadership. The French expression *faux pas,* which means "false step," describes transitional leadership perfectly. Faux pas occur in social situations all the time, so you don't have to imagine too hard to envision leadership situations where false steps lead to a hasty exit for the leader.

In early 1996, Gil Amelio was hired to become the fourth chief executive of Apple Computer. At the time, the company was suffering from flat sales, steep operating losses, and an apparent lack of direction. Amelio, who had come over from National Semiconductor, had overseen a recovery of that company, including a fourfold run-up of its stock price, resulting in the creation of more than $3.5 billion in shareholder equity. On paper, Amelio was the right man at the right time. But he had not counted on the persistent interference and sideline carping of Steve Jobs, one of the cofounders of Apple and a member of its board of directors. As months rolled by after Amelio's appointment as chief executive, Apple's fortunes failed to improve, and Amelio became more interested in retaining his post than in leading the company out of its morass. Jobs finally replaced Amelio, introduced the iMac computer, and put Apple on the road to recovery. Amelio's sin: He failed to listen to the one person who knew more than anyone else about Apple and its unique culture.

Amelio, despite his vast skills, became that endangered species, the *transitional leader.* The time was right for Amelio: Apple desperately needed leadership. But the fit — the circumstances — were wrong. As Amelio says of his very first meeting with the athletic Steve Jobs, "I remember glancing down at my shined black wing tips and thinking of loosening my tie. My typically pragmatic mind had veered into visual superficialities." Looking back, Amelio realized at the outset that he was the wrong person to fix Apple — he simply didn't fit into the company's highly informal culture — but, as he says, "as Apple's CEO, I would be made to feel like a superstar." Amelio was concentrating on the appearance of leadership, not on the problems and tasks.

## Misusing all the right stuff

The transitional leader may be highly competent, and he or she may have all the skills of a leader — the willingness to accept responsibility, the ability to elicit cooperation from others, the ability to listen, and the ability to place the needs of others above oneself. Those skills, however, are often skewed. If you read *Superman* comics when you were a kid, you may remember Bizarro, a creature from another dimension who looked like Superman and had all of his attributes but with everything slightly skewed. In one episode, Bizarro tore down a leaky dam. Instead of repairing the leak with his super-strength and super-speed, his action subsequently flooded out a town downstream. Transitional leaders are similar: They are selected because somewhere along the line they manifested all of the traits of leadership — Amelio at National Semiconductor, for example — but develop a tin ear in their new role.

## Fearing risk

Transitional leaders are often afraid of risk. Why does that happen? According to top headhunter Lester Korn, leaders change from situational leaders to transitional leaders when they become risk-averse, and refuse to pursue their point of view. In his book, *The Success Profile* (Simon & Schuster), Korn has a table titled "Factors Involved In Career Turning Point." The most important factor in determining career success, says Korn, is "Right Place, Right Time," which about half the executives, in a survey by his firm, Korn/Ferry International, said was the critical factor in their move to the top.

The third most important factor, according to Korn's table, is "High-Risk Project," at about a third of the sample. Often, the element that forces potential leaders into transitional roles is an unwillingness to confront risk when confrontation is the exact requirement. In Amelio's case, Jobs had argued from the outset that Apple needed a computer that would take the company beyond its popular Macintosh. (The Macintosh, though more powerful and much faster than any Windows/Intel PC, had failed to establish itself within the business community.) Amelio's strategy was to try to provide price incentives for companies to buy Macs — a strategy that did nothing but lower Apple's already dwindling profitability. Job's solution, — developing a new, low-cost home computer — was far riskier — but risk was the required action in a dire situation.

As William Glavin, a former chief executive of Xerox, puts it, "You've got to have enough confidence in yourself that you're not worried about being fired for saying or doing the wrong thing. You cannot let anything scare you. If you really have confidence that you can always get another job, then you will do the right things."

## Hierarchical Leadership

If transitional leadership is leadership that takes place when the time is right but the circumstances are wrong, then hierarchical leadership is the opposite: The circumstances are right, but the time is wrong. The hierarchical leader typically is someone who assumes a leadership role because it is "their turn," by right of promotion or longevity in a job (or, in the case of monarchy, because of death and birth order).

Hierarchical leaders face a problem: They're "it" whether they want the job of leader or not. For example, King George III was not fit to lead England during the Seven Years War — what Americans call the French and Indian War. His father, George II, however, died in 1760 — in the midst of the conflict. England won the war, but lost the peace, by heavily taxing the American colonies it had fought so hard to keep. George III was never a healthy man and suffered from increasing bouts of madness and depression. He was thus incapable of making rational decisions about what his Prime Minister, William Pitt, considered the legitimate demands of colonial Englishmen. By 1776, the question of colonial rights had come to a head, and the hierarchical leader, unable to step aside or admit that he may be wrong, forced the issue by sending troops to the Colonies and refusing to negotiate with his colonial subjects. The colonists rebelled and the rest, as they say, is history.

The preceding example illustrates the essence of hierarchical leaders — they often "lose the moment" because they are tone deaf to the time imperatives of leadership. Hierarchical leaders are in their position because circumstances have put them there, and nothing short of a revolution can dislodge them. In fact, think of every revolution — in Russia, against a weak czar Nicholas II; in China, against an aging and corrupt Manchu empress; in France, against a timid and slightly addled Louis XVI — and you can understand the failure of hierarchical leadership.

Hierarchical leaders can and do rise to the occasion and become situational leaders. Think of George VI, the father of England's Queen Elizabeth II. He was forced into his job as king by the abdication of his elder brother Edward VIII, on the eve of World War II. George VI, a shy, retiring man, assumed a role he never wanted (one that caused his premature death from accumulated stress). But the king used his hierarchical status to create the British monarchy as we know it — a monarchy dedicated, despite its petty family squabbles, to public service and the cause of the common British subjects.

Many students of history credit Winston Churchill's rousing speeches with giving the British people the will to resist Nazi aggression. The average Briton who lived through that terrible period, however, will tell you unequivocally that it was the King — moving among his subjects at hospitals, orphanages, bomb sites, and war factories and rallying people with his calm voice and words of encouragement — who made the real difference.

# Chapter 3

# Building Your Leadership Muscles

*Leadership and learning are indispensable to each other.*
—John F. Kennedy

You may wonder why some people seem to become leaders naturally and effortlessly, whereas others don't. You've probably heard reverent whispers that so-and-so is a *natural leader,* but (as we point out in Chapters 1 and 2) leadership is situational, not hereditary. Believing that certain people are destined for leadership is easy, however, if those people have personality traits that lend themselves to leadership.

Although some come naturally by personality traits common to leaders, personality traits can be developed, too. Think of it this way: Some people have to work hard to develop a good golf swing, while others seem to naturally have a knack for it. Similarly, with perseverance and work, anyone can develop his or her own leadership traits. (And people who work diligently to develop an ability often end up better than those who just "get by" on their natural abilities.)

In this chapter, we focus on ten of the most important traits common to great leaders. Developing these traits in your everyday life tells everyone you meet that you have the capability to lead.

# Putting Your Brain to Work

To make use of the cliché, you don't have to be a rocket scientist or a brain surgeon to be a leader. Many leaders are not highly schooled, but they are intelligent, and one of the most interesting things about their intelligence is that they can take a limited amount of information and translate it into a workable set of skills. Think of leaders as something like MacGyver, the television character that Richard Dean Anderson played for several years. No matter what situation he got himself into, he was able to find a way to use little more than his handy Swiss Army knife and a roll of duct tape to improvise a solution. His skill was that he could imagine the things at hand to be other things.

## Using what you have

Intelligence is critical to leadership because synthesizing information is often necessary in order to create a vision. When a group comes to you for leadership, their goals are often unformed or poorly formed. When God chose Moses to lead the Hebrew people out of bondage, they didn't know that such a thing was even possible, and many of them initially resisted the idea. In fact, the entire biblical story of Moses — not the movie version — is filled with the constant doubt of the people being led. But intelligence enables you to start from a set of unknowns or with very limited information and proceed to a known outcome — leaving Egypt and finding a new homeland, in this case.

The quarterback of a football team is usually the leader of the team. Some quarterbacks, such as John Elway or Doug Flutie, distinguish themselves with their improvisational skill. They can direct traffic on the field while linebackers are rushing at them, and set up a receiver for a critical play with nothing more than hand signals and eye movements even after the set play has fallen apart. They use the information at hand to create something new and move their teams forward toward the goal line.

In biblical days, when the lines of communication between God and Man were more direct, visions came to people as the word of God. Nowadays, a leader is required to have a vision, which is a fancy word for a purpose and a goal or goals for followers. Creating that vision means recognizing what is possible for the group you are leading, which itself requires intelligence in the form of the ability to assess the skills of the group.

## Test your leadership IQ

Here's a little quiz. Look at the following list and ask yourself whether you do these things often, sometimes, or never. Give yourself a point if you do them all the time, add no points if you do them sometimes, and take away a point if you never do them. Ready?

1. **I respond to situations very flexibly.**

2. **I take advantage of fortuitous circumstances.**

3. **I can make sense out of ambiguous or contradictory messages.**

4. **I can recognize the importance of different elements of a situation.**

5. **I can find similarities between situations** despite differences that may separate them.

6. **I can draw distinctions between situations despite similarities that may link them.**

7. **I can synthesize new concepts by taking old concepts and putting them together in new ways.**

8. **I can come up with new ideas.**

If you've scored four or more points, you are probably already known as a leader. If you've scored two or three points, you have good leadership potential. If you score one or fewer, you have some work to do on your leadership intelligence skills.

## Responding to situations flexibly

Taking in new information and adjusting your response to a particular situation requires intelligence. Instead of responding in a knee-jerk way, an intelligent person responds flexibly, based on circumstances and needs.

Here's a situation: You own a vacation house and you've been away from it for a while. Your brother-in-law, who is looking after the house, has turned down the heat in the wintertime to save you money, even though the area where your house is located is prone to short-term power outages. The power has gone off in your house, the pipes have frozen, and then the power has come back on. By the time you arrive, the frozen pipes have burst, and the furnace is merrily pumping hot water through all the leaks and flooding your house. What do you do?

If your first response is "I scream and curse the Fates," you are not responding to the situation very flexibly. If you threaten to divorce your spouse, who brought into your life the idiot who did this to you, you're not doing yourself any good, either. But if you open the door and a river pours out, along with a cloud of steam, and you run downstairs to the basement to shut off the furnace and then go out and find a couple of pails and mops and begin cleaning up, you are responding to the situation flexibly.

The goal is to prevent further damage. The effort requires that you elicit cooperation from your spouse, so you can't yell or make sarcastic remarks. And you need to listen to your spouse, who probably knows better than you do where the mops and towels are, and who may have some additional ideas to contribute to drying out the house.

The flooded house example is leadership at a very local, personal level, to be sure, but it is no different from the situation that faced Robert Saldick. In 1988, Saldick became president of Raychem, then a $2 billion California manufacturer of electronics products, after spending more than 20 years rising through the ranks of the company. One of the products that Saldick had been a champion of before he became the president was Raytel, a connection system for linking fiber-optic cables to the home. On the surface, Raytel was just the kind of product that could propel Raychem forward at a critical time when its sales were flagging.

As president, Saldick knew he couldn't push Raytel through the company just because it was his right to do so. He began to look at Raytel through leader's eyes, and his analysis was that the project would cost more than the company could afford before it might be successful, it might take too long to bring to the marketplace, and it could be superseded by other approaches from competitors. So he killed the Raytel project, took a $200 million write-down, and moved on to rebuild the company by cutting costs and adding other new products. Said Saldick about his move, "When you are a product champion, you look at projects one way. But when you become responsible for the fortunes of the whole company, you have to reassess everything. You have to be flexible in the face of new circumstances."

## Taking advantage of fortuitous circumstances

The Roman poet and playwright Virgil once said that fortune favors the brave. He didn't mean bravery in the heroic sense, but rather in the opportunistic sense. You not only have to be smart enough to adapt to new information with flexibility, but you also have to have the courage to seize opportunities when they present themselves. Often, the opportunity appears when you do nothing more than reshuffle existing information.

Take, for example, Sam Walton, the founder of Wal-Mart. When he was working for the Ben Franklin stores, that chain served areas that were economically marginal, or what demographers call "C" counties. Walton noticed that a lot of the customers of the stores were from out of the area, from towns and villages that were even more disadvantaged than the towns Ben Franklin stores served. So he asked permission to open a store in a "D" county — a place that is the bottom of the barrel economically. When the company denied Walton's request, he quit and opened his first Wal-Mart. He reasoned, rightly, that no matter where people live, they have the same needs. They have to buy toothpaste and shaving cream and shoelaces and all of the other little things that go into making life normal. If they could buy them without traveling a great distance or paying more money, they would become loyal customers.

Walton took advantage of a lack of flexibility on the part of his employer to create the largest retailing empire in history. He also listened to his customers and created a circumstance for them to cooperate with him — his store opened in their town in return for their patronage. And finally, he put his customers above himself by not charging a premium price even though it cost him more to get his goods to more remote locations. By opening several stores in an area at once, Walton was able to get manufacturers to absorb the extra costs through bulk-order discounts.

## *Making sense of ambiguous or contradictory messages*

In Greek mythology, one of the great tests of leadership was a visit to the Delphic oracle. The oracle was a prophetess of the Temple of Apollo. This temple, at the foot of the steep slope of Mount Parnassus, was considered the center of the universe. When a leader or a warrior went to the oracle, she would descend into the basement of the temple and chew on the leaves of the laurel plant until she went into a trance. Her priests then translated her trance words into what was often highly ambiguous verse.

How the hero or leader interpreted the riddle determined whether he succeeded or failed. So it is with modern leaders. They get information from many sources. Much of it is contradictory, hazy, or ambiguous at best. Modern leaders may hear many messages from a group waiting to be led, including the hostile "Who are you to think you can lead us?" message.

A good leader listens to all the information and then sorts through it. You test contradictory messages by asking for more information in order to find the truth. Martin Puris, the chairman of the advertising agency Ammirati Puris Lintas, calls this concept "piercing the fog," and Lintas believes that a leader's most important job is "the relentless search for the truth."

Often, in order to get at the truth, a leader has to elicit the cooperation of people who don't necessarily want to provide the answers. Working with uncooperative people may require leaders to restrain a natural tendency toward anger and place the need to solve the group's problems ahead of their own personal egos. Leaders use their intelligence to interpret riddles and to come up with the correct answers.

## Ranking the importance of different elements

What happens when you are given all the information you need and all the information is truthful, but the problem itself is breathtakingly complex? Again, a trip back to mythology is in order. In 333 B.C.E., while Alexander the Great was marching through Anatolia — what is today the Asian part of Turkey — he reached the gates of Gordium, the ancient capital of Phrygia. There, he was shown the chariot of the city's founder, Gordius, with the chariot's yoke lashed to a pole of the city's gate by means of an intricate knot with its end hidden. According to local legend, this knot could be untied only by the future conqueror of Asia. Alexander drew his sword and sliced the knot in half. The phrase "cutting the Gordian knot" has come to mean a bold-stroke solution to a complicated problem.

The story of a quick cut to the Gordian knot is entertaining, and although quick thinking is often called for in real crises, bold strokes often end in disaster. A true leader knows how to rapidly sort through the disparate elements of a problem and focus in on the most important component of a complex and interlocking set of facts.

Rather than slice through the Gordian knot, a strong leader often asks for yet more information. When Louis V. Gerstner, Jr., left McKinsey to join American Express as executive vice president of its Travel Related Services (TRS) Division, he already knew a lot about the core of its business — credit cards. At McKinsey, he had spent almost five years consulting with TRS. Yet when he landed at American Express, according to Harvard Business School professor John P. Kotter, he "shocked the people running the card organization by bringing them together within a week of his appointment . . . and then proceeding to question all of the principles by which they conducted their business."

Gerstner used that same procedure when he became president of the TRS Division and later vice chairman of American Express, and again at RJR Nabisco, when he became chairman in 1989, and yet again at IBM, when he became CEO in 1993. Gerstner is insistent that senior management provide him with as much information as possible, and he frequently asks questions much farther down in the ranks of management in order to round out his knowledge of a problem. When Gerstner acts, he is much more likely to be decisive, because he has listened to everything rather than just what was told to him.

# *Finding similarities in apparently different situations*

One of the normal characteristics of intelligence is a talent for analogies. You may remember these exercises from when you were taking the Scholastic Aptitude Test (SAT) in high school. Analogies compare pairs of words, such as black::white as Evil::?. Analogous intelligence in leaders is the ability to draw on prior experience, no matter how tenuous the connection is, to find a similarity that you can use to solve a problem.

You are often a leader in your everyday life, even though you don't realize it. You can draw upon your everyday experiences and use analogies to lend insight into more complicated problems. People call this skill *common sense*. Here is an example of what we mean: If you've planned a wedding and your boss asks you to plan a meeting, draw on the wedding experience to make the meeting successful. If you are asked to head a task force and you have been a Little League coach, remember that the members of your task force are looking to you for the same kind of coaching as your players did. We take up the different roles of leadership in Chapter 4.

# *Drawing distinctions between seemingly similar situations*

You can find differences among situations just as often as you can find similarities, and a good leader learns to recognize when A is not like B and emphasize the differences over what the two have in common. For example, humans and chimpanzees have more than 98 percent of their DNA in common, yet you wouldn't put a chimp in charge of getting a rocket to the moon. Conversely, human beings share more than 99.999 percent of their DNA with each other, yet the most minute differences give us our individuality and act as a yawning chasm between people. The same thing is true of situations: Every situation you encounter is the same, yet different.

As the great engineer and thinker Buckminster Fuller once said, "Unity is plural and, at minimum, is two." Situations are similar to people. You can do the same thing a hundred times, but the moment you begin to treat it as routine, something can change and gum up the works. For example, a physician who has done a thousand heart bypass operations may begin to work on automatic pilot. Maybe on the next chest, the doctor could face a heart that's in reversed position. Failing to recognize the difference could lead to disaster.

An effective leader recognizes that situations rarely repeat themselves exactly, and so will make minor adjustments and not always do whatever was done before, "because it worked so well at the time."

In 1992, Rally's, a small hamburger chain located in the Midwest and the South, began to expand nationally. The company needed a way to emphasize the differences between its generic burger and the generic burgers sold by the two giants. Ed McCabe, the brilliant advertising executive who has created many memorable campaigns, analyzed the fast-food market and concluded that the menus at McDonald's and Burger King had become too complicated and too expensive. In a brilliant series of commercials that drew on the differences between Rally's simple, inexpensive menu and the large chains' complicated, expensive menus, McCabe helped propel Rally's sales from a negligible amount to more than 5 percent of the total burger market. The commercials also forced the two chains into a price war that was ultimately detrimental to Rally's, which could not absorb the losses.

What is important in this area of leadership is not the ultimate consequence, but the ability to find the minute differences that can give you an advantage, even a temporary one.

## Putting concepts together in new ways

Along with analogies, one of the components of intelligence is the ability to synthesize new knowledge by putting together time-tested concepts in new ways. Take, for example, the *80-20 rule*, which says that 20 percent of your customers account for 80 percent of your business. In the 1990s, Mercer Management Consulting used that old idea to help its clients examine their retailing relationships, helping manufacturers realign their marketing channels to make them more efficient and more profitable.

The 80-20 idea is an old one, but when combined with a new idea — channel relationships — it takes on a whole new life. Out of Mercer's take on the 80-20 rule has come the idea of selling into the channels where you sell the most. Many Mercer clients have withdrawn from small mom-and-pop retailers and cut more profitable deals with large "category-killer" retailers, trading per item profit for much larger unit volumes.

Leaders are often expected to synthesize goals. In fact, much of what people who write about leadership call *vision* is really about the synthesis of ideas and information into a new direction. We take up the idea of vision in Part V, "Leadership and Vision: I Had a Dream," where you can gain a better understanding of how to synthesize knowledge into visions.

## Coming up with novel ideas

According to Ecclesiastes, "There is no new thing under the sun," yet sometimes leadership calls for *inspiration,* the novel thinking that enables you to strike off in a new direction, even more than it calls for vision. When you are faced with a situation in which no existing solution will provide you with a clear advantage, you have to invent something entirely new. In 1988, with the Cold War more than 40 years old, "everything that could have been thought of had been thought of and tried," said one German diplomat with regard to the question of German reunification. But remember: Leadership is situational, and situations change.

In 1988, Helmut Kohl, West Germany's Chancellor, recognized that the Soviet Union was in serious danger of riots from food shortages because of a series of harsh winters and the economic hardship caused by Russia's prolonged war with Afghanistan. Kohl proposed a simple solution: He would deliver several hundred million dollars' worth of food, especially meat, to the Russians if they would allow reunification talks with East Germany to proceed without further hindrance. Mikhail Gorbachev, who needed peace in Russia more than he needed East Germany, took the opportunity, and the result was an almost overnight end to nearly 45 years of Soviet control of the eastern half of Germany. Kohl came up with a novel idea, and the world changed.

# *Communicating Effectively*

First and foremost, a leader has to keep the vision in the minds of his or her followers in every conversation, whether in a spoken or unspoken manner. When a leader is speaking as a leader, and not as a friend or confidante, he or she needs to remind people in a simple and straightforward manner and without a lot of additional explanation why they are being asked to turn the vision into reality.

In his book, *Leadership IQ: A Personal Development Process Based on a Scientific Study of a New Generation of Leaders* (John Wiley and Sons), Emmett C. Murphy says that the leaders he has researched have mastered the art of conversation.

> *As we eavesdropped on their conversations with the stakeholders in their organizations — a high-tech marketing manager talking with a recently hired sales associate, a cardiac care nurse conversing with her supervisor, a team of municipal council members discussing economic development with local businesspeople — we saw that they had followed well-crafted scripts in all their communications.*

Murphy doesn't mean literal scripts. Instead, he means that there is a structure to communication between leaders and followers that tends to remain the same even when the circumstances or situation changes. What are the components of communication by leaders?

In other words, a leader has to find a kind of shorthand to remind the group of what the goal is. Often, such shorthand appears in our everyday lives as slogans. The problem with slogans is that they have been overused by advertising, so people tend to distrust them. Consumers may want to be sold on something, but they want to know the difference between a lofty goal and an impetus to purchase.

The responsibility of leadership is to communicate the vision so clearly that no room is left for doubt among those who must execute it. In the Old Testament, in Exodus, God lays out detailed instructions for building the Tabernacle, which are then handed off to Joshua, a 13-year-old boy, to execute. Why someone so young? Because God's instructions are so clear that even a child can understand and fulfill them. That is what we mean by communicating clearly and well.

Leaders must not only explain, but they must also motivate their followers. In ancient Greece, when Aeschines finished speaking, people said, "He spoke well." But after Demosthenes spoke to them, they cried, "Let us march (into battle against Philip of Macedon's army)!" In order to inspire people enthusiastically to do what is necessary to ensure success, a business leader must articulate the very reasons the people have gathered together to form an enterprise. A community leader must do the same thing, and you — no matter what kind of role you play — certainly need to motivate people in your everyday life.

How do you learn to speak to motivate? It all starts with our primary building blocks — eliciting the cooperation of others, listening well, and placing others above yourself. We look at these issues in the following sections.

## Speaking begins with listening

A good speaker almost invariably is someone who can listen to or "read" the mood or tenor of an audience, even when the audience is not communicating verbally. Good speakers can sense nervousness, restlessness, or hostility among a group, and they learn to use the mood of the crowd to their own advantage. Listening also involves asking questions and paying attention to the answers. If the first characteristic of leadership is high intelligence, then that intelligence must be applied. We discuss the relentless search for the truth that a leader goes through when crafting a vision or goals for the group earlier in this chapter. That search is a combination of asking questions, listening to the answers, and then processing the information.

## Eliciting the cooperation of others

Eliciting the cooperation of others is the process of offering something for something. As a song from the 1960s says, "Nothing from nothing leaves nothing. You gotta have something if you want to be with me." Implicit in what a leader does is trading a goal or vision focused on the future for struggle and hard work in the present. The goal has to be real and attainable, and it must fit the needs of the people being led.

# Fixing the problem rather than fixing the blame

You can think of the difference between focusing on goals and focusing on faults in this way: In the developing world of Internet commerce, transactions can be online or off-line. In an *online* transaction, you complete the transaction at the moment you sign off. Buying an airline ticket on the Web, for example, is an online transaction. Your seat has to be locked up by the reservations computer at the time the transaction is completed. But buying a book on the Web is an off-line transaction. The sale looks exactly the same, but no book is instantly pulled from a shelf. Instead, at the end of the day, perhaps hours after you've signed off, your order goes to a warehouse, where it is then pulled and processed.

Solving problems and assigning blame operate the same way. When you find a problem and solve it, you are completing an online transaction because you have not interrupted the flow of events. You are working to keep movement toward the vision going along a smooth trajectory with a minor course adjustment. The determination of who exactly was responsible for the mistake that led to your vision going off course can be handled off-line after the goal has been achieved. Stopping what you're doing to assign blame is one of the most dangerous things a leader can do, because it breaks the flow of events, and controlling the flow is one of the things that a leader needs to do in order to maintain leadership of a group.

For example, when a company is losing money and the rest of its industry is growing by 15 percent a year, it does no good for a CEO to set 20 percent growth as next year's goal. First, the executive has to find out why the company is losing money while its competitors are profiting — that's listening. Then the chief has to set an attainable goal, which may be stopping the hemorrhaging of cash. Then and only then can the company think about moving forward, which becomes a next goal. Even then, the goal cannot be outlandish; it needs to be attainable.

How does a speaker put the needs of others above his or her own? By speaking to the concerns and needs of the person you are talking to rather than your own. You have to acknowledge how hard a person is working toward a shared goal or vision early on, not your own difficulty in leading. You must focus on the group's sacrifices and the importance of the mission, and you have to discover how to refrain from finding fault even while you are looking for the source of the roadblocks to completing the mission. This method sounds contradictory, but it isn't. Blaming people is distracting; finding the fault, correcting it, and moving on is not.

## Milk or buttermilk

To see what can happen when a leader learns confidence, consider Malcolm Forbes. Before Forbes became the editor and publisher of *Forbes Magazine,* he was known, and ridiculed, for his indecisiveness. During Forbes's unsuccessful run for Governor of New Jersey, his opponent said that Forbes was so wishy-washy that he couldn't decide whether to have milk or buttermilk for breakfast. When Forbes took over the magazine his father had founded, it was deeply in the red and needed self-confident leadership. Forbes literally created a persona, a public image of self-confidence — with his motorcycles and ballooning — that helped remake the magazine as "The Capitalist Tool " and made it highly successful. In private, he remained a shy and hesitant speaker all his life, but whenever Malcolm Forbes was in the public eye, he moved with ease and confidence.

# Driving Yourself

The drive to succeed is composed of aggressiveness, self-confidence, and the ability to communicate. All these traits have to be present, balanced, and focused on the problem at hand, or the result can be a disaster. A leader who is only aggressive often substitutes short-term tactical advantage for a longer-term gain, to the company's disadvantage, whereas someone who lacks confidence is likely to reverse a decision or look for another course of action at the first sign of trouble.

Originally, MCI was conceived as a microwave radio system that would allow truckers to communicate with each other while they were on the road. But making the system work required a connection to AT&T's lines, permission that the telephone company refused to give. Almost any other person would have given up in the face of AT&T's clear monopoly power, but William McGowan, a consultant to MCI, insisted that the fledgling company's headquarters be moved to Washington so that he could lobby MCI's case with the Federal Communications Commission (FCC) and Congress. As a result, McGowan thought of MCI less as a phone company and more as "a law firm with an antenna on top." McGowan's drive to succeed not only made MCI successful, but it also completely changed the nature of telephone service in the United States.

# Developing a Sense of Urgency

Generally, business visions are born of a change in the marketplace that suddenly creates an opportunity. What separates a more successful company from a less successful one? The better leader has a sense of urgency about translating the vision into a business (see Chapter 7). A good leader doesn't wait for information, but instead seeks it out. A great leader begins assembling a team and determining what resources are necessary to make the idea a success even while information is still coming in.

## Don't wait

At Chrysler, prior to its merger with Daimler-Benz, the top leadership would meet together for lunch nearly every day. The purpose of the lunch was not to talk about company problems, but rather to shoot the breeze. However, within these informal conversations were often heated discussions about how people were using their cars and what types of vehicles people may want next.

Bob Lutz, then president and vice chairman of Chrysler, says that the give-and-take in these meetings was far more important than any formal market research study because it focused the best and brightest minds in the company on the future without putting anything at stake. "There's a lot you can do informally to move your company forward," says Lutz. "By the time an idea gets to the formal proposal stage, we ought to be able to say yes, because everybody already knows everything they need to know. Once a proposal is formally approved, then we move as rapidly as possible to getting the car into production."

Just because a leader has a sense of urgency does not mean that a good leader like Lutz or Chrysler chairman Bob Eaton relies on hunches or intuition. Some leaders do, but the better leaders depend on systematic planning to guide them. Once a Chrysler car has moved beyond informal discussions and into the formal planning process, the planning process takes over, and every car is planned out in exactly the same way. Systematic planning is also required to start a business. Though businesses may be different, starting all businesses requires most of the same steps — planning, determining needs, and raising or allocating money.

## Form a "kitchen cabinet"

The best way to stay on top of information so that you can maintain your focus on goals and maintain your sense of urgency about reaching them is to form what President Andrew Jackson called a "kitchen cabinet" of advisors. These advisors are people who can not only act as a sounding board for ideas but can also form the nucleus of a team after all the information for making a go-ahead decision is available. This committee is not a clique or an elite palace guard, but a wide-ranging group of people who have ideas and knowledge in diverse areas. You can call upon them for advice and, when necessary, for help in making the connections that will help you reach your goal.

---

## Take your time: Think it over

Intellectual honesty is perhaps the toughest trait for a leader to acquire. If you are at the top and you truly believe Harry Truman's old maxim, "The buck stops here," you may well believe that you have to have all the answers because you have the final say. Not so. A leader is allowed to say "I don't know" and ask for as many options as are needed to arrive at the best answer. After a decision is made and action is set in motion, it is too late for new information, so take the time to be rigorous in your search for the truth and discover how to recognize it when you see or hear it.

---

# Being Honest and Searching for the Truth

Leading well requires that people be honest when they look at information and resist their own biases, even when they think they already know the answer.

Since its founding at the end of the 1960s, Leon Hirsch had been the near dictatorial owner of U.S. Surgical. He had relied almost solely on his own ideas of where the market for surgical staplers was going, but in 1994, faced with a sharp downturn in sales and mounting losses, Hirsch did an uncharacteristic thing. He went to his employees and asked them for ideas on how to fix the company. He asked each section head to come up with ways to save money, and he formed a team of senior executives to explore new avenues for the company. The result was a remarkable turnaround in sales and profitability. Hirsch could not have accomplished his turnaround without being intellectually honest to an extreme (in this case, admitting that he didn't have all the answers) and without surrendering his own long-held beliefs about the future of U.S. Surgical.

# Displaying Good Judgment

Leaders are generally pretty responsible people. One of the things that people look for in a leader is his or her willingness to accept responsibility from early on, and people tend to judge potential leaders by how well they meet their responsibilities. Continuing to rise as a leader means that you continually exercise prudent judgment and don't allow yourself to fall into extreme situations. It means that you always keep the needs of the group in mind and that you don't commit the group to a potentially disastrous course of action. That's what we meant before, when we talked about sizing your vision to the capabilities of the group. If you gamble everything, you risk losing everything. But if you gamble a little and lose a little, you can figure out what you've done wrong and try again.

Good judgment goes out the window only in the most dire life-and-death circumstances when failing to take a chance may result in the demise of the group. As a leader, even then you must communicate the options available to the group and persuade them that gambling everything is in their best interests.

# Being Dependable and Consistent

Woody Allen once opined, "Ninety percent of success is simply showing up." He meant that in order to reach a goal, you have to attack it consistently. A leader cannot be mercurial, whimsical, or wishy-washy. After a vision or goal has been selected and clearly articulated, you do not serve the needs of the group by altering course. Such indecision leads only to confusion and consternation among your followers.

Dependability is itself a form of good judgment. Of course, because a leader is dependable doesn't mean that a leader needs to be stubborn. Circumstances change constantly, and today's decision, made with the best information available, can mean tomorrow's disaster if external events change significantly. But consistency means that you follow the rules of leadership in a regular way. You are always searching for the truth, always listening, always working on the things necessary to keep your group cooperating toward its goal. You do not withdraw support from people on whom you depend.

# Creating an Atmosphere of Trust

Consistency and dependability, especially when they accompany the basic requirements of leadership, breed trust among followers. If you know that the leader of your group is always going to listen to what you have to say — he or she may not follow your advice but you know you'll get a full and fair hearing — and that your leader is always going to find a way to elicit your cooperation, you are far more likely to trust that person than someone who doesn't communicate this way.

## Trust is sacred

How does a leader create an atmosphere of trust? Perhaps the most important way is to learn how to keep confidences. There is a saying that, if you are told something, that isn't really meant to be kept secret, you have to learn to keep conversations as privileged information unless you are told otherwise. In intelligence agencies, the rigid classification system is based upon a "need to know."

Conversely, you also have to learn how to disseminate information in a way that keeps all your followers completely in the loop. At Colgate-Palmolive, CEO Reuben Mark knows that it is impossible to personally tell all of his thousands of employees what the company is planning to do next, so he prepares meticulously detailed briefings for key executives. He gives them briefing materials so that they can brief the next level of executives down, and so on, until everybody in the company who may be affected by a decision has been told. Employees are told exactly what they need to know by the leader above them, and no communication is missed. Colgate uses that system successfully to launch its products on a worldwide basis.

As parents are fond of telling their children, trust is earned. However, as parents often find out — to their chagrin — trust is a two-way street. The parents' actions must be consistent if a developing child is going to learn to trust his or her parents. A parent who constantly changes the rules regarding what is expected and what rewards and punishments are meted out is a parent who is discouraging a child's trust. Conversely, children have to turn the lessons their parents teach them into instinctive behavior before a parent can learn to fully trust the child and extend privileges and responsibilities.

## *Encouraging a Learning Environment*

Perhaps the most important thing that a leader can do to ensure that a goal or vision is achieved over a long term is to promote group learning. *Group learning* is one of those terms that management consultants like to throw around, but it really means that as whole group gets smarter, the leader makes better decisions. When a leader makes the effort to keep everyone informed, to communicate new information rather than hoard it — in other words, when the leader places the needs of the group above his or her own — the entire group benefits in ways that cannot be calculated. In turn, the leader benefits, because with better information, members of the group are far more likely to come up with new ideas for solving problems that were previously thought to be intractable.

## Share information

Group learning means that the leader has to learn from the group as well as being a teacher. Because leaders often respond to the needs of multiple groups, the information the leader learns from one group can often be conveyed to another, which improves the knowledge of all. The leader becomes a conduit for information so that all groups understand a problem from the same perspective. In order for this kind of give-and-take to happen, the leader must be a fast learner who is able to absorb new lessons and then apply them in the service of reaching a goal.

# Looking for Common Ground — The "Type O" Personality

A curious thing about good leaders is that they are generally likable. They know how to get along with people — not just the people who follow them or admire them, but people who have every reason to despise them. They do not rise to the bait and fight with their enemies; rather, they seek to find common ground with their foes, knowing that a well-considered compromise can benefit both sides.

A poor leader will push opponents until they are forced to respond, often with disastrous consequences to both the person doing the pushing and the group they are leading. Saddam Hussein is a perfect example of a leader who has pushed too far too many times. Though Saddam has not been dislodged, he has caused the Iraqi people untold suffering while achieving little of benefit.

At times, of course, a leader cannot get along with everyone. When you make the judgment that someone in the group is seriously impairing the group's ability to move forward, you need to take corrective action, which may mean putting the needs of the group above the process of cooperation. You may also have to lead your group into battle for its survival if your enemies will not allow you to find a middle ground. But in non-war situations, you can usually find a field for compromise and cooperation.

## Learn to like people

How do you find common ground with anyone? You can start by taking Will Rogers' maxim "I never met a man I didn't like" to heart. Liking people makes listening to what they have to say possible. When you begin to really listen, you'll see that with the exception of dealing with madmen, a grain of reason and legitimacy is evident in nearly any position.

Your job as a leader is to offer a point of retreat or an out for your opponent at the place where his or her position is least reasonable. If an opponent attacks your leadership, you are pulled away from reaching the goal of the group. You descend into a fight to maintain your leadership, and you wind up sacrificing the group's needs to your own.

# Chapter 4

# Which Hat Do I Wear? The Roles That Leaders Play

● ● ● ● ● ● ● ● ● ● ● ● ● ● ● ● ● ● ● ● ● ● ● ● ● ● ● ● ● ● ● ● ● ● ● ● ● ● ● ● ● ● ● ●

## *In This Chapter*

▶ Understanding how leaders take on many different roles

▶ Becoming a truth-seeker

▶ Blazing trails as a direction-setter

▶ Being a catalyst for change

▶ Talking it up as a spokesperson

▶ Rallying the troops as coach/team builder

● ● ● ● ● ● ● ● ● ● ● ● ● ● ● ● ● ● ● ● ● ● ● ● ● ● ● ● ● ● ● ● ● ● ● ● ● ● ● ● ● ● ● ●

*He wears his faith but as the fashion of his hat.*
—William Shakespeare

**I**n his book, *Visionary Leadership* (Jossey-Bass), Burt Nanus says that a leader may have to assume various roles to turn a vision into reality. In the course of achieving a goal, small problems are likely to get in the way, and a good leader needs to be able to respond to each problem appropriately. Problems may be internal or external; the group may lose its way, or it may race toward its goal without heeding changes going on outside of the group. Sometimes the leader needs to assume a role solely for the purpose of getting the maximum amount of cooperation from a group. Other times, a leader needs so much to place the needs of the group above his or her own that he or she appears to be a martyr for the group.

We're not saying that a leader needs to have multiple-personality disorder — nothing could be farther from the truth. Leaders always need to be well-grounded in reality and true to their own personalities. But most leaders also have the ability to adopt a new persona that gives the group the push it needs to move forward, playing the character the way an actor plays a role. You can think of adopting this persona as putting on a different hat that allows you to become a different person, doing a kind of leadership improvisational act.

A leader can play probably an infinite number of roles, but we have defined five roles that we believe are critical to effective leadership. At one time or another, a good leader will be all these things. Some leaders will be more of one than another. But you cannot be a good leader if you don't play some of these roles at least part of the time. In this chapter we show you each role in some detail so that you can get an idea what the role involves and how the basic leadership skills come into play.

# Bareheaded before God: The Truth-Seeker

A leader is like the head of a pilgrimage on a journey of discovery. As the head of the pilgrimage, the leader needs to know where the group is going and must have a general sense of how to get there. But just like the pioneers setting out into the American wilderness, much of the way is labeled Terra Incognito — unknown territory. Like U.S. history's Lewis and Clark exploring for the Northwest Passage, a leader is constantly trading for information to illuminate the road ahead. Because much of the information is likely to come from unreliable sources, the good leader must be a diviner of the truth and have the ability to test the information that is given.

## Triangulating information

When journalists receive a piece of information, they attempt to verify it. Journalists call this verification process *triangulation,* a name borrowed from airplane pilots, who use it to mean the process of locating a radio beacon. Journalists use triangulation to corroborate the information from at least two, but preferably three, independent sources. An independent source is a source that does not know the first person who gave you the information. For example, if someone tells a journalist that he has evidence of a crime, the journalist listens to the allegation. But before the story ever finds its way into print, a diligent, responsible journalist looks for a piece of information that proves a crime may actually have been committed. This supporting information could come from a victim or (if the crime is an illegal environmental discharge) could be the results of water samples that the journalist had drawn and had tested.

## Gathering intelligence

Good leaders, like good journalists, need to accurately judge the worthiness of their sources. An effective method for evaluating information is the standard model that intelligence agencies use for evaluating both information and the source from which information comes. The intelligence agencies assign a letter grade to the source and a number grade to the value of the information. Table 4-1 shows what the model looks like.

| Table 4-1 | | Information Indicator | |
|---|---|---|---|
| Source's Rating | Meaning | Information's Number Grade | Value |
| A | Always reliable | 1 | Stands without further corroboration |
| B | Highly reliable | 2 | Stands with minimum confirmation |
| C | Reliable | 3 | Stands with some confirmation — requires additional research |
| D | Usually reliable | 4 | Requires re-reporting |
| E | Unreliable | 5 | Does not stand after re-reporting |

Effective leaders seek the truth and adjust their sights according to what they learn. These leaders know to listen to the meanings of words rather than simply to the words themselves, and to extract additional information from between the lines.

# Pith Helmet: The Direction-Setter

After you have the information you need to proceed along a route, you need to make certain that the destination you already have in mind is worth going to. We call that destination a vision or a goal. The leader's job is to select and articulate the target in the future toward which the organization should direct its energies. Yitzhak Rabin's decision to make peace with the Palestine Liberation Organization in 1993 after decades of Arab-Israeli strife is one example of how a vision can set an entire nation on an entirely new course. In business, Lee Iacocca's decision to build the Chrysler minivan is a powerful example of how the selection of a vision can change the course of a company's destiny.

To be a good direction setter you must be able to set a course toward a destination that others will recognize as representing real progress for the organization. Progress may mean

- ✔ Taking a clear step ahead in effectiveness or efficiency.
- ✔ Adding the ability to serve a new set of customers.
- ✔ Gaining recognition as the leader in a new technology or product area.

If you are successful as a direction setter, you will have established a vision so compelling that everyone in the organization will want to help make the vision a reality.

# Pulled-Down Fedora: The Agent from C.H.A.N.G.E.

For a leader to merely articulate a vision isn't enough. A good leader also is responsible for being the catalyst in making changes in an organization's internal environment. The changes make it possible for the organization to achieve its vision or reach its goals. Being an agent of change can mean taking on the responsibility for making adjustments in personnel, resources, or facilities to make the vision achievable. Often, being a change agent is the least glamorous part of being a leader because the efforts are trench work that has no clear payoff.

Articulating a goal is easy, but the process of achieving it is tough work for a leader. Your challenges can vary: forming a new team, pushing through a budgetary increase to buy new software that will raise the company's productivity, or persuading your firm to open a new office or marketing channel. The goal can be accomplished only if you can link the proposed change to an end benefit.

To illustrate how making the link between an investment — in this case money — and end is beneficial, consider a recent IBM television commercial about electronic commerce. In it, a senior manager asks a subordinate what he is going to tell the board about the company's Internet investment. The employee sits in nervous silence and then blurts out, "Tell them that each dollar we spend will return two dollars by the end of the year." The boss smiles because his employee has demonstrated a linkage between a current decision and a future goal — increased profitability. With that linkage, the manager knows he can sell his board.

ANECDOTE

## Leading with someone else's vision

Jack Maple, a New York City Transit Police lieutenant, had a vision: Changes in the deployment of police around the city — *active policing,* he called it — could make a substantial dent in the crime rate. Maple's idea was simple. A study of the arrests made on buses and subways showed him that people who were being arrested for simple crimes such as fare jumping were often found to have outstanding arrest warrants against them. These people often had committed other, more serious crimes, and were wanted by the authorities for arrest and trial.

Maple made a detailed proposal to then-Chief of Transit William Bratton and persuaded Bratton that the system could work if given a chance. With the assent of New York's new mayor, Rudolph Giuliani, Bratton (who by then was New York City Police Commissioner)

promoted Maple to deputy commissioner. Bratton allowed Maple to change the nature of the crimes people were arrested for — an increase in arrests for so-called "quality of life crimes" such as fare jumping and running red lights — and then carefully searching the records to determine whether those arrested had outstanding warrants.

The result was a startling drop in New York's crime rate, which allowed Mayor Giuliani to do something that no New York City mayor had been able to do in more than 30 years — make good on a promise to reduce crime.

In this example, the *vision* belonged to Maple, but the *leadership* belonged to the mayor and the police chief.

# *A Talking Hat: The Spokesperson*

Everybody thinks of Lee Iacocca as the spokesman for Chrysler, with his tough talking, "If you can find a better car, buy it." But being a talking hat isn't being a leader, and a dare isn't a vision. What made Iacocca a respected leader was that he forced Chrysler to do the hard work of rebuilding itself.

Being a spokesperson is often a necessary role for a leader of a new enterprise. Consider Steve Jobs, one of the cofounders of Apple. Jobs had the vision of a personal computer that everyone, even without any knowledge of computers, would be able to use to improve their work performance. Both internally, to his team, and externally, to the public, Jobs tirelessly promoted the vision of the personal computer, keeping his team focused when most people thought that creating such a device would be impossible.

Jobs wasn't talking through his hat. He had thought through the idea of the personal computer at every level, so he could sell the idea to anyone he needed to speak with. Jobs needed to persuade venture capitalists, as well as ranks of engineers, programmers, and chip designers who actually built the first machines. All these people had to be *evangelized (*to use a term common at Apple) to the belief that they could actually achieve Jobs's vision and that the effort was worthwhile.

How does a leader motivate people who are skeptical? Part of the task involves making the impossible seem merely difficult, and the very difficult seem to be just another day's work. This approach doesn't mean that a leader should lie or misstate the difficulty of achieving a goal. Rather, a good leader:

✔ Is both frank and honest in describing the difficulties, but optimistic in his or her faith in the team's ability to overcome obstacles to reach the goal.

✔ Usually has a well-thought-through plan for moving from a vision to an implemented goal, and an unshakable determination to reach the desired goal.

# Baseball Cap and Whistle: The Coach/Teambuilder

Because every team has its problems maintaining focus in the face of internal conflicts and external pressures — especially the competitive pressures of the marketplace — a good leader needs to take on yet one more role to help the team along — the role of coach.

The most successful coaches, it is often said, live their jobs. George Siefert, who was the coach of the San Francisco 49ers and the winningest coach in NFL history, spent countless hours in the film room, watching tape of upcoming opponents, looking for any edge that he could turn into a winning play for the team. By game time, Siefert had reduced his entire game plan to a small series of set plays, which he unleashed on the opposition, as much in the hopes of demoralizing them as of scoring. Each play exploited a specific weakness and made the point that the 49ers could score at will.

To be an effective coach, you have to let your team know where you stand, what the vision means to you, and what you will do to make it happen. You must also be committed to the success of everyone in the organization, respecting them, helping them learn and grow, and teaching them how to improve constantly their ability to achieve the vision.

# Living the vision

Not only is it necessary for great leaders to live their jobs, it is also often necessary for them to "live the vision," serving as the living embodiment of what an enterprise's goals are and as an example for those whose efforts are necessary to get the job done.

Chief executive officer Tom Chappell and his wife Kate, who run Tom's of Maine, are a good example of living the vision. They test their personal-care products on themselves and their children long before they let other people test them. Before Tom's of Maine products are introduced to the public, successive levels of employees have tested the products, starting with Tom himself. Only when they are fully approved by all employees are the products marketed.

Martin Luther King, Jr, was another effective leader who lived his vision. It wasn't enough for King to tell other people to resist. He took part in numerous civil rights demonstrations and spent countless nights in Southern jails, where he ran the personal risk of being murdered in his cell or lynched by an angry mob just outside. King believed that he had to be a personal witness for civil rights, and that he could not ask anyone to take any risk that he wouldn't take for himself.

# Part II
## Leadership Is a Process

**The 5th Wave**  By Rich Tennant

"Great! The scarecrow and I get coffee makers, the Lion gets an Instamatic camera and Tin Man gets RayBan sun glasses. Next time we get in there, let me do the talking!"

# In this part . . .

Preparation is the key to leadership, and before you can begin to lead, you have to ask yourself a few critical questions. Do you have the skills necessary to be a successful leader? Do you know what you're expected to do? Do you really know the people you're supposed to be leading, and what they want? Is their mission different from the people who put you in charge? In this part, we cover the steps to preparation that will set you apart from average leaders and help you become more effective at accepting a leadership role.

# Chapter 5

# Take the Lead? Me?

• • • • • • • • • • • • • • • • • • • • • • • • • • • • • • • • • • • • • • • • • •

• • • • • • • • • • • • • • • • • • • • • • • • • • • • • • • • • • • • • • • • • •

*Jobs should be selected, not accepted.*
—Lester Korn

**Y**ou're a middle manager sitting in your office working away at a project when the telephone rings. The chief executive of the company wants to see you immediately. You know that you haven't embezzled from the company and that everything in your department is working well. So you feel just a little flutter of nervous energy and expectation as you stop in the bathroom to smooth your clothes, check your hair, and make sure you don't have oregano from your lunchtime pizza stuck between your teeth. Then you head upstairs to the corner office.

The chief executive greets you with a warm handshake. Also at the meeting is the manager of another division. After exchanging pleasantries, your CEO gets right to the point: The division manager is taking another post within the company, and you're being promoted over your boss into a new, more senior position. What do you say? How do you react? What questions do you ask? Should you even take the promotion?

In this chapter, we give you the tools to answer such questions and determine whether you and your skills are a good match for a leadership position, and whether accepting a particular position will help you.

# *Now What Do I Do?*

Many managers expect to be promoted, but few are prepared for what's expected of them after they're in a position of real leadership. Right behind the elation that accompanies a promotion, the feeling of well-being that goes along with a raise, and the satisfaction of receiving additional perks and benefits often comes a sense of unease. What exactly is expected from you in your new position, and is it one in which you can make a genuine contribution?

Chances are that when you're offered a promotion, you won't turn it down. It is the rare executive, says top executive recruiter Lester Korn, who rejects a promotion in the hope that something better will come along. But, Korn notes, you sometimes want to take a promotion that no one else will because it provides an unusual opportunity to show off your talents and skills.

When you're promoted to a position of senior responsibility, either on the job or outside work, how do you deal with this new situation in the most effective way? You have to ask yourself three questions:

- ✔ Why did they pick me?
- ✔ What is my mission?
- ✔ Who are the people I'm supposed to be leading?

The following sections explain these questions in detail.

# *Why Did They Pick Me?*

Retreat into your office and close the door while you read this section or pick a quiet place in your house, because understanding why your superiors chose you to lead is vital to planning your course of action. The possibility that your selection to a leadership position isn't necessarily a reflection of total trust in your abilities to get the job done may deflate your ego, but assuming your new position with your eyes open can help you assess your situation realistically.

Your selection for a leadership position comes for one of three reasons:

- ✔ Your superiors expect you to succeed.
- ✔ Your superiors expect you to fail. (They're testing you.)
- ✔ Your superiors picked you by default.

These reasons correspond nicely with situational leadership, transitional leadership, and hierarchical leadership (we explain these in detail in Chapter 2). In the case of a promotion to leadership, we add you to the equation:

- ✔ **Situational Leadership:** You're the right person in the right circumstances at the right time. They expect you to succeed.

- ✔ **Transitional Leadership:** You're the right person in the right circumstances at the wrong time. They expect you to fail.

- ✔ **Hierarchical Leadership:** You're the right person in the wrong circumstances at the right time. You are there by default.

All prospective leaders want to believe themselves to be situational leaders, and management textbooks overflow with examples of chief executives who made their careers by being in place when good things were about to happen. Certainly, most companies expect that the leaders they choose are the right people for the circumstances and the time: Nobody enjoys failure. But you have to consider the possibility that you may be a bad fit for the job, or that the new job may be a bad fit for you.

> *A company controls the job. You control your career.*
> —Lester Korn

## Assessing your situation

One of the central components of leadership is listening, so the first thing to do is listen to what you're being told about the position. You need to gather information about the responsibilities your superiors are asking you to assume.

> *Leaders, especially chief executives, are calculated risk takers. They get ahead by knowing when to say yes, and they stay ahead by knowing when to say no.*
> —Quinn Kroll, chief executive of Pull Technologies, Inc.

If you're accepting a leadership position, the first thing you need is information, and lots of it. Long before you meet your team, you need to make a quick but detailed examination of the group you're expected to lead. The questions to ask are these:

✔ **What has the group's past performance been?** In American corporations, senior managers are often promoted every two or three years, and each new leader brings his or her own goals to the group. Often, a manager may move on before the group reaches a stated goal. When he or she is promoted or leaves, you have to ask, "Does the goal the group is working toward have the approval of the most senior current management?"

✔ **Does management care about my group?** Finding out whether the group's goals have remained constant or are constantly changing gives you a pretty good idea of where the group stands in the eyes of senior management. If each successive manager was given leeway to pick his or her own goals, that indicates that management probably doesn't know what to do with the department. In this situation, you're not exactly expected to fail, but there isn't much commitment to your success, either.

✔ **Has the group's success or failure been short term or long term?** Because managers move around so much, it's easy for them to evade blame for long-term failure and accept the accolades for short-term success. Have the division's accomplishments matched the accomplishments of the people who have been promoted out of it, or is the department seen mainly as a training ground?

✔ **Have there been many personnel changes in the team or is it stable?** This question is another way of asking about the group's knowledge base. Frequent personnel changes prohibit any kind of collective group memory, which not only wastes time, but can force mistakes. Is there anyone in the group — in any position — with enough institutional memory for you to rely upon in a pinch?

✔ **What are the group's goals?** Is there a pre-existing vision that you are being asked to make good on, or are you being asked to supply a new vision to the group? If you are new to leadership, taking on the responsibility of supplying a vision makes your task more difficult.

✔ **How does the group compare to similar groups in its ability to command resources?** You're going to be competing for resources when you become a leader. If you're taking over a company division, you compete with other division heads for personnel, resources, and attention. If you're running a charitable organization, you compete with other charitable organizations for money and people willing to commit to your cause. You have to make a sober assessment of your group's ability to capture the resources it needs to achieve its goals.

✔ **What is the commitment of the larger organization to the group?** Ultimately, how strongly and definitively does your group fit into the organization's plans for the future? If you are expected to succeed, the expectation and commitment may be high. But if you are getting your new position by default, or because nobody expects much from you, the organization may not make much of a commitment to you in your new position.

## Being ignored isn't necessarily bad

When Bob Lutz first came to Chrysler, hired away from Ford by Lee Iacocca, he didn't have any formal responsibilities. Ultimately, he was given charge of a newly formed "platform team," which would have complete responsibility for designing, engineering, and budgeting a new car, and was told that he could have anybody he wanted from any of the divisions. In reality, division managers at Chrysler allowed Lutz to pick only the people they regarded as castoffs.

Instead of being defeated by the situation, Lutz turned his group into a kind of "skunk works," a car designing and building organization that was out of the mainstream of Chrysler's traditional design ethos and was free to develop what they thought would succeed, with few marketing constraints. The cars they came up with became Chrysler's big sedans. The success of the skunk works platform approach was so evident that it spread throughout the company, and Lutz was made president of Chrysler.

## Doing a personal inventory

Presumably, if you are being selected for a leadership role, whoever does the selecting is impressed by some component of your character or work history. Try to draw out this information during your conversation with senior management about the new assignment. The answer to a question like "What qualities do you think are most important for managing this group?" can tell you both why you were selected and what's expected of you. Your seniors owe it to you to tell you the problems and pitfalls that may arise. However, there is no such thing as a perfectly honest person, so you're always at risk of being blindsided by some bit of information you weren't privy to.

Before you accept a new position, match your skills against the job. What areas are you good in and where are you weak? Are your skills practical or are they based on using your intellectual abilities?

What goes into your personal inventory? First, you have to rate yourself on the three main leadership skills: the ability to elicit cooperation, the ability to listen, and the ability to place others above yourself. No one is equally good at all three. Rate yourself on a 1 to 5 basis for each, with 1 being the lowest and 5 being the highest. You are looking for your weaknesses as well as your strengths, so if you are truthful and you rate low on your ability to place others above yourself, for example, then you will have to manage through a buffer, someone who can counsel you to go gently on team members who don't measure up to your high standards.

More than likely, on a scale of 0 to 15, your total score is about ten, with outstanding skills in at least one leadership component, and better than average skills in the other two. If you score above 10, you have strong potential as a leader. Scoring below ten indicates that you still have a way to go.

If you rate low on

- ✔ **Listening,** work to develop a more organized system for extracting information by having your group make regular presentations to you, in writing and orally. You should have people report to you on the status of the group's mission, and how well it's on target towards achieving its goals.

- ✔ **Eliciting cooperation,** you probably got where you are by prodigious personal effort, but you may not be able to go much farther. Trying to make all decisions yourself just bogs you down and may lead to anything from the resentment of your subordinates to loss of your job. Work to correct this by picking a small task and surrendering control of it to a subordinate. After you see that the task can be done without failure, pick something else, and keep enlarging the scope until you reach a level you are comfortable with.

- ✔ **Putting others' needs above your own, keep this in mind:** In some religions, the head priest will wash the feet of his acolytes as a symbol of humility. That may be a bit much, but you can do lots of little things as a leader to show that you are at least symbolically willing to put the needs of the group above your own. Bringing the morning donuts, or making coffee for the meeting instead of asking your secretary to do it, are examples of symbolic humility. Forming a committee to review personnel practices and figuring out better ways to compensate people for their work — with comp time, extra vacations, bonuses, and so on — is another.

### Assess your functional skills

After you know where you stand on leadership skills, use your personal inventory to assess functional skills. For example, when Philip Smith was president and CEO of General Foods, he willingly told people that he wasn't good at details. "I knew this about myself a long time ago," he said. "In business school I took a lot of math and accounting, and it was nearly the death of me. The whole early part of my career was spent fighting to make sure I didn't screw up the details, and doing things over and over again to make sure I did them right." When Smith was first made a brand manager and given his first leadership responsibility, he traded one of his assistant brand managers for a statistical clerk, and let somebody else on his team worry about the details. By finding a way to compensate for this leadership deficiency, he was able to accept a promotion to chief financial officer of the company, despite his weak math background.

Just as you rated your leadership skills, rate your functional skills with an eye toward your weaknesses as well as your strengths. As you put together what is, in fact, a personal *depth chart* of the same type that a football coach uses to man his team, you will be putting together the nucleus of a template for forming your own team after you assume your new role. (A depth chart is a handy tool that rates each player on the team on some scale — say one to five — that tells the coach where the strengths and weaknesses lie on the team.) How so? A smart leader fills a team with individuals who are strong where the leader is weak, and delegates responsibility to those people.

### Rate yourself on vision, creativity, and goal-setting

If you ask senior management the right questions about your new position, you ought to get a pretty good idea of their expectations for you in this role. Can you deliver? Can you come up with the new ideas that are required to make your position a success? Well, what have you done in the past that counts as creative, or visionary, or that showed an ability to reach a goal? Whatever it was that management saw in you, you have to learn to see also, and then magnify that quality. So, if you came up with a suggestion to streamline the operations of your last team, start by looking for ways to streamline your new group. If you had a great idea for boosting sales, see if something like it works in your new position.

*Remember:* A new idea doesn't have to be unique. It just has to be something that works.

William Smithburg, former chairman of Quaker Oats, tells the story of a brand manager responsible for Cap'n Crunch cereal who used a telephone promotion to boost sales. After he moved up to a higher position, the next three brand managers failed to use the promotion because they thought that duplicating their predecessor showed a lack of imagination. As a consequence, the brand began to erode until finally, a fourth brand manager was promoted into the job. That manager used the telephone promotion again, but in a completely different way, restoring the brand to its former competitive position. The lesson: Don't worry about being original. Being effective is more important.

# What Is My Mission?

A *mission* is the plan of action for reaching a goal. It sums up the tasks at hand and their expected outcomes. There are two components to your personal mission: The first involves your job; the second, your career. Basically, you can break it down to the following questions:

✔ **What am I expected to accomplish?** If you want to be well thought of in your new position, you have to do the task you've been assigned, whether it's taking a hill in combat, meeting a sales target as a brand manager, boosting your division's profitability, finding new markets for your company, or turning out happy, satisfied players (and parents) as a Little League coach. If you inherit a demoralized group, or one whose skill levels are low, it may be enough to turn the group around and bring them up to a standard equal to other groups.

✔ **What can I accomplish that is unexpected?** You need to constantly think about what *more* you can do, how you can go beyond the expected. During World War II, General George S. Patton was given control of the center of the Allied Forces in their push against Germany. Instead of moving in lockstep with the rest of the armies, Patton pushed his troops — who were no different from other troops in terms of fighting experience — harder and faster into German territory, thereby changing the shape of the battlefield, and preventing Russia from occupying even larger parts of Germany after the war. By exceeding expectations and doing the unexpected, Patton not only shortened the war in Europe, he affected the peace settlement afterward.

Anything unexpected that moves your group well beyond the minimums attracts attention. And because success follows success, it also attracts resources and talented new members to your team. Think of it this way: As a leader, your mission is to make your group a winner, not just a contender.

# Who Are These People I'm Supposed to Be Leading?

In American work life, most leadership situations are not organic. Before you say yes to a new leadership role, it's helpful to meet the group you're expected to lead, or at least some of its key players. At a minimum, try to meet with the heads of all the departments reporting to you: If you're a new brand manager, meet all the assistant brand managers and the marketing people. If you're a rookie Little League coach, meet the assistant coaches who are still with the team as well as your players.

What do you want to accomplish in this initial meeting?

✔ Tell your assistants that you're up to (and up for) the responsibility of leading them.

✔ Ask for their cooperation.

✔ Listen to what they have to say.

✔ Promise to put the group's needs above your own.

Meeting with people before you actually accept the leadership mantle gives you a head start in recognizing trouble areas, and identifying your probable allies and enemies (for more on this, see Chapter 28). This first meeting also gives you the opportunity to assess the team's style, and to glean critical information that may not have been supplied when you were offered your new position.

If your promotion is to a lower- or mid-level position, you may simply be told when and where to show up to assume your new duties. In cases in which you don't have much time to prepare or to meet the people you'll be leading, you have to manage your own expectations. You may be very excited by the prospect of leading, but you have to "hold back" and allow situations to develop. You want to communicate enthusiasm, to be sure, but you don't want to be engulfed by the needs of your new group.

Above all, go into the situation with your eyes open. Use these questions to do your own evaluation of the job:

- ✔ **Does this new promotion fit in with your career plans?** If you've had three assignments in marketing and your new promotion is another marketing job, do you want the position, or do you want to round out your experience with a tour in finance or strategic planning? If you want to get out of your rut, find out whether you can turn down the new job without penalty or perhaps win a promise of a rotation to a different area following this assignment. If you can't negotiate a concession, it's probably time to look elsewhere.

- ✔ **Does the new promotion place you in a hostile work environment?** Will your new team react to you as a leader, or will they look at you as an obstacle to overcome? Issues related to race, religion, nationality, and gender can act as a barrier to leadership. You have the right to expect a fair chance to succeed, except in a situation where it's understood that your promotion is the (hopefully) short-term solution to a company emergency.

- ✔ **Does the new promotion have potential job satisfaction?** During the information-gathering process, have you found an area where you believe you can excel? If not, take another look before concluding that the opportunity just isn't there. If you're expected to do nothing more than mark time, maybe it's time to say no and look elsewhere.

# Chapter 6

# The Missions of the Leader

> *He had decided to live forever or die in the attempt, and his only mission each time he went up was to come down alive.*
>
> —Joseph Heller

*A* mission answers two questions:

✔ What am I expected to accomplish?

✔ What can I accomplish that is not expected?

The first question deals with clarifying goals or objectives. Often, when you are given a mission, there seems to be an obvious goal, but the real goal or objective remains hidden underneath. That's because *mission* combines an objective or a goal with the reason for going there. Because people are often unclear about their reasons, the mission becomes unclear as well. Clarifying a mission, either by setting a strategy or by finding out why a particular objective was chosen, helps you meet the expectations of your superiors. In addition, having a clear sense of your mission also opens up the possibility of accomplishing something that is unexpected.

In this chapter, we take up the first question — "What am I expected to accomplish?" — in much greater detail. If you've been doing the listening and information seeking that good leaders do and you are now about to take over a team, you have to know what is expected of you.

# Defining Missions and Goals

*A mission* is, in effect, the battle plan for accomplishing a goal. People work toward a goal when their lives or livelihoods depend upon it, but they never reach their goal unless they have an understanding of how to get there.

A mission is a statement of what you're trying to accomplish as you struggle toward your goal, and it goes beyond the goal itself. Not only is a mission what you have to do to get to your goal, but it also encapsulates the reasons that the goal is worthwhile. A true leader makes the mission the greatest single thing in his or her life and is someone who says, "I will make this my priority. I will commit myself to put my energy and my time into making this project a success."

Often, goals are misstated so that the mission isn't obvious. *We want you to raise sales by 15 percent a year, and increase profitability by 10 percent* sounds like a pretty clear mission; but in fact, it isn't. The numbers are *goals* to be reached, but the *mission* hasn't been defined. The preceding goal statement also doesn't take into account the possibility that you may want to do something completely different, such as create a new product or acquire a company that will boost your sales. A misstated goal not only impedes your ability to define the mission, but also reduces your ability to be creative and daring.

The definition of the mission is different depending upon your position in an organization:

- ✔ **The leadership perspective:** From a leader's perspective, vision comes first. *We want to become the number-one widget seller.* From that vision, the leader defines the goals: *In order to make the vision into a reality, we have to overtake Acme, which enjoys a 25 percent share of the market and gets 50 percent more for its widgets than we do.* Finally, comes the mission: *If we're going to overtake Acme, we have to make a better widget, which will sell better, get better price appreciation in the marketplace, and allow us to achieve our vision and goal.*

- ✔ **The management perspective:** Management typically works from a goal outward. *We want to overtake Acme in the sales of widgets* is a goal. To achieve this goal, management sets a mission to achieve a 15 percent sales increase and a 10 percent rise in profits over the next year. From management's perspective, if you're successful in your mission, then the goal can be attained.

Labor-management relations have traditionally been poor in the United States partly because workers have participated very little in goal-setting and defining the mission of the company. Conversely, entrepreneurial firms work so well because a close relationship exists between the leader, the group being led, the mission, and the ultimate goals of the group.

When people speak about "a sense of mission," what they mean is the ability to formulate a plan toward a goal as well as explain the reasons for an unwavering commitment to reach that goal, even when tactics and plans change. A football coach's mission is to win the game. He may pull his quarterback, change plays at halftime, or substitute players, but he won't throw in the towel when his team is severely behind at the end of the third quarter. His mission is to find a way to win, no matter how adverse the circumstances. And if he loses, then his fallback goal is to find a way to win the following week, in order to finish high enough in the standings to make the playoffs.

Because most leaders don't have their missions as clearly defined as a football coach does, we decided to break down the different types of missions into three basic categories. Whether you are in charge of a company unit, running a church fund-raiser, or managing a kid's soccer team, your mission fits into one of three categories — chief strategist, chief marketing officer, or savior — and calls forth different roles from you as a leader.

# Chief Strategist

The chief strategist is the clearest and most conventional mission-setting role. Your goals are crystal clear and well-articulated, and your responsibilities involve careful planning that takes into account all possible hindrances and missteps.

## Searching for the facts

At Chrysler Corporation, as at many other companies, a formal executive planning process takes place every five years. The senior management has an off-site retreat for about one week at which they create a list of categories — sales, marketing, manufacturing, quality, dealer relations, design, external demand, demographics, and so on — that explain the reasons why people purchase cars.

The senior management then discusses the factors in each category that Chrysler can control and the factors that are beyond its control. For example, factors that Chrysler can control may be the design of the brochures and the co-op advertising that it extends to dealers. Factors beyond its control may be heavy layoffs in an area where traditionally a lot of Chrysler products are sold. After all the factors are laid out, strategy-setting becomes an exercise in enhancing the things that Chrysler does right and minimizing the things that it does wrong, coupled with squeezing the "luck" factor out of the equation to the greatest extent possible (see the section, "Eliminating the luck factor," later in this chapter).

## *Eliminating mistakes*

Eliminating mistakes is a critical job for the chief strategist because mistakes cause you to skew your response to problems. To give you an idea of how mistaken beliefs can change a situation, consider the story of the B-24 Liberator, one of the warhorse bombers of World War II. When used in raids over Europe, planes would come back all shot up from German anti-aircraft fire, with heavy casualties. In meetings to discuss ways of making the airplane safer, safety committees came up with the idea of analyzing the bullet holes in the returning planes and heavily reinforcing those areas. This reinforcing added weight to the B-24, so it became necessary to retrofit the B-24 with larger engines. This step took the planes out of service and caused the Eighth Air Force to choose more close-in targets.

After several months of this cycle of change responding to change, someone realized that the first idea was wrong. Reinforcing the shot-up areas did nothing for the safety of the crews, because it was the other unreinforced areas that were the problems. Nobody had bothered to analyze the planes that had been shot down. When the extra armor was taken off the planes and relocated, the B-24s were able to resume long-range bombing missions, after months of delay.

That example of how bad information can cause mistakes is just one reason why, as chief strategist, you have to pay attention to the things that other people ordinarily consign to luck. The more randomness you can wring out of your business plan and the more mistakes you can eliminate, the better your chances of success.

In the Chrysler case (see the previous section, "Searching for the facts"), the leadership involved worked on a strategic mission. The goals were loosely defined improvements; the mission was to devise a strategy to reach the goals. After all the members of the team understood what the mission was, everyone could take individual responsibility for reaching the mission's goals.

Setting a strategy depends largely on the first two roles of leadership, The Truth Seeker and The Direction Setter (see Chapter 4). Note that for Chrysler, the leaders pulled in information on everything they could think of, including so-called luck factors, in order to develop the clearest portrait of what was actually happening. Also, direction flowed naturally out of the information received and the way it was structured. The system wasn't any more complicated than 3-x-5 cards tacked onto a bulletin board used to assemble all the data. What did take place, however, was that the leader challenged the group to come up with all the factors and did not impose any mission on the group until everyone agreed on all the facts. Finally, the group leader said the obvious — strengthen what makes us good, fix what makes us bad, and find a way to reduce the influence of extraneous events on what happens.

# Eliminating the luck factor

How do you accomplish a mission as a chief strategist? You are in charge of selecting the mission, so you can choose a slow, steady course (which has minimal risks) or a bold stroke (which has a higher risk but helps you reach your goal faster). You have to soberly assess what you know about the information you've been given. One of the easiest ways to do this is with a SWOT chart. SWOT stands for Strengths and Weaknesses, Opportunities and Threats. When you put them together on a grid, they give you a powerful tool for assessing your mission. Figure 6-1 shows a SWOT chart. From this SWOT, you can see that Team X needs to keep opposing players from hitting, following the old baseball maxim, "Good pitching beats good hitting."

Suppose that you are assessing the competitive position of your division vis à vis competitors at other companies. List all the factors that can contribute to the strength of your division — its people, manufacturing, distribution, marketing channels, customer base, product quality, innovation, and so on — and determine which factors are strengths and which are weaknesses. Now do the same for each of your competitors. If you put your charts onto transparencies, you can put one on top of another. By doing this for two or three competitors, you can see where the opportunities and threats are. For example, you may not have as complete a product line as your competitors, but your product quality is better. If you increase product variety while maintaining quality, you have an opportunity to increase sales.

# Plot your SWOT

You can take the same SWOT chart we introduce in the previous section to plot the strengths and weaknesses of a Little League team. You are assessing the level of skill of your players, the abilities of your assistant coaches, your players' knowledge of baseball in game situations, and a host of other things.

Next, plot a SWOT chart for each of your opponents. If you have been coaching in a league for a number of years, you will have seen many of the same players year after year, which makes plotting the other teams' charts easy to do. If you have just accepted the coach's position, you will have to do some substantial information gathering, including talking to parents, who probably have a good working knowledge of all the kids in the league.

After you put together your SWOT chart, you have a pretty good idea of your team's chances against any given opponent. But more importantly, you know which skills and attitudes you need to work on to improve your players' abilities and help make them winners.

| X = Team X<br>O = Team O | Opportunities | Threats |
|---|---|---|
| **Strengths** | X = Excellent defensive team | X = Three best pitchers in league<br>O = Powerful cleanup hitter<br>O = Good shortstop<br>O = Good pitcher |
| **Weaknesses** | O = Lack of range of outfielders<br>O = First baseman can't catch | X = No consistency in hitting<br>X = Team demoralizes easily |

**Figure 6-1:**
**A SWOT chart is a powerful mission-assessment tool.**

With your SWOT chart in hand, you can devise a strategy that helps your team reach the goals expected of it. You might not do the unexpected, but you should have a clear picture of how to achieve your mission. Brilliance, if necessary, can wait until you are better prepared.

# The Chief Marketing Officer

The chief marketing officer mission-setting description combines the roles of the spokesperson — the person who articulates the mission of the company and its value to the group and outsiders — and the coach/team builder — the leader who encourages the group members to do their best work, and provides the mentoring and teaching help so they can. Often, your new group does not possess the skills to reach the goal it's been given, and may need some encouragement to achieve it, even if the goal is easily achievable. So your primary mission is selling the goal to the group members and then teaching them how to achieve it.

## Selling a down team on a brighter tomorrow

At Lee Iacocca's Chrysler, it would have been impossible to execute the sort of strategy that Bob Eaton regularly does. When Iacocca went to Chrysler from Ford in 1979, he found a completely dispirited company whose engineers weren't talking to each other, much less talking to the people in marketing. He also found a company with little cash in the till and enormous debts. All the company had was a small, fuel-efficient automobile dubbed the K-car, which it couldn't produce because it lacked the cash needed for retooling.

Iacocca, who is a consummate salesman, went to work selling "the new Chrysler," to his engineers and marketing people, to the unions whose cooperation and funds he needed to borrow, and to Congress and the President, who were fearful that a failed Chrysler would spell the beginning of the end for the beleaguered U.S. automobile industry. Iacocca was autocratic and often dictatorial in his decision-making processes, but no one marketed the idea that Chrysler could resurrect itself more effectively than Iacocca, both internally and externally. By the mid-1980s, the company was swimming in cash, and Iacocca was being hailed as one of the most brilliant leaders of the 20th century.

Long before you can teach a team how to win and devise strategies and plays, your job as a leader is *selling* your team members on the expectation that they *can* win and that winning is their sole mission. Selling is an intangible. You may have your SWOT charts in hand, but selling requires that you be able to convince people that they *can* do something that they believe they can't do.

You can't lie to people when you sell to them, because that raises their expectations, makes failure all the more crushing when your group doesn't meet its newly acquired expectations, and engenders bitterness directed at you, the leader, for sending the group on a doomed mission.

When you have done your SWOT analysis and picked a mission, the leader's role as chief marketing officer is to ensure that the mission is possible. Often, that means selling the mission to people outside the group. Not only was Iacocca the best salesman inside Chrysler, he was the best outside salesman as well, actively lobbying Congress and the President with his view of a reinvigorated company. His job as chief marketing officer was to get the resources the company needed to go forth on its mission.

## Leaders sell potential

As a coach, selling the future — the potential success of the group, its vision, and its goals — is also your job, and that's why coaches are so heavily involved in recruitment. You aren't simply selling a winning vision to your existing team; you're selling this vision to potential members. The same holds true when you take part in a charitable activity, such as fund-raising, for your church or school. Your job as chief marketing officer is to inspire people to want to do the hard work of calling on their friends, relatives, neighbors, and local businesses to ask them for money. You must have a clear sense of what will be accomplished if the group succeeds — a new ball field for the school, a wheelchair ramp for the church — and it has to be a goal that others will find worthwhile.

One of the hardest things to do as a leader is to match up a group's internal goals with the expectations of a larger, wider group. Why do I care if you are raising money so your elementary school can have computers, if my school is never going to get them? Widening your group may be the first thing that you have to do as a leader to build a greater sense of mission. If every school in the district benefits from a fund drive for new computers, the entire community is more likely to participate.

The role of the chief strategist is to select a mission, and the role of the chief marketer is to decide to whom it must be sold, and how.

# The Savior

The role of the savior is like *Mission Impossible,* so if you find yourself in this role, you should constantly have the theme music from the series going through your head as you set about performing this most daring kind of leadership. Leaders set out on mission impossible when they are expected to fail, or at least are not expected to have a complete success.

## Failure is not an option

Head coach Bill Parcells inherited the New York Jets when they were one of the worst teams in football. Far beyond the team's 1-15 record the season before Parcells arrived, the Jets (under Rich Kotite's leadership and for years prior to that) had a long history of inconsistency, the worst injury record in the entire NFL, a poor draft record, and a large number of players who exhibited erratic behavior, disregarded their coaches, or were outright indifferent. Most of the New York sportswriters, while praising Parcells as a savior because of his work with the New York Giants and the New England Patriots, were nevertheless convinced that Parcells was doomed to the same failures as his predecessors.

They became even more convinced that Parcells would fail when he didn't make any substantive changes in the team, bringing over only a handful of players he had worked with at both New England and the Giants, such as linebacker Pepper Johnson, running back Dave Meggett, and one-time center

Jumbo Elliott. Parcells then picked up a cast-off quarterback, Vinny Testaverde, whose reputation was for making dumb plays and throwing interceptions at critical moments.

Despite these negatives, Parcells placed the Jets in the playoffs after only two seasons and helped the team to its best record since 1969, the year it won the Super Bowl under Joe Namath, another mission impossible personality.

If anything distinguishes mission impossible leaders from chief strategists and chief marketers, it is their personalities. Whereas the strategist is cool and analytical, and the marketer is warm and outgoing, the mission impossible leader is often abrasive and self-absorbed. It's not that this type of leader listens to no one; it is that he or she takes in information very rapidly, makes quick decisions, and lays out the options for the teams in simple terms. In order to win, Parcells had to sell his team on the idea that simplifying the offense for Testaverde — giving him fewer, more direct choices — would lead to fewer interceptions and more scoring. He then had to sell his running backs on the idea that more completions would open up the running game and create more scoring opportunities for the running backs. Parcells will be remembered for simplifying a complex situation and then selling it to the Jets, and providing the team with a clear road to their championship.

## Changing for the better

Creating positive change is the brilliance of mission impossible leaders. Their plans are not complex, but often are breathtakingly simple. If you remember back to the kinds of hats that leaders wore (we explain the roles of leaders in Chapter 4), the one hat we haven't mentioned is the Pulled-Down Fedora: The Agent from C.H.A.N.G.E. C.H.A.N.G.E. means that the action you take Can Have A New Great Effect. This action is the bold stroke that yields the biggest bang and causes people to rethink their positions. Most of the people we consider to be great historical figures were agents of change. Their ideas were often startlingly simple — that all men should be free, that women should have the right to vote, that everyone should be able to afford a personal computer, for example — and they were people who, after they outlined their mission, were willing to pledge everything in order to get the mission accomplished.

The agent of change is a rare individual, it would seem — the genuinely creative person who transcends ordinary leaders to do great things, while the rest of us work to become dependable. But just as everyone has the potential to be a leader and nearly everyone exhibits some leadership skills in their everyday lives, almost everyone has the potential to become an agent of change. The question is not how hard you work to become a leader or how well you develop your skills. The question is what you do when the situation arises and you are the person on the spot.

# Finding your niche

Sometimes, rather than making a change for the better, the savior identifies something that isn't being done and takes responsibility for it. Lester Korn, one of the world's great executive recruiters, in his book, *The Success Profile,* writes:

"Sometimes the way to break out doesn't involve doing something better; it involves doing something that isn't being done at all. Many successful executives begin to move up the corporate ladder when they stop trying to outdo their peers in their assigned responsibilities. They accept that everybody is doing his or her job well, and that it may be difficult to do one's job so much better than one's peers that one would stand out from the pack. So (while continuing to do their own jobs well), they looked for something else that needed to be done."

Gary Wilson, midway through his career, was chief financial officer of Marriott and was responsible for the company's real estate development program, as well. "We developed one billion dollars' worth of hotels a year, so that was by far the most important thing I did." And how had he been assigned this crucial corporate role? He hadn't. He found a vacant niche and moved into it. "Part of the strategic plan in 1975-1976 was that we were going to expand the hotel business, and to expand the hotel business, you had to build hotels. So I started. I just did it. Nobody else knew how to do it. I didn't either, but I did it." Bill Marriott backed him, and the company thrived.

How can you turn yourself from a strategist or a marketer into a savior? As you can see from the Gary Wilson example, it didn't take any special talent — just the ability to know what was critical to the company's future and the willingness to put himself in the future's path by accepting responsibility for Marriott's growth. Often, though, it doesn't even take *that* much effort.

If you've been managing your mission as chief strategist, and you have your SWOT chart handy, you have within your mission the potential to do the unexpected. If you've carefully analyzed threats and opportunities, you can find an opportunity that, by exerting some effort, results in a return that is many times greater than that effort.

# Chapter 7

# The Responsibilities of a Leader

*In dreams begins responsibility.*

—William Butler Yeats

**W**e explain in Chapter 1 that leadership begins with the willingness to accept responsibility. But to what end? Does responsibility mean, for example, that you have to involve yourself in the personal lives of the people you're leading? Do you have to be all things to your group, wearing all the hats at all times? Accepting and dealing with responsibility are so fundamental to leadership that we devote more attention to the responsibilities of a leader in this chapter.

The central responsibility of a leader is to provide the climate necessary for creating growth and success. You can do many things as a leader, but ultimately, if your group's mission isn't successful and you don't manage to grow something — whether it's the skill and knowledge in a group of kids you're mentoring or the profits of a major enterprise — then you have failed in your most basic responsibilities as a leader.

Defining the central responsibility is simple. But for your group to be a success and to accomplish growth of some sort, you'll have to do a lot of other things along the way. In this chapter, we explain those things that leaders absolutely must do, everything from developing a vision and goals for your group to motivating your team and getting them to work together toward those goals.

# Developing a Vision

A *vision* is a doable dream — a distant goal that's worth pursuing because it involves growth and success and provides the binding energy to bring a group together to accomplish great things. It doesn't matter whether you are running an existing enterprise or starting a completely new one; visions are necessary to your ultimate success as a leader.

> ✔ **A vision can be an idea for a product.** When chemist Edwin Land was walking in the desert with his daughter and taking photographs of cactus flowers, she asked him why they had to wait so long to see the pictures. Land's daughter provided him with the vision to invent Polaroid film and cameras. As fantastic as the idea must have sounded at the time, the vision was a doable dream for Land, whose specialty was polarizing light and capturing light in chemical colloids. Land knew that with time, money, and a good team, he could develop instant pictures — and he did.

> ✔ **A vision can be an idea for a service.** Carl Weiss worked in New York's garment district. His job took him on many fabric-buying trips to Italy. While he was there, he spent many hours in small cafés, sipping cappuccino and espresso. Back in New York, Carl began to toy with the idea of developing the quintessential Italian café experience in New York. In 1978, he opened Caffe Bianco on New York's Upper East Side. It has been a success since the day it opened, helped along by Carl's relentless perfectionism in pursuit of his vision.

> ✔ **A vision can be a way to make the world a better place.** A vision can be a way to improve a neighborhood or to help people live longer.

The important thing about vision is that you be able to visualize the outcome of your work and the work of your team in the form of a world that has been changed in some way.

# Putting Together a Plan

Neither the grandest vision nor the simplest one materializes by itself. Nearly anything that you want to do and that is worth accomplishing takes time and effort. It also requires careful planning so that you can determine exactly what resources your team needs, when it needs them, where they will get them, and what outcomes are expected at each step along the way. No one goes from an idea directly to a finished product with no intermediate steps, so you have to learn how to develop plans that can translate visions into goals.

# Turning a vision into a plan

Defining your vision through a plan helps you define the scope of your vision. Your chances of success will be that much greater if you invest some initial time, effort, research, and study into building a solid plan.

The size of the plan and the amount of detail depends to a great extent on the size of the project, the complexity of the undertaking, the available resources, and the difficulties you're likely to encounter along the way. Writing a *visionary plan* (a plan that sketches out the major goals to accomplishing your vision) may take anywhere from a few weeks to a few months, and launching a successful enterprise can take anywhere from weeks to years.

When you are looking to turn your vision into a plan, you have to decide what size enterprise your resources, knowledge, and commitments can support. Consider the following three factors in determining the initial size and scope of your enterprise:

✔ **The critical size for a plan to be considered a success:** Starting an electronics company in a garage is a lot harder today, even though Hewlett and Packard did it 60 years ago, and the 2 Steves — Jobs and Wozniak — did it more than 20 years ago. The electronics hardware business today is a commodity business in which unit profits are quite low and high volume is necessary for profitability. That's the virtual definition of a large, expensive operation.

On the other hand, you don't need much more than a computer, an idea, and some skill with programming languages to write a software program and start a software business. Scott Cook wrote the basic program for Quicken at his kitchen table and started Intuit in the early 1980s. Lots of people have followed his example and built successful businesses. So, size your idea to reality — and the resources it will actually take to bring your vision to reality.

✔ **Critical size compared to your competition:** Here's a simple rule: If you're starting a business within an established industry, then, generally, the more competitive the marketplace for your product is, the larger your start-up has to be. This doesn't hold true for restaurants, of course. Size won't matter if you have excellent cuisine, the right market, the right location, and great reviews. But for practically any other enterprise, size matters. If, for example, two bands play music in one small town and both bands are raising money for trips, the band that's going to the more interesting location — size here translates to audacity — is likelier to get the majority of the funds.

✔ **Critical size determined by resources:** You can start a one-person employment agency or any number of small service businesses with a few employees, but starting a semiconductor company takes enormous resources. The key is to know what the critical size for success is going to be so that you can acquire the resources to launch the enterprise and maintain it until it becomes self-supporting. Visions lose focus when they are beyond the scope of the people trying to turn them into reality. By starting small, you do not compromise your vision. Instead, you give yourself the chance to learn and grow. Starting small keeps you below the competition's radar, allows you to gain a foothold in a market, commits you to using available resources, and focuses your thinking on market niches, which may become market leadership positions as you grow.

## Learning by doing

How do you go about learning by doing? Basically, you can do this in two ways. The first is to learn the skill of planning as a formal discipline. You can take courses within an MBA program and learn what things are required to make a plan go forward. But the cheaper, simpler way is to go out and gain experience in the field. Opening a restaurant if you've never been a chef, a restaurant manager, or someone who has worked the front room as a maitre d' makes no sense. Generally, you ought to do a couple of rotations working different jobs within a particular field in order to learn it from several different perspectives. This experience introduces you to the pitfalls as well as the potentials of an idea.

## Writing the plan

Writing a good plan takes more time than you may imagine. Fred Smith's business plan for Federal Express began as a term paper at Yale, for which he received a C grade. Smith spent two years writing and rewriting his plan and nearly four years raising money from family, private investors, and banks, before he launched Federal Express in 1973.

As Ernest Hemingway said about writing, every story begins the same: with a single, blank sheet of paper. So does every vision, and ultimately, so do the plans that visions require to turn into reality.

To start the planning process, write down four things on a single sheet of paper:

✔ **The idea behind your business:** Try to describe the idea behind a business, preferably in 25 words or less, that says what the business is all about. For example:

- *I want to market a new software product that reduces accounting time for small businesses by 25 percent (or that eliminates viruses or specializes in overseas banking, for example).*

- *I want to open a trendy new restaurant serving exciting, low-fat food, with great service, in an affluent neighborhood.*

- *I want to open an employment agency for information technology people, working mostly with Fortune 1000 companies.*

✔ **The vision that drives the idea:** Walt Disney's original vision for Disneyland was articulated in two paragraphs. It was a simply stated, fully articulated set of goals and expectations — who would go there, what benefits they would derive, and why they would choose to return. Your vision has to state all those things and provide the motivation for turning the idea into a reality. Vision focuses on the benefits that the customer, your group, and society will get from you bringing your vision forward to reality.

✔ **Why it will be successful:** Whether you plan a new product, a new service, a distribution business, a professional office, a manufacturing company, a charitable project, or a sports program for kids — be clear about why people will want to commit their time or money to your idea — and why they will come back again in the future.

In the case of a software product, you could have the idea for a unique design based on your special knowledge of the accounting needs of small businesses. In the case of a restaurant, you could see that no great restaurants are in the area and have the idea for starting one yourself. Or maybe you've seen a wonderful model in Paris that you think will work equally well in an area that already has several different restaurants. In the case of an employment agency, you may already be a manager in the high-tech field and know how hard it is to find good people. The need you have for good employees may give you the idea of starting your own agency to surpass the present agencies, which aren't doing a good enough job.

✔ **Why and how *you* can make it successful:** Even the simplest vision requires strong leadership to succeed in its marketplace. Successful enterprises of all types are developed skillfully, carefully, and energetically. Describe your leadership roles in achieving your vision, the strengths you can build on, the resources you can draw on, and the commitments you're willing to make to give the enterprise the best chance of becoming a success.

Planning a new enterprise requires knowledge, skill, research, and a large number of assumptions. Most people find it difficult to estimate sales, costs, personnel, and the length of time it takes to get all the tasks done — beginning with writing the plan itself. Don't be afraid to make assumptions and, wherever possible, look at existing enterprises similar to your own to see how reasonable your assumptions are.

The actual results you see may often be 50 percent lower than your plan, or (rarely) 50 percent higher than what you originally called for — and there may be great differences between the plan you've made and the reality of developing your idea. Your assumptions won't be perfect, but they're better than no assumptions at all.

Write the plan so that you can take it seriously. Stick to the plan as much as possible, but analyze when you stray from the plan and why. Understand that you'll have to update your plan when the business starts.

After you have your plan, you have to do three things:

- **Be thorough.** Putting together the best plan possible is important, but don't overwrite. Give yourself a realistic time limit, and force yourself to get the plan completed. If the concept is good, the mere logic of the idea should help you put a good plan together. If the concept is poor, no amount of preparation or paperwork will improve the outcome.

- **Be cautious.** Make provisions from the beginning for possible errors in judgment, unanticipated problems and reversals, larger lead times than expected, greater costs, and sometimes radical changes in execution.

- **Be timely.** Putting your business plan together is the first task in your new enterprise. How quickly and how well you get it done will tell you a lot about your approach to your enterprise and the group you are leading. Your time is a precious resource that cannot be expanded. Set yourself a time limit and then try to deliver the best possible plan, on time.

# Identifying Goals

Your plan will help turn your vision into a mission, but you can't lose sight of the goal of your vision. Many an enterprise has planned itself into confusion by becoming overly obsessed with the details. Plan-obsessed leaders see not only the forest, but also the trees, the bark, the needles and leaves on the forest floor, and the tiny insects boring under the tree bark. And worse, they attach equal importance to each object in the forest and fail to notice that the forest is on fire. Make it a practice to review the goals set forth in your plan with regularity, so that you never forget what your goal is.

# Creating a Cohesive Team

You as the leader will supply the vision, but it takes followers to make your vision a reality. You have to nurture a cohesive team that works together toward a common goal. Here are the important factors in creating an effective team:

✔ **Motivate and encourage your followers:** A good leader is responsible to his or her followers. A leader must do everything possible to bring out the best in a group. Motivating people is a responsibility of leadership because it is the most expeditious way to achieve a goal. If everybody is focused on the same goal, you waste a minimum amount of energy, and you reach the goal faster and better. In today's competitive environment, the best leaders are those who can keep their groups focused and motivated.

✔ **Create teamwork throughout the ranks:** Good leaders can't do everything, so they have to take a group that is usually unformed and wield it into a team that is tightly focused on accomplishing a specific goal. Teams are orderly and disciplined; groups are not. So building team spirit is crucial if leaders are to succeed in helping a group achieve its goals. Conversely, in order for a vision to succeed, the team must know that a leader is enthusiastic about their efforts and that their persistence will be rewarded.

✔ **Create an orderly atmosphere:** No team runs well all the time. Even in the most enlightened company, or the most democratically run volunteer group, situations will always arise in which people are unhappy. You can reduce tension in a group by creating order. Order gives each member of a group an assigned task and makes them part of a team with a focus. Order establishes roles and rules, but a group can quickly become bogged down by procedures unless a leader learns to use the process of order. A leader is responsible for finding ways to eliminate problems as they arise.

A good leader can minimize problems by establishing ways for complaints to find their way quickly to the people who have the power to resolve them. A good leader also minimizes dissent by making the team's goals and values so clear that team members don't feel any sense of ambiguity about what is expected of them.

# Providing the Resources Your Team Needs

A leader is responsible for making sure that the team either has or can get the resources necessary to achieve its goal. The resource needed most often may be money, but it can be time, a person with a critical piece of knowledge, a location where a group can meet, organizational skills, or any one of dozens of things that, if lacking, keep the group from doing its best work. The leader's job is to provide these things, even if the leader asks the group to engage in an exercise of Stone Soup, in which each member of the group is asked to contribute something that the entire group needs for its nourishment.

The idea that leaders are responsible for providing the group's resources is somewhat new. Until well into the late 19th century, companies expected that workers would bring their own tools to the workplace. Not until the age of mass production and standardization did companies begin to recognize the value of providing the workplace resources so that work output would be consistent and uniform. As work has grown more money-focused and more complex, expecting that team members are responsible for bringing their tools along with them has become increasingly unreasonable.

After a team is formed, the leader is also responsible for providing other things that are not ordinarily thought of as resources but actually are vitally important to the future cohesiveness of your team. In a company, these things include competitive wages and benefits. But in all environments, things not normally thought of as resources also include the encouragement, promotion pathways, and bonuses that are the rewards for doing well. Leaders should learn to plan for all resources; otherwise these resources may be overlooked when the company has become successful.

# Holding People Accountable

Part of being decisive as a leader and, equally, part of being consistent, is that leadership establishes firm policies and directions for achieving goals and then adheres to those policies. That is what mission is about — the how-to component of achieving a goal. After a mission is established, and everyone in the group understands exactly what it is, the definition of success and failure becomes how tightly team members adhere to the mission in accomplishing a goal. In combat, for example, taking a hill when everyone is killed in the process does no good, especially if the mission was to take the hill with a minimal loss of life.

In business, holding people accountable often means rewarding those who are successful and firing those who fail. But if the leader deals with accountability in that way, he partially evades his responsibility. When you are a leader, you are putting together your team. You are deciding upon the roles that members of your team are going to play in achieving a common goal. And you are responsible for moving people into the positions where they are capable of doing their best work so that failure becomes improbable.

# Part III
# The Art of Leadership

The 5th Wave    By Rich Tennant

SQUARE DANCE PICNIC

"...pretty soon we realized we were lost. That's when Frank, the band's Caller, took charge, and before you knew it, we dosey-doed our way through the woods and back to civilization."

# In this part . . .

**W**elcome to the nitty gritty of leadership. Now that you know more about yourself, you need to know what skills you'll need in order to become a dynamic leader. You have to learn how to harness your strengths and your weaknesses and to differentiate leading from merely managing. Perhaps the most important thing you can find out in this part is that often, you don't have to wait for a title to become a leader.

# Chapter 8

# What Are the Skills of a Leader?

*I find the great thing in this world is not so much where we stand, as in what direction we are moving.*
—Oliver Wendell Holmes

*L*eaders are constantly being asked to make choices. These choices generally fall into three categories: choosing among goals, choosing among missions, and choosing among people. The first two are fairly straight-forward. But whenever people come into the equation, the choices you make automatically become more complex. Choosing among people not only means mediating the conflicting claims that people have on a leader's time, but it also means making a personal choice about how much involvement you want to have with your group.

This chapter helps you understand the skills that allow you to make good choices and shows you, step-by-step, how to apply your skills in real-life situations.

## Understanding Leadership Concepts

You can't really begin to put the skills of a leader into practice before you understand what they are. And often, the words that we use in describing these skills seem close together in meaning.

To help you keep these terms and concepts separate and distinct in your mind, look at Table 8-1.

| Table 8-1 | Concepts in Leadership |
|---|---|
| *Leadership Concept* | *What It Means* |
| Vision | An overarching idea or doable dream |
| Mission | A statement that summarizes goals that, when accomplished, fulfill the vision |
| Direction | A changeable goal or set of goals that responds to the current situation or best information; the path from where you are now toward accomplishing the mission |
| Goal | An intermediate step that responds to the current situation that, when taken with other goals, accomplishes the mission |

# Leadership on the Oregon trail

*Oregon Trail,* a popular computer game widely played in elementary schools, provides a good way to think about many of the skills necessary for leadership. The object of the game is to get your wagon train from St. Louis to Oregon. Along the way you encounter all sorts of problems, from storms to hostile natives to sickness and accidents. Your task is to make enough right choices so that the greatest number of your party makes it all the way to Oregon.

Your first choice in the game is picking a direction. Oregon is your goal, but how are you going to get there? Are you going to go in summer or in winter, in the autumn or the spring? Are you going to take a northerly route or a southern path? Sometimes, you're better off going to California first and then to Oregon. These types of decisions are known as *direction setting.*

Next, you make a *strategic plan.* You decide what supplies you need and how much to take:

ax handles, wheels and axles, food and clothing, and ammunition and weapons, for example. This provisioning is for your *mission,* which is the detailed plan to get to Oregon. The provisions are supposed to account for all sorts of circumstances, foreseen and unforeseen, that you may encounter during the trip.

Along the way, you have to make decisions that rely on your interpretation of information. When you come to a river, the computer tells you how deep the river is and what your prospects for fording the stream are. You can choose to take a risk and cut off some time, or you can choose to go farther up or downstream and ensure that your group gets past its problem safely. In real life, you'll encounter those fast-moving streams all the time. They are the obstacles that appear seemingly out of nowhere after you've done what you thought was careful planning.

# Making Leadership Decisions

Decision making is the most important day-to-day job of a leader. We use the term *decision making* here in a very specific sense: making decisions that focus on your resources, plans, mission, and goals. You create a plan and turn it into a mission ("This is how we are going to get to our goal. . . ."); you check it constantly, and then make small course corrections as new information comes in or as the unexpected pops up.

The only way that you can make decisions well is if you have information — and lots of it. If you are the leader of a volunteer group, then you may set a mission of raising 10 percent more money than in the previous year of fundraising. In this case, your goals may center around having one or two very successful fund-raising events. To make decisions, you need to know the schedules not only of your volunteers, but more importantly, of the people whom you expect to contribute. You would want to be in constant contact with insiders of all the groups that you think would be potential donors and know their schedules. You would want to know about the most effective means of contacting potential donors so that you can decide how much of your budget needs to go to advertising your event. You need to know about the availability of hotel ballrooms, meeting rooms, and caterers at sites that would appeal to your potential donors. All this information is necessary for you to make effective decisions as to the right date, time, activity, and means of publicizing the events that will allow you to accomplish your mission.

The 20th-century Danish mathematician Piet Hein coined the phrase, "Knowing what thou knowest not is in a sense omniscience." The phrase means that you should concentrate on finding out what you don't know instead of showing off what you do know, and then make the effort to fill in those gaps in your knowledge. If you are going to be a leader, your decisions are always going to be called into question by someone, so the better informed you are every step of the way, the greater the likelihood that you will make the right choice.

After the battle of Vicksburg during the Civil War, the victorious General Sherman wrote in his memoirs:

> The campaign of Vicksburg, in its conception and execution, belonged exclusively to General Grant, not only in the great whole, but also in the thousands of its details. I still retain many of his letters and notes, all in his own handwriting, prescribing the routes of march for divisions and detachments, specifying even the amounts of food and tools to be carried along. . . . No commanding general of an army ever gave more of his personal attention to details.

# Setting a Direction

*Direction setting* means choosing among various goals. Perhaps direction setting really should be called destination choosing, because the point of making the choice is to get somewhere, to reach a goal. You haven't been given your position of leadership because you are the most popular person. Your group has a strong expectation that you are going to take them someplace that they don't think they can get to without your guidance — your leadership.

If you know that your group can't reach a goal in the near term or if attaining the goal costs too much in human terms — the amount of sacrifice is not worth the effort — then it's your responsibility as a leader to explain your decision to your group and to persuade them to accept a more practical, near-term goal.

In day-to-day terms, direction setting means making practical decisions about the goals the group wants to reach. You will always feel some pressure to reach for the stars — to go for the highest possible goal. But you need to consider a few factors as you make your decisions about the goals your team can reach without undo stress:

- ✔ The skills of your group
- ✔ Their ability to work together as a team
- ✔ The resources you have available
- ✔ The competition for those resources elsewhere

# Arbitration and Mediation

As a leader, you have to settle arguments within your group. These arguments cannot be about goals — it is your job as a leader to select the goals for the group. But group members will argue with you about your mission; about the roles you've chosen for them to play; and about whether each person is pulling his or her weight within the group, either in terms of work or in terms of personality (often, a team member's personality determines how much they can accomplish because it has an impact on their effectiveness of getting people to cooperate with them). Groups that become teams accept that each person has an assigned role, and that their turn to perform will come. Poor leaders, such as a head coach with an unruly team, have not been able to get their players to accept their individual roles.

A leader's job is to listen to team members before making decisions. If one person comes to you with a complaint about the performance of another team member, don't shrug it off. You need to gather information — about the work itself, the kinds of interaction between the two team members with a conflict, and about how the work and the conflict affect others. When you focus on the complaint of a single person, don't solicit input from other members of the group, but rather, spend your time observing.

When you have enough information to make a decision, it is time for mediation. As the word implies, you look for a middle ground that satisfies both parties in the dispute, with the proviso that your decision doesn't take either party away from their mission, which is driving toward a goal. Try to avoid mediated solutions that involve changing the roles of team members by adding to one person's responsibilities and taking away from another's. Look instead for ways to get two people working on the same task so that they share the load.

Often, your attempts to mediate are going to be unsuccessful. Many decisions don't have a middle road. The situation could require you to choose between the needs of one person and another, or between the needs of a single person and the group. When you have to choose between the needs of an individual and the group, your choice should always be for the group. If you have to choose between one person and another, however, you will have to either find a new role for the person you've chosen against, or find yourself with a dissatisfied (and potentially subversive) subordinate.

When you make a discretionary decision, the person whom the decision affects deserves to know the exact reasons why he or she is being targeted. This is one of those times when you need a script. In this example, we first show you what you may typically say, and then we'll pick it apart so that you know what is really being said:

*John, I'm replacing you as head of manufacturing. Our goal is to increase quality by an order of magnitude this year and to increase throughput by 10 percent. We all agreed that we were going to do that by concentrating on our rework rate. Quality control has told me that we continue to have a high number of parts rejects coming through, so as you know, we began looking into the problem last month. It is not a machinery problem, and it is not a problem with any of the line workers. The problem, I am sorry to say, is that you have not put a sufficient effort into prechecking tolerances during each assembly stage. I have to get someone who can do the job.*

Now, let's deconstruct that dialogue and show you what each one of the sentences means. Here's how it sounds in the language of leaders:

*John, I'm taking you out of the role I've chosen you for. We had a goal, which we are not going to be able to reach within the allotted time, even though we have all agreed upon the mission. The information I have received is that we are not working effectively on the mission. As a group, we began looking into this problem last month, and the solution is not to change or increase resources or to make changes among the other roles being played by members of the team. You have not been able to meet your agreed-upon responsibilities, so I have to get a new person for that role.*

As you can see, there is nothing arbitrary in the decision. You have explained your decision in terms of goals and missions, and how you went about making your decision. You have given John all of the information he needs in order to accept your decision, and you have given him no grounds to question it.

You can apply the following dialogue structure to all sorts of situations where you have to explain a tough decision:

1. **State the action you are taking.**

2. **Explain how your action fits in with the goal you are trying to reach.**

3. **Explain how your action fits in with the mission.**

4. **Explain the agreed-upon tasks of the mission, and each person's role.**

5. **Explain what is going wrong and why.**

6. **Explain how focusing on the individual is the solution.**

Whenever you make a discretionary decision, the two things you can't say are, "Because this is the way things have always been done," and "Because I said so." Such statements are arbitrary, and contribute nothing to a person's understanding of what they've done wrong. Being arbitrary hinders a leader's ability to find a new way to help the team and engenders bad feelings if the person is removed from the team.

# Facilitating

*Facilitating* is a fancy word for the things you do to make it possible for other people to do what they need to do. In a crisis, such as a flood, the facilitators may be the people who bring the sand, the sandbags, and the coffee to the front-line workers who are actually filling the bags to shore up the levee. Facilitating is another way of saying "providing support," and a good facilitator looks for ways to make other people's lives easier (the word itself comes from the Latin *facile,* which means easy).

Often, facilitating is the process of challenging, stimulating, and rewarding team members for doing the best for themselves. For example, when Carlo DeBenedetti was CEO of Olivetti, an Italian office equipment company, he took the door off of his office so that people at his headquarters knew they could always walk in on the boss. When that didn't work, DeBenedetti invented what business author Tom Peters later termed "management by walking around." DeBenedetti would simply take himself into the office of a middle manager and ask him what he was doing at that moment. The two would then talk, DeBenedetti would make some suggestions and offer encouragement, and then leave. People who worked at Olivetti in the early and mid-1980s, when DeBenedetti was chief executive, reported feeling exhilarated, supercharged, but most of all, unthreatened, when their shirt-sleeved CEO stopped in to help them out. His words of encouragement and suggestions were facilitation at and from the highest level.

A good facilitator does not necessarily need to have all the skills needed to solve a problem. You simply need to be able to remind your team member, in the most unthreatening way, about the goal toward which you are both striving, and the mission by which you've agreed to reach the goal. Often, while in discussion, you discover things that are blocking your team member from accomplishing his or her task, and you can then focus together on finding an appropriate solution.

# *Cheerleading*

A leader has to decide how involved he or she wants to become with a team. This decision is important because the higher up you go, the more indirect your leadership is likely to be in day-to-day events, and the more likely that you will not have contact with many of the people you lead. An army general rarely sees the men and women he leads into combat, except, perhaps, at a parade ground review. He does not look into the eyes of the people he is about to send into battle, perhaps to their deaths.

## Facilitating can lead you in new directions

Even if you are the leader of a large enterprise, it often pays to be a facilitator at the most local level. The best politicians, the late House of Representatives Speaker Tip O'Neill, used to say, are "retail" politicians — the members of Congress and senators with strong local staffs who get small problems solved for their constituents. In the process, a leader can achieve greatness.

Take, for example, Senator Alphonse D'Amato. Long known in New York as "Pot Hole Al," D'Amato was the consummate retail politician.

No job for a constituent was too small for his staff. But D'Amato never got the respect of New Yorkers until he tried to solve the problem of an old woman, a Holocaust survivor. The woman claimed that Swiss bank secrecy laws defeated her efforts to secure her father's money from the Swiss bank that held it. D'Amato launched an investigation that ultimately yielded a major settlement between Holocaust survivors and the banks, and brought about a change in the way Swiss banks monitor their accounts.

How, then, does a remote leader inspire a team to meet its goals and to find the mission worthwhile? Part of the answer is honesty, but a large part of the answer is cheerleading. Any leader has to be able to instill confidence in a group and do it in such a way that the group strongly wants to meet the goal, even though the risks are high. Leaders must not only explain, they must motivate their followers. A leader must articulate the very reasons people have gathered together to form an enterprise, to inspire them enthusiastically to do what is necessary to make it a success.

Often, leaders motivate with the promise of rewards. In ancient times, the rewards of war were the spoils of battle, but finding appropriate rewards is still a task of motivational leadership. At many high-technology companies, leaders reward the efforts of their followers with special grants of stock to employees who create marked improvements in productivity, or to teams who solve a particularly thorny problem in a timely manner. A rising stock price represents the efforts and productivity of everyone in the company. If you go into the lobby of almost any large company, whether it is British Airways' headquarters, Speedbird House, near Heathrow Airport, or K-Mart's linked cubes near Detroit, you'll see a common factor. One of the first things you notice in each lobby is an electronic tote board that shows the stock price and the daily number (for example, the load factor at British Airways or the rate of inventory turns at K-Mart) that is critical to success in that given industry.

Your job as a leader is to make a fence-sitter want to follow you, through the right combination of stimulation and rewards. That's what cheerleading is.

# Chapter 9

# Harnessing Your Strengths and Weaknesses

*In This Chapter*

▶ Leadership *jujitsu*

▶ Leadership *karate*

*You gain strength, courage, and confidence by every experience in which you really stop to look fear in the face. You are able to say to yourself, "I lived through this horror. I can take the next thing that comes along." You must do the thing you cannot do.*

—Anna Eleanor Roosevelt

Not everyone has the same leadership skills or even the necessary skills in equal measure. That imbalance doesn't matter. If you have been chosen to lead, you have to figure out how to overcome the weaknesses in your leadership tools and how to turn them into strong points. In order to do this, you have to understand the difference between *jujitsu* and *karate*.

Both are Asian forms of martial arts, and both look good when you watch a Bruce Lee or Jackie Chan "chop socky" movie. But the two forms of combat couldn't be more different. *Jujitsu* takes its name from two Japanese words, *ju*, which means weakness, and *jitsu*, which means skill or art. *Jujitsu* emphasizes the exploitation of an opponent's strengths, which you are taught to turn into your own. *Karate*, another Japanese word, literally means empty hand, and it was meant to be an offensive method of fighting when a warrior was rendered weaponless on the battlefield. *Karate* is a method that relies upon your own strength to help you cripple or disable an opponent.

*Karate* depends on the forward thrust, *jujitsu* on using your opponent's strength as you retreat. *Karate* leaders push at problems. *Jujitsu* leaders let the problem come to them. Every leader needs to know when to be a *karate* leader and lead with strength, and when to use weakness to its best advantage. Not every problem can be solved with only one method or the other. In this chapter, we tell you the characteristics of each form of leadership as it applies to the basic leadership skills so that you can determine how it fits with your own needs and personality.

# Keeping Your Balance

The key difference between *karate* and *jujitsu* is in the way you hold your body. In *jujitsu*, to exploit an opponent's strength and your own weakness, you have to allow your opponent to lunge at you, which puts him off balance. Because you're moving backwards at the same time as your opponent, the combined movement produces a seemingly effortless throw, where your foe is sent head over heels behind you. In *karate*, you have to step in towards your opponent, in order to deliver your blow with maximum force.

Leadership works in much the same way. When you are weak in a particular leadership skill, you must allow the situation to come to you. Where you are strong and in control, you must handle the situation. Take a look at how weakness and strength create different situations in the three key components of leadership: eliciting the cooperation of others, listening, and placing others above yourself.

# Cooperating

Cooperation is important to any enterprise because few things of size or consequence can be accomplished rapidly by a single individual. In Amish country, people know all about cooperation whenever a neighbor gets into trouble. If a barn burns down, people show up spontaneously and help to build their neighbor a new barn. Each of the men and boys in the group has all the skills needed to do the job, and all the women band together to facilitate their work, bringing tools, nails and pegs, food, and drink to the work site so that the frame of a large barn can be raised in a single day.

Leaders have to be able to get their followers to cooperate in order to accomplish the goals of the group and to realize the leader's vision. But cooperation is a skill that needs to be drawn out of individuals in order to turn them into groups. A leader can elicit cooperation in several ways, which we discuss in the following sections.

## Cooperation karate

If you have a natural talent at eliciting the cooperation of others and it's one of your major strengths, the reason can be that you have good selling skills. You are bold and unafraid to pick up the phone to ask someone to help you or to do the same thing in person. You are concise in your thoughts, a natural conversationalist, someone who can articulate the goals and visions of a group in a direct, even obvious way. You instinctively put people at ease when you speak to them, and you have a quiet confidence that automatically elicits trust from people.

You are the first person to record the goals of the group on paper, the first one to organize a discussion of how to develop a mission, the first to take responsibility. If you were a soldier during World War I, you'd be the first over the trench wall, yelling, "Follow me," and everyone would, confident that you knew what you were doing and that you weren't about to be mowed down by a machine gun.

## Cooperation jujitsu

What does the soft, *jujitsu* version of getting people to cooperate with you look like? You are a quiet consensus builder. You ask others for their opinions and keep silent about your own. You gather information and intelligence and carefully put it together. Only then do you make your presentation, relying more on the facts to help you make your case than on an appeal to vision.

People trust you precisely because they know that you are not likely to lead them into a minefield, and that you will proceed cautiously, making certain that the way is clear before bringing your group along. In this, you are more like a platoon leader in the jungle, taking the point, map in one hand and radio in the other, eyes keenly focused on the underbrush ahead. When a surprise springs out of the undergrowth, you are prepared. Your people are properly deployed to deal with almost any threat, because you have spent much of your free time teaching them how to respond and preparing them for the fact that there is no such thing as the unexpected, only the unanticipated.

The difference between the two styles is that the person who's strong at eliciting cooperation from others appeals to vision and goals and relies on trust, likability, self-confidence, and instinct to move the group forward. The person who is weak on eliciting cooperation appeals to the sense of mission and relies on preparation, information-gathering skills, consensus-building, and keeping the group informed of every move in order to maintain group cohesiveness, trust, and confidence.

# Listening

If you don't make listening a critical skill, you can never be a leader. Leaders can only take people where they want to go, and if a leader can't hear the mood of his or her group, it is impossible to take them anywhere. Listening provides advance warning about problems at all levels, and helps a leader to become more effective at defining the possibilities of goals and missions. But how you listen is just as important as what you hear, as the examples of *karate* and *jujitsu* in the following sections explain.

## Karate listening

The *karate* listener says, "Tell me. I want to know." He or she actively hunts out information and intelligence and does not wait for bad news to find its way to his or her doorstep. The *karate* listener has people inside the organization or group whose primary responsibility it is to keep the leader informed. The *karate* listener, however, then goes out and gets *more* information so that he or she does not become a victim of a staff that filters out information that they don't think the leader wants to hear.

## Jujitsu listening

The *jujitsu* listener says "I hear that. . . ." or "People tell me that. . . ." The *jujitsu* listener listens by walking around, by taking in and monitoring the flow of memos and e-mail by which members of a group communicate, and by constantly evaluating situations and people within the group. If you are a weak listener, then you need to develop systems that allow you to hear more. For example, the National Security Agency has satellites and receivers that scan every known radio frequency so that its analysts can find even a hint of a message and then decode it. The weak listener has to build the kind of listening organization that a strong listener probably already possesses.

How do you build a listening organization? You begin by building listening posts across your entire organization and, especially, at every point where your group interfaces with the outside world. For example, if you have a business organization, you have a post at every point of customer contact. If you're running the Little League team, your phone list has the names and numbers of every parent and all the league officials.

After your listening posts are active, you have to get every person in your organization involved. Often, somebody won't tell you, the leader, when something is wrong, but he or she will tell a friend or colleague. The colleague has to be encouraged to report the information to you for the good of the mission and for the good of the goals of the group.

# Placing Others above Yourself

Whether you're facilitating or working on developing a plan that will take a group where it wants to go, to be effective as a leader requires that you be altruistic, placing the needs of the group above your own needs. The leader who concentrates on the trappings and perks of leadership rarely survives for long, while the leader who sees to the needs of the group in an effective manner will prevail whenever there is a crisis.

You can meet the challenges of altruism head on, by going up to people and asking what they need, and then getting it for them, or you can act as a facilitator, patiently listening to their complaints, and easing their burdens when they are still small problems instead of larger, more complex problems. Both ways work, as you can see in the following sections.

## Altruistic karate

The *karate* leader is the hostess at the party who grabs the tray of hors d'oeuvres and offers it up to each new guest, taking their drink order as she passes out canapés. She is the person who takes it upon herself to introduce strangers to each other — on the grounds that if they are at her party and friends of hers, then they ought to be friends of each other. She takes the initiative in saying, "Get together and do something."

In the January 11, 1999, issue of *The New Yorker,* author Malcolm Gladwell writes, in "Six Degrees of Lois Weisberg," the story of a private citizen in Chicago who has vast amounts of personal influence: "Lois is a type — a particularly rare and extraordinary type, but a type nonetheless. She's the type of person who seems to know everybody, and this type can be found in every walk of life. . . . You start to suspect that he or she may be far more important than we would ever have imagined — that the people who know everyone, in some oblique way, may actually run the world. I don't mean that they are the sort who head up the Fed or General Motors or Microsoft, but that, in a very down-to-earth, day-to-day way, they make the world work. They spread ideas and information. They connect varied and isolated parts of society. A Chicago government official describes Lois as 'the epicenter of the city administration,' which is the right way to put it. Lois is far from the most powerful person in Chicago. But if you connect all the dots that constitute the vast apparatus of government and influence and interest groups in the city of Chicago, you'll end up coming back to Lois again and again. Lois is a connector."

## *Altruistic jujitsu*

The *jujitsu* leader says, "How can I help? What can I do to make your life easier?" The *jujitsu* leader is Bobby Kotick, the dynamic CEO of Activision, a large manufacturer of computer games based in Santa Monica, California. Bobby and Howard Marks (his University of Michigan roommate and business partner) first got into the computer business in 1984 with a program, called Jane, which improved the performance of small Apple computers. Howard had all of the programming knowledge and ideas, but it was Bobby who became the CEO of the fledgling enterprise.

What did Bobby Kotick do while the programmers were writing code? "Anything they needed to keep them happy and productive," he says. "My job was to go out and get them pizza at 3 a.m. and to feed their cats and walk their dogs. I was the chief facilitator of the company." In other words, Bobby provided the "glue" that held the enterprise together until it could become successful, resolving small internal conflicts while keeping everybody on track. Bobby used his weakness — a total ignorance of the computer industry — to his best advantage, and, in doing so, helped his company grow.

As you can see, you don't have to have strengths to be a leader. Your weaknesses can be exploited to the benefit of others — and to the enterprise you are leading.

# Chapter 10

# What about Expectations?

*Oft expectation fails, and most oft there. Where it most promises.*
—William Shakespeare, *Measure for Measure*

Expectations are key to leadership. After you find yourself in a leadership position, you have to manage several sets of expectations. Not only do *you* have expectations, but so do the people you are leading. Moreover, if you have been chosen to lead a group by someone outside the group — a senior management team, for example — you have to deal with their expectations as well.

Your job as a leader is to bring your expectations, the expectations of your superiors, and your team's expectations into line, creating trust among all the parties and minimizing conflicts so that everyone remains focused on achieving the overall goals. If you fail to bring these expectations into line, you may get caught in that most unhappy of triangles, in which you, your group, and your superiors see things differently.

Your greatest enemy is unrealistic expectations. Your goals have to be realistic and doable, and they have to be communicated upward to senior management and downward to your team. This chapter shows you how to ensure that expectations are realistic and that everyone has a clear understanding of the goals. Managing expectations makes leading a joy rather than a chore.

# Mapping Out Your Expectations

Your *expectations* are the minimum list of things you expect your team to do in order to accomplish the mission, after you have defined the vision or goal for them. In a way, your expectations are a kind of "Leader's Bill of Rights" — the things you consider reasonable about the interactions between you and the people you are leading. Your list of expectations is the mirror image of the responsibilities of leadership. For every responsibility, there is an expectation that goes along with it. For example, if it is your responsibility to have a vision, it is your expectation that, having communicated it well to your team members, they will go along with your vision. (See Chapter 7 for more information on the responsibilities of leadership.)

## Believing in your vision

You have been made a leader because you were presumed by someone or by a group of people to have the ability to think on a larger scale than simply accomplishing a single task. You have been chosen to lead because you were able to articulate a vision that made sense, or at least demonstrate that you could achieve a desired end or goal. Now you have to go out and sell that vision or goal to the group you are actually leading.

William Rogers was Secretary of State through much of the Vietnam era under President Nixon. Rogers's State Department was a freewheeling place, where debate was not only tolerated but also encouraged. Even so, Rogers had one firm policy: After a decision had been made about a foreign policy goal or objective, after all voices had been heard, everybody at the State Department had to either adhere to that policy or resign. Rogers listened to everyone, which made him a good leader, but he also had the expectation that he would be listened to after he told team members his goals.

## Accepting your goals as realistic and doable

After your team accepts your vision in the largest sense, they have to accept that your goals are both realistic and doable. No one wants to believe that he is being sent off to do an impossible job. In the Army, making goals realistic and doable is the heart of *doctrine*. An old story relates that soldiers, faced with a formidable foe, will flee rather than fight, unless they believe that some combination of superiority in strength, weapons, generalship, or cause gives them a reason to stand and fight. The idea of doctrine is to persuade armies to stand and fight — and possibly die — when it makes more sense, from a short-term survival perspective, to run away.

## Making others believe

Convincing your team members that success is possible is a key element to succeeding. During World War II, the U.S. Army Office of Information hired Hollywood director Frank Capra to do a series of doctrinal movies titled *Why We Fight,* which were shown to all soldiers in order to give them a reason to go into battle. But such films were not persuasive by themselves. Generals Eisenhower and Bradley believed that American soldiers were not as well trained as German soldiers, and certainly not as battle hardened. In order to convince American troops to go into battle, the military leadership had to devise a new kind of warfighting doctrine, one that would accomplish the mission of winning the war, and at the same time persuade American soldiers that the war was winnable.

Eisenhower and Bradley decided to overwhelm the Germans with equipment and logistical support, so that what they lacked in experience could be made up for with sheer numbers and overwhelming presence. Moreover, Bradley and Eisenhower wanted their soldiers to concentrate on fighting, and not on the other problems of war, such as getting fed, or getting the wounded attended to. So, for every combat soldier who served in the European front, eight support troops were assigned the tasks of bringing up fresh equipment, food, ammunition, and medical supplies to the front lines and carrying away the wounded. The German army, by contrast, had barely any support units. This convinced American soldiers that the war was winnable, even against heavy odds.

A leader has to tell his team exactly what the problems in achieving a goal are, and what he or she is going to do to overcome those problems. Only then will a group accept that the goal they've been given is doable and realistic.

## Believing in your mission and collective goals

You have the right to assume that your team will accept your plan for accomplishing the mission that will get them to a goal, if you have taken the time to listen to them and answer their questions at the planning stage, and to collect the information that will allow you to pick the right method of getting everyone to a collective goal.

If you are a persuasive leader and can inspire trust in your new group, you can ask that the group accept your judgment of where the group needs to go and how they will get there. You will put your guide's hat on and, having carefully explained all phases of your mission and every team member's role, encourage them to get to work.

# Coming to you for leadership, motivation, and encouragement

After you've got the team going, you have to let them know that your role as leader is not just to give them marching orders. You have to tell them that they must come to you immediately if things are not going according to plan, so that you and they together can figure out what needs to be done to get back on track. Establish a weekly or monthly reporting system so that you can keep track of your goals and whether you are on target. Also, parcel out work by establishing committees, and then work with and motivate your committees, encouraging them and helping them to solve their problems through your direct intervention.

In other words, you have to act like a leader in the most personal sense. If you want people to trust your judgment about where you are taking them, you have to remain highly visible to your team as you move toward a goal.

# Working as a team

Most teams are made up of people who are *not* all voluntarily in agreement about a vision, or a goal, or even how to accomplish a mission. Even after the team has reached general agreement, one or two people, or even whole factions, inevitably will continue to disagree with you. Those people go along with the process of achieving a particular goal because it suits their own ends, but not their own motivations. This situation is especially true in politics, where coalition building is a way of life, and where people who ordinarily disagree can come together to achieve something useful once in a while. As a leader, you need to make sure that unhappy campers do not become disruptive.

# Cooperating to accomplish the goal

Often, getting your team to cooperate to accomplish a goal is just the first step. If the goal is sufficiently difficult to attain, you also have to gain *commitment,* the willingness of the team to work as hard for a goal as the leader who is supposed to help them attain it. Just as you have the right to expect commitment to the goals and mission of the team, you have the right to expect that, after you have all gone to work on a problem, distractions will be minimal. In Tracy Kidder's excellent book from the early 1980s, *The Soul of a New Machine* (published by Avon Books), team esprit — the commitment to the team that is more than just spirit — was so high that several people sacrificed completely their personal lives to get a new computer developed on time. CEO Edson de Castro had given them such an overwhelming sense of mission that they believed they were saving the company, and they were willing to make personal sacrifices to do exactly that.

Most situations don't rise to the level of *complete* commitment. People have personal lives — wives, husbands, children, parents, bills to pay, credit problems, health problems, and a host of personal woes. They have issues about personal self-esteem and whether they are more or less valuable to an organization than their team members, and they have personal aspirations and ambitions as well. None of those problems goes away when you are in the midst of accomplishing a task. Your responsibility, as the leader of the group, is to find ways to help your team members solve their external problems before they interfere with the team's ability to accomplish its mission. But you do have the right to ask team members to keep their minds on the mission and to focus on working through the mission in an orderly fashion.

## Informing your team of resource requirements

You may be the leader of a group, and you may have the world's best tracking system, but you are not a mind reader, and even the best laid plans can develop unforeseen problems. You have the right to tell your team members that it is their responsibility to the mission that they let you know about problems, and about the resources they need to fix those problems, before they become so serious that they derail the entire team.

In other words, you have the right to ask your team members to be responsible — to the mission, and to each other. No leader can be expected to do everything.

## Being accountable and not blaming each other

Things do go wrong, even on the best team, and you have the right to hold people accountable for their mistakes. But accountability does not give you the right to single out people for blame or finger-pointing. Those behaviors are useless and even counterproductive, and they take you away from accomplishing your mission and cause uncertainty among your team. Accountability means finding out what is going wrong and then figuring out a way to fix the problem. Accountability also entails asking that the person who created the problem either take responsibility for getting it fixed or explain to the team why that can't happen. Accountability does not mean assigning blame.

At NASA, when a launch goes awry and a rocket has to be destroyed, they create a committee to assess what went wrong with the mission. People are not penalized for coming forward and explaining what they did that was a deviation from accepted norms and procedures, because the assessment is meant to ensure that the next mission will eliminate the problems that caused the previous mission to fail. The same rule applies at "mortality and morbidity" conferences, which all hospitals hold whenever there is an unexpected patient death. The central idea behind these conferences is that doctors learn from the mistakes of their colleagues, not that blame be assigned.

# Understanding Your Team's Expectations

You, as a leader, have expectations for how your team is going to behave, but your group or team also has expectations about their new leader. Every team member will be a little nervous when you make your first appearance, because each person has an unspoken or unwritten agenda for what he or she wants to accomplish personally and is unsure that you'll be able to provide them with that opportunity. As a leader, you are going to make the effort to listen to everyone to find out what those hidden goals are, whether they are personal or on behalf of the organization, but in the end you are either going to pick one of them or choose your own path, and inevitably disappoint a lot of your team members.

If you accept that leadership doesn't exist by divine right and that command authority extends only to the point where people are willing to rebel against what they perceive to be poor or unjust leadership, then what expectations is a group or a team entitled to have about its new leader? Your team's expectations closely mirror the traits of a leader's personality (see Chapter 3 for more on personality traits of leaders). The following sections cover those expectations.

## Having intelligence

Team members have the right to expect intelligence from their leaders. They don't want to put their fate in the hands of an idiot. But it's more than that. Intelligence, combined with experience and resourcefulness, means that when things go wrong, their leader is far more likely to find a new path for the team to take that will still allow the team to reach the goal it has chosen for itself.

# Communicating thoughts and ideas well

Being smart and having good ideas isn't enough. Effective leadership depends on the maintenance of a bond between leaders and followers, and that bond is best served by communication. Your team has a right to expect that you will keep them in the loop, communicating not only the changes that need to take place but also the reasons behind those changes. Great leaders are often highly eloquent, but eloquence is required only when the task before the group is especially difficult. In most situations, a leader who communicates clearly, succinctly, and swiftly is doing a good job. The timing and speed of a message is as important as what is said or written. People become uncertain when they feel that they are being left in the dark, and they become distrustful of you, their leader when that happens.

# Having a drive to succeed

Your group has the right to expect that your thirst to accomplish a goal is at least as large as theirs, or larger. You are being counted upon to provide the motivation for the group, and the greatest motivator is success. You cannot appear to be lukewarm about the goals or the mission. If you are, rethink them before you take your team or group down a new path. Your team members will appreciate your foresight far more than if you realize that your goal needs to be changed suddenly, or too late.

# Demonstrating a sense of urgency about the mission

Along with the drive to succeed, which is about reaching an endpoint, goes a sense of urgency about mission. People respond to leaders who are constantly motivated. In the midst of a flood, the leader of the sandbagging operation shouldn't suddenly call a two-hour lunch break as the water continues to rise. If the leader did that, everybody would jump in their cars and take off before the flood spilled over the levee, leaving the leader there with sandwich in hand. Most people have a reasonable amount of common sense and understand that work needs to be done within a certain amount of time in order for it to be most effective. A leader is expected to communicate this urgency when the group feels like slacking off.

# Being intellectually honest and rigorous in searching for the truth

Team members have a high expectation that you, their leader, will make every effort to find the truth in any situation, rather than fix blame, or make excuses for why things have gone wrong. You, in turn, have the right to expect them to cooperate in the search for the truth. You also have the right to expect them to bring problems to the attention of leadership early on, so that small problems don't become large ones, or large problems don't become insurmountable. The search for the truth is often difficult, because there is often pressure to find a partial solution so that the team can continue to move forward. But in times of crisis, you want to be the kind of leader who is absolutely rigorous in his or her fact-finding, and who has the courage to make tough changes and choices when they have to be made.

# Exercising good judgment

What constitutes good judgment is anything but straightforward. You don't have to be a moral exemplar. But you are responsible for not putting your followers unnecessarily in harm's way or asking them to do anything that may cause the group as a whole to question either the goal, the mission, or your commitment to either. Good judgment means doing the things that keep a team focused on its goals, but it also means not doing the things that distract the team from those goals.

# Being dependable and consistent in your behavior

With good judgment goes consistency and dependability, but only in the constructive sense. Attila the Hun was consistent, but his behavior was bloodthirsty and caused fear even among his own people. Today, leaders must lead by example and by creating trust among their followers. So dependable behavior means doing the things that keep communication open between leaders and followers, and not behaving in an arbitrary or negative manner when things go wrong. Your team members have the right to expect that you won't act with arbitrary favoritism toward other members of the group, or take action at their expense, without an explanation that is consistent with the mission and goals of the group.

# Creating an atmosphere of trust

Good judgment, consistency of behavior, and dependability lead to trust, and your team members expect that you will trust them, and that you will be worthy of their trust, individually and as a group. In order for that to happen, you must be open and communicative, and not secretive or shut off from the rest of the group. Your team members have the right to expect that you will be solicitous of the needs and welfare of the group and of individual members, that you will provide them with the things you need to accomplish your mission, and that you will not give any excuses for why you haven't followed through on your word.

# Creating a learning environment

You and your team members are going to make mistakes, as we all do. But instead of being punished for your mistakes or doing the same to your team members, you need to show them a better way to get your task accomplished. You also need to give them the opportunity to learn not only from your leadership, but from the group as a whole. The best groups are learning environments, where new information is taken in, fit into a framework of existing knowledge, and then disseminated to the group as a whole, so that the mission can be adjusted long before a problem becomes critical. Your job is to create and maintain that learning environment, and to become involved in bringing team members into the learning process at every phase of a mission.

# Looking for common ground to minimize conflict

"Curse you and the horse you rode in on" is an old maxim for new leaders. Many of your team members, faced with you, a new leader, ask the same questions you may have asked yourself, though with a different cast and in a different tone of voice. Why did they choose you? Who are you to tell me what to do? Why should I follow you? Members of a team are naturally skeptical of any new leader, especially an organizational leader imposed from outside the group (the headmaster of a school, hired by a committee of faculty and parents, for example). No matter how careful the selection process, some team members will question you and your role as leader.

What do you do under the circumstances? Your group has the right to expect that you will not become the group's major source of conflict, which is a polite way of saying that they expect you to reach out to them to find ways to create consensus. Even the most skeptical person wants to be convinced and sold on the idea that you are the right choice to lead them. After all, the imposition of a leader upon a group is something like the arrangement between a teacher and a student. The teacher has a group of kids he or she has been assigned to teach, and it is the student's job to be in class. As each depends upon the other, the atmosphere in class becomes easier to tolerate, and real learning eventually takes place.

After you and your team have joined together, your team has the right to continue to expect that you will take the lead in resolving and minimizing conflicts among team members, and between yourself and other members of the group. You will never please everyone, but you can at least get the most difficult members of your group to concede that your goal and mission are worthwhile and that they have a vested interest — their career growth, perhaps — in seeing it completed.

# Living Up to the Expectations of Your Superiors

You may have been selected for a leadership position and then imposed upon a team or a group and told to lead them toward a goal. Sometimes, the goal will be one of your own choosing, but in highly structured, multilayered organizations, the most you can hope for is that you will be given a reasonable amount of freedom in selecting your mission.

The people who selected you to lead have expectations, too, and you are going to have to balance their expectations against your own and those of your group. Just as your group may be initially skeptical of you and your ability to lead, even the most enthusiastic and encouraging executive team will have you "on probation" until you prove yourself. So you have to know what the expectations of upper management are, if you are going to meet them.

## Establishing goals and missions quickly

Most people who place individuals in positions of leadership, whether they are assigning someone to run a division of a company or to serve as the head coach of a team, have an expectation that you will do whatever it is you were hired to do — and do it quickly. Team owners don't like to hear about five-year rebuilding programs. Even if they know that it will take a full five years to reach a championship level, they expect to see continual year-to-year improvement. If you are made the head of a division, and you are given a three-year window to improve profits, your superiors will still expect you to have some effect on profitability within a quarter or two of your arrival. If you don't at least appear to be making changes, you will be called in quickly and be expected to give an accounting of what you've been doing with your time.

# Marshalling your resources to the maximum benefit

Getting off the dime quickly means that you have to be expeditious about learning what resources are available and then getting the resources you need. If you are a head coach, that means making a quick but detailed assessment of your existing team, determining the players' strengths and weaknesses, figuring out who is tradable and who is going to retire, and then going out and drafting and training new players, who will fit an offensive or defensive scheme that makes sense to them.

Marshalling resources does not just mean throwing money or people at a problem. It means teaching people so that they are more capable of doing what you need them to do with the resources you have at your disposal. If you are a newly appointed division manager, marshalling your resources may mean looking at the plant, equipment, personnel, your existing brands, and your research and development effort, and then reworking each within the budget you've been given to find the combination that delivers the best prospects of growth.

# Keeping senior management from being surprised

Even more than quick positive results, senior managers are obsessed with not being blindsided by negative results. If you find that the division you've just been appointed to head is in much more serious trouble than you were lead to believe, even if you made a detailed preliminary examination of the situation, do not hesitate to report this fact back to the senior management, along with recommendations for fixing the problem. Be prepared to defend your assessment. After all, you will be telling management that your predecessor blindsided them. So be certain that you understand your problems at every level.

Likewise, if you are a new head coach, and you've been given five years to get to a championship, and you discover that your team is even worse than their existing record indicates, you'd better rethink your plans and find a way to get more out of the people you have. This strategy may mean hiring more assistant coaches, but it may also mean devising a completely new style of play that has little to do with the way you have previously coached. No matter what, one of the most important jobs you have in keeping senior management informed is managing their expectations. A little honesty early on in the game goes a long way toward giving yourself the room you need to make effective changes.

## *Building an effective team that can operate without you*

Leadership is always temporary, and nowhere is this more true than in situations where you have been appointed as a leader from outside the group. You know that, succeed or fail, you are going to be replaced at some point, either because you are going to be rewarded with additional responsibility and more authority, or because you were ineffective and are going to be looking for a new career somewhere else. Under the circumstances, senior management expects you not only to achieve your mission and goals but also to build an effective and cohesive team in the process, so that your successor's job will be a little easier.

Building a cohesive team does not mean building a cult atmosphere that will send your team into terminal mourning upon your departure. It means delegating authority and responsibility early in your leadership tenure and teaching your team how to achieve its goals no matter who is leading them. It also means explaining the role of your group to the larger organization, so that they think of your job as worthwhile (which, in turn, gives you a little job security in the future).

# Chapter 11

# The Axioms of Leadership

● ● ● ● ● ● ● ● ● ● ● ● ● ● ● ● ● ● ● ● ● ● ● ● ● ● ● ● ● ● ● ● ● ● ●

## In This Chapter

▶ What leaders do

▶ How they do it

● ● ● ● ● ● ● ● ● ● ● ● ● ● ● ● ● ● ● ● ● ● ● ● ● ● ● ● ● ● ● ● ● ● ●

> *The genius of a good leader is to leave behind him a situation which common sense, without the trace of genius, can deal with successfully.*
> —Walter Lippmann

The German word for "management" is *Fuehrungskunst,* which doesn't mean management at all, but rather "the art of leadership." In most countries, however, leadership and management are two very different things. Most European and Asian companies have active boards of directors, who provide the hands-on decision making and leadership for their companies. Managers, on the other hand, simply execute the missions they have been given by the board.

In the United States, leadership is more democratic, and leadership and management are more integrated. Most corporate boards of directors are advisory, and do not provide direction. The board's major functions are to hire a chief executive officer and then to review periodically his success or failure. The chief executive, who is the primary executive leader, then hires his own cadre of leaders and managers, without the advice or consent of the board. Goals and visions are approved by the board, as are the decisions to allocate major resources. But by and large, American CEOs are left free to lead and manage.

The American structure blurs the line between leadership and management. (And confusion that results from the gray areas often causes difficulties for American managers.) Make no mistake, however: Leadership and management are different entities:

> ✔ Leadership sets the style and tone for achieving a vision and motivates people to sacrifice for the attainment of the vision.
>
> ✔ Management is the *tactical process* of executing and achieving the mission: Management's concerns lie with the details and the day-to-day grind without which a vision can't become a reality.

Leadership is about vision, and management is about execution. This chapter shows you the differences between leaders and managers and what these differences can mean to you.

# What Leaders Do

Leadership and management overlap in that they both require you to embrace responsibility in order to be successful. The leader is responsible for his or her followers. The manager has to be willingly responsible for the details of the mission. Because missions are often highly detail-oriented, it is easy to become obsessed with the day-to-day aspects of a mission, and in the process, lose a goal or vision. There is a song that asks the question, "Where were they going without ever knowing the way?" Managers will go forward without knowing the way, whereas leaders are supposed to be scouting the path ahead. The following sections concentrate on how leaders and managers differ.

## Leaders provide a check and balance on managers

One of a leader's most important jobs is to prevent management from overrunning an enterprise, and to keep management's responsibilities properly aligned with that of the leader's vision. Left to their own devices, managers will always micromanage, worrying about small details and missing the big picture. Because much of management is rule-based, managers left to their own devices will bury an enterprise in endless red tape and rules. As a leader, you have to ask yourself constantly what the systems and structures that make up your enterprise are doing to help the enterprise achieve its vision, and which things are unnecessary to the smooth operation of your group. The systems and structures can include finance, personnel, research and development, marketing, operations, manufacturing, and distribution. Next, ask the managers of those departments the same question. You may find differences between your expectations and their answers. In that case, your role as a leader calls for you to do what is necessary to bring your systems back on track.

# Use common sense

You'd be surprised how easily some people complicate the tasks they've been given. People will take simple responsibilities that are crystal clear and proceed to muddy the waters. Several factors can do battle with your common sense:

- A lack of the knowledge that comes from the experience of doing
- A desire to impress someone with how smart you are
- Becoming overwhelmed by a task

If you want to lead, start with normal, sensible things, things that seem to obviously relate to reaching a goal.

What is a sensible thing? Take the story of a paper products company that decided to produce a super-strong, super-absorbent paper towel during the early 1970s. The division head delivered the mission to his R&D team, which came up with a towel that was paper laid over a web of nylon fibers. The product was a marketer's dream when it was tested, and the company spent millions introducing the product. The problem was, it was sold mostly in the suburbs, where many houses had in-sink waste disposal systems. The nylon fibers wouldn't shred and instead clogged the disposals and burned out their motors. After the company received several hundred complaints in the space of the first month, they killed the product — and the division head's career.

If you think that the division head made a sensible product and the customers were wrong for not using common sense, think again! If people are getting mad at the product, they're not going to buy it. Nothing else matters.

# Hang your goals on the wall

In almost every enterprise, leaders develop plans, present them to senior management, and then go off to execute after approval. How do you remember what the goal is? Take the page out of your presentation that states the goal and have it blown up to poster size. Make enough copies for yourself and every member of your team, and then hang the poster on the wall that you face every day. If you see the goal, and your people see the goal, it's hard to say later, "Uh, I forgot."

# Make a contract with your team

Looking at a poster of your goal doesn't provide enough impetus on its own. Everyone has to pledge to implement the goal and to not lose sight of the goal while undertaking the tasks of the mission. After everyone agrees on a goal, sit down and write an agreement between you and all the members of your team. State clearly what the goal is and loosely define the mission. Give everyone a copy, and ask each person to sign it and return it to you. Make copies, sign them all, and return the two-signature copies to each person. Then, when you have meetings, refer to that contract whenever problems arise. The contract keeps people focused.

## Keep the task simple and obvious

Good engineers live by what's called the "K.I.S.S." rule, which means, "Keep it simple, stupid." Everything you do as a leader should be oriented toward finding simpler, clearer, more direct ways of doing things — not just clearer to you, but clearer to anyone who is going to be executing the plan. If you are writing a manual or a set of instructions, it has to be written so that a person with little or no education or experience with your product can figure out what to do.

## Change your criteria for selecting managers

If you want to build better managers, look for people who are capable of becoming leaders. Most of the time, companies select managers based on their professional know-how. If you have a research laboratory, you hire a Ph.D. to run it. If you have a marketing organization, you promote the top sales or marketing person into the job.

That manager may indeed be the most competent person in terms of job experience, but the best person for any management spot has other qualities:

✔ **An ability to move the group forward.** The manager you want has the creativity to come up with a vision of her own. She has the commitment to the goal that will lead her to come to you in the early stages of developing problems. You don't want someone who will simply move ahead blindly, taking her mission so literally that she actually argues with you when an obvious change needs to be made.

✔ **The knack for focusing on the tasks at hand.** An effective manager reminds his people that their future depends on their ability to meet the goals upon which they've agreed, and that playing office politics is a waste of time. In many companies, and in many other situations where leadership is diffused, people will look for allies outside their team, or try to influence a manager by attempting to exert influence on the people above him. As a leader, a good manager always keeps the people above him intimately informed about what is going on with his team. He doesn't allow himself to be blindsided.

✔ **Courage and good, steady nerves.** You want your managers to come to you early and first if the mission begins to stray off course, and you want them to be unafraid when they come to you. If you have been listening to them and building trust, your team will develop courage, even in the face of adversity.

# Focus on people, not on systems

We can't think of any way to get around the fact that organizations need, well, organization, to run properly. Organization means creating systems and imposing structures and rules that govern the interrelationships between the different parts of an organization. As the organization becomes larger, the rules become more complex and case-driven. (*Case-driven* is a fancy way of saying that in large organizations, what you are allowed to do in the future is often based upon what was done in the past.)

So people in large organizations tend to find a level of comfort and approval simply by obeying the rules. "Go along to get along" is a commonly heard phrase in many rule-driven organizations. That phrase shouldn't apply, even to the lowest-level worker. Your goal as a leader should be to eliminate unnecessary rules. Question everything, and question it with the needs of your team in mind.

Straying too far in the rule-unmaking direction is just as easy as making too many rules. Never, never, never unmake any rule that may lead to the harm of any teammate or worker, even if the rule appears to be trivial and represents a case that rarely happens. Bad things do happen, and you don't want to be the subject of a review that asks the question, "Who was the moron who did away with that rule?"

The lowest levels of management most often are the people who deal directly with your customers or your customers' customers. Make the effort to teach those managers the same flexibility about rule-making, with the emphasis — like Webster Bank — on building customer trust.

# Take the long view

Nobody, not even a savior, can improve an organization overnight. If you happen to be an extremely charismatic and effective leader, your presence may improve morale quickly and allow previously dispirited managers and lower level leaders to face problems they may have previously avoided. But such improvements are short-term gains, much the way that an initial dose of medicine may have a short-term effect on a sick patient. One of the reasons your doctor tells you to take a course of antibiotics for a week or more is that the process of becoming well takes time.

ANECDOTE

## Make the rules serve the organization, not vice versa

During the Great Depression, a lumber mill owner founded Webster Bank, now a medium-sized banking group in Connecticut. The owner reasoned that if people couldn't get mortgages from conventional banks, they wouldn't build houses, which would mean that they wouldn't buy his lumber. So Webster Smith, after whom the bank is named, made a point of keeping the bank's mortgage decision-making rules to a minimum. Under the bank's current CEO, Jim Smith, the bank continues to follow that policy and has long been considered a leader in customer relations. All managers have the discretion to bend the bank's rules, and that discretion extends down to the teller level. Because the bank actively works to build trust with its customers, the customers respond with lower-than-normal loan-delinquency rates.

What works for Webster Bank should work in any organization. As a leader, ask your managers to review, on a regular basis, all policies and rules for which they are directly responsible. Tell them that as a goal, they must eliminate one rule per quarter. Your managers must explain the rule, why it existed, and why it is no longer necessary. That exercise will put them into the right mental framework for focusing on people.

But the bureaucratic mentality dies hard, so you have to do more, and so do your managers. Make a policy: No new rule can be implemented without review by the responsible leader, and all rules made will have a time limit. So-called "sunset laws" have worked well in government to streamline policy-making. Sunset laws limit the amount of time rules can be in effect without coming up for review. Your organization should figure out how to do the same thing.

The same holds true for any organization. When an organization responds quickly to your leadership, you can easily persuade yourself that you have done the right things. Remember that responsiveness, while gratifying to your ego, is just a tiny step in moving your organization toward its goals. Don't lose sight of the big picture.

## Break goals down to a manageable size

The easiest way to keep your team on an upward path is to take your long-range goal and break it down into a series of smaller, more manageable goals, each of which leads logically to the next goal.

Dividing large goals into smaller, more manageable objectives:

- ✔ Gives you time to assess your situation and readjust your mission.
- ✔ Enables you to assess the capabilities of your team.

✔ Provides you the time to bring new learning to the group at each stage, so they don't have to absorb too much new knowledge at once.

✔ Gives you time to build trust between you and your team.

✔ Encourages your team with a series of small, morale-building successes, instead of a single make-or-break event.

## Never miss an opportunity to rethink

Leaders plan and work toward today's goals, but the job doesn't stop there. You also must think about the future needs of your enterprise and what the morrow may bring in the way of threats and opportunities. Any opportunity that requires you to think about a current goal or mission should also be an opportunity for you to think about the future — your enterprise's and your own.

Rethinking requires that you identify the root of problems and solve them. Say you are a division-level leader and you are attempting to wring off a couple of percentage points from your general, selling, and administrative GSA expenses — the overhead that eats up profits. You examine your costs and you find that personnel costs tie up a lot of your GSA. If that expense applies to you, then it's probably true for other division leaders as well. Your first step should be to informally poll your peers, the other division managers. Tell them that your personnel costs are high, and ask them about their own costs. If you find one manager whose costs are more than 10 percent lower than yours are, find out why. Your solution may be to emulate what he or she is doing — a kind of "best practice" exercise — and you can achieve a benefit in the short term.

## Coach your team to victory

In order to get into the mentality of learning how to take a long-range view, put on your Coach's Hat. Take your ultimate goal and think of it as akin to reaching the Super Bowl or the NCAA Final Four. Call your time horizon for achieving the ultimate goal your "season." Break your long-term goal into short-term goals and call each short-term goal a "game." If you win the first game, proceed on to the second. If you lose the first game, do what the coaches do. Watch film and adjust your strategy, which means, review your mission and make changes in it, in team members, in the commitment of resources, or whatever else you need to win the next game. Follow that formula until you start winning — achieving or exceeding each short-term goal — and then repeat what you've done for the entire "season," and you will achieve your long-term goal.

But if everyone has costs that are out of line, ask the other division managers to a meeting, which you should chair, to discuss the problem. Invite the head of personnel to join your meeting, and propose that you set up a task force to look into the problem. Don't say that you want to cut your costs, because that translates to the head of the personnel department as "cut the budget" or "shrink the personnel department." Instead, your goal is to enable personnel to be more productive on your behalf — it will produce the same savings as cutting the budget — and allow them to do more.

The exercise may lead you into an entirely new set of experiences, and may help shape your career in an entirely new direction.

Robert Walker had been Hewlett-Packard's chief information officer for several years when he began to consider rethinking HP's entire approach to information management. "We asked ourselves the question," says Walker, "How do you propagate knowledge?" To answer that question, he put together a band of experts from all parts of the company. His team quickly found, in discussion, that every division had some problems in common, so they figured that if they could get these people to come up with a solution, it would be a solution that would satisfy the great majority of users. They also reasoned as a group that because the ideas were coming from the division level, they would meet less resistance than if a corporate information systems department imposed them.

One of the first ideas the group came up with was that information and communication standards had to improve service. "One of the big mistakes that people make is to view a standard as an end in itself rather than as a means for improving service or lowering cost," says Walker. "We decided that anything we were going to do had to result in a measurable service improvement to all users." Walker chuckles at his own statement. "Hewlett-Packard, you have to remember, is a measurement company, so when we say *measurable service improvement,* we really mean it. We were looking at issues such as how many calls people were making to the help desk, how long it took to get a fix, how long it took to get new hardware and software installed, you name it, we were measuring it from a service perspective."

The first chunk of the problem was solved in 1989, when the entire company decided to create a global network based on the Internet, using the Internet standard communications protocols for relaying information back and forth among HP employees. In retrospect, HP's decision to do that became significant because it predated the rollout of the World Wide Web. Had the Web been brought public using a different communication standard, it may have cost HP millions of dollars to change its network, because HP employees would be able to communicate by computer with each other, but not with the outside world. With the network protocols established, local managers began exchanging information over the network a year later, in 1990.

Putting HP's internal communication on the Internet solved many problems for about two years, but the goal of providing better service kept the group looking for solutions, and what they finally came up with is something they call a *common operating environment.*

Although the process of creating a uniform operating environment was considerable, Walker says that the company does not have an IT budget. "If you have a budget," Walker says, "the first thing any manager does is try to keep expenses down. That immediately changes the focus of the problem, which should really be, 'How do you get the maximum utility value out of your information infrastructure?' If you focus on money and cost savings, you're always going to sacrifice service, and that's easy to do, because often, you can't measure the productivity gains you make from better service. But they are there, and they do add up."

# Every enterprise stands on its own

As a leader, you hold your people accountable, and accountability sometimes means that you must recognize failure as well as success. When a group you are leading or are responsible for consistently fails to meet its goals, you have to soberly assess the leadership — your own and that of the people who report to you — and the commitment of resources you are making to that group. In companies, this is one of the hardest things to do, because almost every business unit has long-established, well-entrenched interests.

If you are making the decision on a group's future, you have to consider the greater good by asking:

- ✔ Will closing down the unit hurt the larger effort?
- ✔ Can work be outsourced with a minimum of disruption?
- ✔ Has the team really been given a fair chance to make improvements?

All these questions are necessary, but you also have to ask yourself what more you could have done to head off the crisis.

# Renovate before you innovate

An old Yankee maxim goes like this: "Buy it new. Wear it out. Make do or do without." Every enterprise could benefit from paying better attention to that maxim. Conventional management theory differs from the old wisdom and insists that you should throw out the old in favor of the new. This theory, known as the *S-curve of investment,* attempts to apply the law of diminishing returns to research and development. It's one of the worst ideas to come out of management theory during the 1960s and 1970s.

Hearkening to the S-curve of investment theory rather than holding onto important patents and reworking technologies, American business ceased innovating in the entire field of consumer electronics and in the auto industry. Thus, while the transistor, television, VCR, and a host of other gadgets were developed in the U.S., the really huge profits were made on these devices by the Japanese, who bought licenses on the original patents — sold cheaply by Americans who didn't believe there was any innovation potential left. The Japanese proceeded to add new features to the devices, and to make them better and less expensive. It was only in the late 1980s — when American industry abandoned the S-curve in favor of the Japanese idea of Continuous Improvement — that American industry suddenly became competitive again.

## Continuous Improvement isn't just for products

Continuous Improvement is a good idea for leaders in all areas, not just technology and products. All leaders should have the idea of Continuous Improvement embedded in their minds; Continuous Improvement should be every leader's goal. Anything you can do, you can do better. If quality is your goal, then you should keep working at it until mistakes are so rare that they are a cause for curiosity. If customer service is your goal, then getting to zero complaints isn't enough. Your goal should be universal customer praise. If you are a Little League coach or a teacher, your role model should be Glenn Holland, the character that Richard Dreyfuss played in the movie *Mr. Holland's Opus*. The film is about a music teacher who is so dedicated and so good that when he retires, virtually every student from his more than 30-year career comes back to the school to wish him well.

# How Leaders Do It

Of all the attributes of leadership, the one thing that leaders do more often than anything else is make decisions. Harry Truman's motto, "The buck stops here," ultimately applies to every leader. That's why you have the marshal's baton. You're in charge, and after all is said and done, you are going to be evaluated, promoted, or fired based on the outcome of your decisions.

## Timing is everything

If you have been listening to your team, eliciting their cooperation, and have your team's trust, what more do you need to do? Principally, you need to be decisive. Your decisions have to be convincing and be made swiftly, after you have all the information you need. One of your primary axioms as a leader should be, "Seize the moment." Time spent hesitating after you are capable of making a decision is time lost. Taking too much time is one factor that will undermine the confidence of your followers, and it is time that will allow a competitor to gain an advantage.

## Focus on vision and goals

The best way to improve your decision-making speed is to keep focused on the vision and goals that you are bringing to the group. If you are leading your group well, they will help you devise a mission and a plan to get started, but remember: Missions and plans change, as they confront a changing set of information and new realities. So don't worry too much about the need for making perfect decisions about plans and missions. If you are a middle-level leader, keep your superiors informed that your mission and plan is subject to adjustment, but that you remain committed to the goals you have agreed upon. Keep an eye on your plan so that you haven't committed too far.

When pilots fly across the ocean, they reach something called "the point of no return." This is the point in the ocean where the combination of the fuel they have on board, the weather conditions, the condition of the plane, and other factors are such that continuing toward a destination is easier than turning back.

The same principle applies to organizations and enterprises. Your ultimate goal, for example, may be to change a money-losing division into one growing at 15 percent a year. After committing resources, it may become clear that you are going to reach only 5 percent. Do you stop and replan and recast the mission to reach 15 percent? If you are early in the mission-execution process, you might, but if you have passed the point of no return — you have committed substantial resources of time, money, and people — it is up to you to help adjust people's expectations. A 5 percent gain is like attempting to fly from New York to Paris and running out of fuel over Ireland. You haven't crashed, and you can refuel after a brief stopover, and then decide to fly on to Paris, or maybe change destinations and go on to Moscow.

How do you improve your timing? Keep three phrases in mind:

✔ **Recognize what is needed early.** No situation exists without a history. Even start-up organizations have the histories of the people on the team and a prior competitive marketplace to guide them. You may have a new technology that you consider revolutionary, but in fact, there is no such thing as new technology without prior art. Most of the time, you will be taking over a group with a long history, one that has a trajectory of events that you are being asked to change. You may be taking over the best fund-raising organization in existence, but if you are its new leader, you are going to be expected to reach new heights. You may be starting up a restaurant, but other restaurants are undoubtedly in the area. You know that those restaurants have enough traffic so you believe the area can sustain another restaurant — yours.

✔ **Take advantage of history.** Use history to truncate your goal-setting and planning processes so that you can get to the mission more quickly. The first thing you should do as the leader of a new group is ask the person in the group with the most history to bring the group — and you — up to speed. Use that meeting to ask questions and increase your store of information, and to help shape a goal. By recognizing early what the problems are, you will have a significant leg up on determining what your goals should be.

✔ **Accelerate the decision-making process.** Set deadlines for information-gathering. The first test of your group's ability to pull together is its ability to put together a situation analysis of its problems. In many organizations, each department leaves such analyses to one person. That's *wrong*. Situation analysis is a group responsibility. If the group does not fully participate, no learning takes place. Your team will either passively accept or reject analysis in which they didn't take part, and they will resent the fact that they were denied a chance for input.

Making everyone responsible for information-gathering shortens the planning process, and it shortens the distance you have to go before you decide on goals.

✔ **Implement decisions quickly.** After you collect all the information you need to make decisions, make the decisions quickly. Don't torture yourself and the people around you with indecisiveness. It is demoralizing for your team if they have to sit around while you slowly and ponderously ponder the future.

# Chapter 12

# Managing as a Leader

· · · · · · · · · · · · · · · · · · · · · · · · · · · · · · · · · · · · · · · · · · · · · · · · · · · · · · · ·

### In This Chapter

▶ Knowing what to delegate

▶ Learning how to delegate

▶ Setting goals and measuring your progress

▶ Settling disputes among team members

▶ Helping your team find its own path

· · · · · · · · · · · · · · · · · · · · · · · · · · · · · · · · · · · · · · · · · · · · · · · · · · · · · · · ·

> *Our life is frittered away by detail . . . simplify, simplify.*
> —Henry David Thoreau

*L*eading is about decision-making, and one of the most important decisions you can make is to let your team make the decisions.

## Setting Reasonable Goals — Forget the Impossible Dream

A leader's primary responsibility is setting goals. The first rule is, "Learn to be realistic about the goals you set." When Peter Derow was president of *Newsweek* back in the early 1970s, a piece of advice he used to hand out was, "Take care in how you set your goals. If you set them too high and don't reach them, you will be seen as a failure. If you set them lower and then exceed your goals, people will look at you as a hero." Derow could have added, "Don't set them too low, or management will think you're too timid."

Matching goals to your group's abilities takes planning and perspective, and it takes a critical and honest evaluation of your team, the resources you have been given, and where in the pack of competitors you currently sit. If your Little League team finished in last place last summer, telling the kids that they

## The theory of relativity

If the senior leaders of your company have given you a Mission Impossible, work with them to readjust their expectations. A marketing executive at a financial services software firm was given the job of growing his company's sales by 30 percent annually. His bonus and stock options depended upon his ability to hit that number. When the stock markets took a tumble during the summer of 1998, it became impossible for him to hit that target. For 1999, the CEO reiterated the target, and said, "Forget about 1998. It was a bad year. I won't pay you a bonus, but I won't fire you, either." The marketing executive said, "You're calculating wrong. We grew sales by 12 percent when the market demand for our product was declining by 20 percent. 'Relative to the market' we grew our sales by 32 percent." His boss thought it over and paid him the bonus.

can win the championship this year is probably unreasonable, and is likely to put too much pressure on them. On the other hand, if your team was in last place and lost the great majority of games by two runs or less, the addition of one more good pitcher and slightly better fielding, along with the maturity, experience, and better coordination that comes with age, may indeed send you to Williamsport, Pennsylvania, the site of the Little League World Series. But that should be a privately held hope, not a goal that you're going to sell to the team. Realistically, you have to believe that with improvement, you can win half of the games that you previously lost.

How do you set reasonable goals? Keep in mind the maxim, "Things take time." Rome wasn't built in a day, and even the most charismatic leader can't improve a bad situation overnight. You should want to, and you should bring the drive and commitment that says you will seize any opportunity to reach your ultimate goal; but you don't want to burn out your team on false hopes and wasted labor before they have reached the ultimate goal. Instead, tell your team what your ultimate goal is and set up a series of milestones, which, if you accomplish them, teammates can look upon as "mini-goals" that they've achieved.

How you measure your goals is as important as the goals themselves. If you pick the wrong targets, or if you allow others to pick your goals for you, you greatly increase your chances that you will not measure up. Conversely, if you take a strong, leadership role in setting your goals, you will show yourself to be accountable for your success or failure up front, but you will also have a better understanding of what is expected of you, because you will have participated in the decision-making process.

✔ As a leader, you never want people to judge you on an absolute basis, but on a relative basis — relative to how your competitors are doing.

✔ As a leader, you want to be able to find multiple measurements of performance rather than a single measurement. Your superiors may have given you a sales target that proves impossible to reach; however, if you can show that you lowered your cost of selling or your cost of new customer acquisition, or increased customer loyalty as measured by a retention rate, you will live to fight another day, because those are all indicators of progress, both to your team and to your superiors.

# Delegating to Your Team

Although many new managers are reluctant to delegate authority, fearing that it may cause them to lose control or that others may perceive them as weak, nothing could be farther from the truth. Delegating authority, when done properly, is one of the most useful tools a leader possesses to build team spirit, motivation, and cohesion.

A good leader spends a lot of time at the beginning of the planning process, ensuring that every team member has a delegated task. Your job is to make team members feel completely wedded to your team's goals (see the section, "Setting Reasonable Goals — Forget the Impossible Dream," earlier in this chapter). Delegating authority is one of the best ways to do that.

## Knowing how to delegate — don't get bogged down by people

So much of delegating is wrapped up with choosing *who* to delegate authority to, that the primary rule of delegating is "Don't get bogged down by people." You are leading people, of course, but as a leader, you have to learn how to avoid the inevitable squabbles that arise out of personality conflicts, charges of favoritism, jealousy, and dishonesty. When we say "don't get bogged down by people," we mean "don't allow yourself to be distracted by all the petty aspects of human behavior."

When you assume a new leadership role, ask for an organizational chart, so that you know what the reporting lines of authority are supposed to be. That's just a start. Also ask around to find out who has the real power, and revise your chart accordingly to reflect the way decisions and resources flow in your area.

### SWOT your staff

Your first step in assuming a new leadership role is to conduct a *SWOT,* which means identifying the strengths, weaknesses, opportunities, and threats of the most important members of your team (for more information about SWOT charts, see Chapter 6). In the beginning, as you review personnel files, forget about job titles. Look instead at strengths and weaknesses.

- ✔ **What do previous leaders say about your team members?** Do they identify particular people as obstacles, or say that your team is easy to work with? Do they identify people with important knowledge, or people who are especially effective? Ask about these things to get a fix on the capabilities of the group.

- ✔ **Do you see any discernible patterns?** Have several previous leaders told you the same things about the group? That could mean that there is an institutionalized pattern of behavior. It could make the group more effective and cohesive, or it could be the group's undoing.

- ✔ **Do any glaring weaknesses stand out?** Does the group consistently meet its goals, or are there constant struggles? If so, where are those struggles focused? Is it particular individuals or is it an entire department?

- ✔ **Does the team member have particular strengths?** Skills such as written and oral presentation skills, analytical capabilities, decisiveness in action, and good judgment may indicate leadership potential, regardless of functional specialty.

- ✔ **Are there team members who are brilliant but don't fit in?** These may be team members to whom you want to delegate a special project in order to give them the encouragement to become a vital member of your team.

You should also complete a sober assessment of your own strengths and weaknesses, and you ought to be looking at people who can fill in for you where you're weak. If you have come this far as a leader, you probably know where you need improvement and what your skills are. Look around your group to find people who complement your strengths and who can help you overcome your weaknesses, and give them responsibility for doing those things you don't do particularly well.

After conducting a SWOT analysis, go through your goal-setting and planning process (Chapter 6 covers goal setting and planning in detail), and at the same time, do a SWOT analysis of your competitive situation. Try to do the analysis in terms of the skills needed to reach the goal. For example, if you're a market laggard with a superior product, your analysis tells you that you have to communicate your message better. Do you have a superior communicator on your team? No matter what that person's functional title is, you want that person sitting in when the marketing department and the advertising agency are planning strategy.

Try to find out from the next level of management above you who is "ear-marked" for promotion. Every organization has people who, fairly or not, are protected and seem to have a clear track for advancement. Compare the actual work performance of such people with what has been said about them. If it is equal, then give them more responsibility. If their work performance is sub par, find something for them to do that has significant ceremonial meaning, but that won't bog down your mission or the team's ability to accomplish its goals. If there is such a person in your organization, the best use of that person will often be as a bridge to higher management, to help buy your team more resources.

## Choosing up sides

The problem for leaders comes when people who want to be chosen for a task besiege the leader. Do you remember when you were a kid and you were choosing up sides for a game? The two people who did the choosing, usually the two best athletes who functioned as team captains, had to make quick decisions about who they wanted for their sides. Not only did they choose on the basis of athletic skills in descending order (the best players were picked first, the worst players were left for last), but they also took into account factors such as trust (whether they had previous playing experience with one person over another), and such convoluted factors as whether, in order to get player A (who was great) you had to pick player B, player A's best friend (who was pretty awful). Finally, after sides were chosen up, the captain then had to find something for each person to do. In softball, that meant that the good hitters were at the top of the lineup and the poor hitters were at the bottom. And the people with good hands played infield, while the clumsiest player got stuck out in right field where he would do the least damage and could spend time praying that no ball would be hit in his direction.

Choosing up sides and assigning positions in a game is a simple leadership experience compared to delegating authority in a large organizational situation, or even in a volunteer setting. You may often manage to others' expectations; therefore, the roles and tasks that you assign and delegate may often seem to be less likely under your control. Delegating authority is something like choosing up sides with someone standing to one side who has both veto and insistence power. "You can have player A, but you can't have player B under any circumstances, even if he or she wants to be on your team and is a perfect fit."

Moreover, many of the people you may deal with already have well-defined jobs. If you're being charged with running a division, the sales people don't want to suddenly have to do finance, and the finance people don't want to get their hands dirty with production, despite the fact that it may actually help the entire organization.

### *Recruit stars when you can; train employees when you can't*

You will inevitably find holes in your team. Like the football coach who needs an extra linebacker or the baseball coach who needs a good shortstop to plug up the gap in the infield, you may find that you need specific "role players" to meet your goals.

Where do you find them? They may exist within another division of your company, but more than likely, they work for your competitors or are people in subordinate positions who want to step up and embrace the challenge of more responsibility. In order to convince such people that they want to work for you, you need to demonstrate to them that your team and your workplace can provide certain advantages. These include the following:

- ✔ **Provide a feeling of participation.** The American workforce is now the best educated in the world. To ignore the talents and knowledge of the people you hire, because of rigid job designs or a tight hierarchical structure, is to throw away a significant resource. The best companies actively seek out the knowledge of their workers to lower costs, to improve the design of their products, to make them more competitive, and to aid in decision-making.

  Any company can get more out of its employees by designing processes that bring worker knowledge to the attention of top management without the filtering that often goes on through middle management. One of the best ways to do this is to reward managers who bring the suggestions and ideas of their workers to the attention of management, and to make it a basis by which their performance is measured.

- ✔ **Provide opportunities for advancement.** Everyone is capable of advancement, under the right circumstances. Great leaders create the mechanisms for all their team members not only to excel but also to find the level at which they can do their best work. Great leaders also add responsibility to their team members when they are ready for it, to keep them involved and committed.

- ✔ **Meet the personal needs of your employees.** Not so long ago, the workplace was homogeneous in almost every way. Not only were all the employees white males, but they lived in similar neighborhoods and had nuclear families with parents who were able to take care of themselves and with children who could be allowed a fair degree of independence because the streets were quiet and safe. The world is different now, and it is unlikely to become so homogeneous ever again. Moreover, the demand for college graduates will continue to outpace supply for the rest of this decade. The demand for skilled workers is insatiable, and virtually every business is hiring, so it is easy to understand why the workplace is going to become increasingly diverse. With that diversity comes a very wide range of work habits and outside-of-work needs.

A company that wants to get the greatest commitment from its workers must be fully prepared to meet those needs and to minimize the inevitable distractions that life now brings to the workplace, by providing day care, a range of health care options, flextime, and job sharing. When you take on the responsibility for a team, you take on the responsibility for people's lives. You have a right to expect discipline and concentration on the job, but you have to do the things necessary to encourage the behavior you expect.

✔ **Encourage diversity.** Diversity is no longer a matter of enlightened social policy. It is a necessity. Not enough talented people are available for any enterprise to cut itself off from any potential pool of applicants. Becoming an equal opportunity employer is a mechanism by which an enterprise gives itself the best chance of remaining competitive. In practice, diversity is harder to achieve than most people believe, because managers tend to hire people whom they are comfortable with. Diversity requires your personal commitment, and the commitment of every leader in your company.

In order to make diversity a success, you also have to commit yourself to

- Training and development from the time new hires enter your company.

- Creating models of appropriate behavior within the company.

- Nudging people into opportunities that they may think are beyond their present skills.

- Providing ongoing training and ongoing support.

✔ **Equip your workplace properly.** In an age of sophisticated machines and computer and communication networks, a company that does not equip its people with the proper tools can't remain competitive. The proper tools include the proper training. Employees should be trained not just to be minimally competent at their jobs but also to excel at them. The pressures of competition are too relentless to lose time to poor training.

✔ **Make your workplace safe.** Workplace safety should never be an afterthought. Safety must be designed into the tools, content, and structure of every job. Whether it is machinery that does not physically threaten the lives of your employees or breaks built into the day to prevent fatigue and stress that may lead to injuries, maintaining a safe workplace has a direct and positive impact on the profitability of your enterprise, as well as an indirect impact in lower insurance premiums charged to your overhead costs. Today, many companies believe that safety is an issue that affects only heavy industrial companies and those that handle hazardous materials. This is simply not so. Any workplace where work is repetitive and where the measurement of productivity is pure throughput is a workplace waiting for an accident or repetitive motion stress injuries to happen.

# Knowing what to delegate — don't get bogged down by details

If you have managed the *who* of delegating and you think your team is in reasonably good shape, it's time to tackle the *what* of delegating. You need to determine how to break your plan down into goals and a mission. (Some call these *strategy* and *tactics,* but strategy is only a component of a goal and does not include the ultimate destination.) Then, delegate everything that has to do with the mission. (See Chapter 6 for more on missions.) Create committees to handle each aspect of the mission, and have the relevant people in these committees report all new information on a timely basis.

Give your subordinates the chance to embrace the responsibilities you have given them. In other words, you want them to lead. Your role, during the development of the mission, involves supervising, mediating, mentoring, and controlling resources. You want your team to demonstrate its ability to execute the mission.

Track how well the team executes the mission. You may have to intervene. To know when you should take this step, sit in on any committee meeting where a problem is beginning to crop up: Listen, help, and, if necessary, take temporary control.

## Rethink your problems

You want your team to be capable of solving its own problems wherever possible. But what do you do when someone comes to you and says, "I've tried everything, but it still doesn't work"?

Often, a problem that stymies everyone is a problem that is stated incorrectly. To quote the Danish mathematician Piet Hein, "The solution to a problem lies in its definition." Hein was once hired by a large Danish department store to work on the problem of moving people quickly in and out of the store's excellent cafeteria. The store could lower the quality of the food, but that could have had an impact on overall store sales. Or, the store could hire ushers to shoo away loiterers. Instead, Hein helped a chair designer develop a dining room chair whose shape would be comfortable for no more than about 20 minutes. If people sat on them any longer, they would begin to suffer excruciating pain in their bottom. The chairs were made, and turnover increased as desired.

You need to think the same way. If you have an intractable problem, go back to the beginning and attempt to recast the problems in terms you may be able to solve, before you begin to think about calling in high-priced consultants. Often, rethinking a problem means accepting responsibility for a new situation. For example, car manufacturers wrestled for years to design better bumpers to protect cars and their drivers in low-speed crashes. It was only when designers began to realize that it was more important to protect the occupant than the car that rethinking led to padded dashboards, recessed instruments, a redesign of the steering wheel to protect the chest, and the addition of seat belts and then air bags to protect drivers and front seat passengers.

How do you go back to the beginning? You can approach an intractable problem in a number of ways. For example:

- ✔ **Reverse engineer.** If you're making a product that isn't selling well, go out and buy a couple of examples of a competitor's product that's out-selling yours. Take it apart. Figure out not only why it's better, but also attempt to figure out how it was made. Almost always, you will gain clues to how your competitor solved a problem that you cannot.

- ✔ **Reverse market.** Perhaps your product isn't selling well because it's being sold in the wrong places, by the wrong people, or in the wrong way. Again, look at what your competitors are doing. Ask around about how your competitor's product is being sold and where. Look at your competitor's brochures and advertising. They'll provide clues about where your competitor thinks the market is heading.

- ✔ **Hold an open competition.** If your own group cannot solve a problem, open it up to other people in your company. Post it on the company bulletin board and offer up a prize for a solution. This will spur people to put in time off the clock to find a solution to your problem, and may flush out someone who should become a member of your team.

- ✔ **Recast the problem.** Often, the way a problem is stated inhibits a solution. For example, if you say that you want to raise your profits by 10 percent, you'll look for areas where you can cut costs or increase sales. But if all those avenues have been tried, and no more profit can be wrung out, you may want to ask the questions, "Which are my most profitable sales channels? Can I create a promotion that's limited to those so that a small incremental gain in sales within those channels yields a large increase in sales and profitability?" This is an example of recasting the problem in a small way, looking at the source of profits rather than the profits themselves.

## Run a "play clock" in your head

As a leader, you ultimately want to be able to delegate anything that doesn't impair or hinder your ability to lead or that will interfere with your ability to make decisions at a critical time. Just as a quarterback keeps a kind of clock in his head that tells him how much time he has to get rid of the ball by throwing it or handing it off, as a leader, you have to keep multiple clocks going in your head to let you know when to intervene in the various components needed for your team to reach its goals.

You can keep the clock a couple of ways. The obvious way is to put up a chart with all of a project's deadlines on your wall, or record them in your diary. But one of the things we have found is that deadlines are artificial, so an effective leader will advance deadlines a bit. If you need a completed marketing plan within a month, give the person who has to complete it three weeks. That way, if problems arise, your team member will have a week for revisions without imperiling other parts of your project.

Moreover, learn to schedule small reviews before projects are to be completed. If a project is especially complex, there should be a schematic that contains all the steps needed for completion and the order in which tasks need to be finished. If you break down the schematic finely enough and then monitor the completion of each piece, you'll quickly notice where problems arise.

This leads inevitably to the question, when do you take over? As the leader, your sense of timing will have almost everything to do with the confidence you have in your team, based on your experience with it, and almost nothing to do with actual schedules. You have to learn to develop a "feel" for when to intervene that's based on observation, conversations with team members, and the needs of the mission. An effective leader tends to intervene early, but not so early that he or she demoralizes the members of the team. ***Remember:*** You want them to do the work. You're there to set the team on its path and to encourage the team members to follow it.

# Settling Disputes within Your Team

As a leader, one of your responsibilities is to maintain an orderly environment. This means listening to and mediating disputes that may arise (some of which concern themselves with the mission, but many more of which are personality-centered) and eliciting the cooperation of your team members to get them to cooperate when they are feeling torn apart from the group by their own concerns. You also need to get team members to act like leaders by asking them to place the needs of the mission above their own.

Your first question in settling any dispute should always be, "Is this about the mission or is it about people?" Many disputes come to you in the form of "Joe is impairing the mission because he's taking too much personal time while the rest of us are sitting here sweating our butts off trying to find an answer to this vexing problem." Before you come down on Joe, here's what you need to do:

1. **Review the work of the team members to try to find out why they are having difficulty.**

This may sound counterintuitive, but it really isn't. Make Joe's presence at the team meeting that you're attending mandatory, as an indication to the team members that they can only talk about the problems in terms of structures — no personalities allowed. If someone insists that Joe's absence is the problem, do not ask Joe to defend himself. Ask that person to demonstrate specifically that Joe's absence has caused a missed deadline or inferior work, or has in some way damaged the mission.

The kinds of questions you need answered are, "What exactly is the problem that cannot be solved?" "Is Joe's presence critical to the solutions?" "Is this a team comfort issue or is it a mission issue?" You can determine quickly whether it is a "Joe" problem — that he is not really pulling his weight — or whether some larger issue exists.

2. **Find out whether you can supply the team with more resources.**

    Because your role as a leader is to keep the team moving toward its goal, helping the team members by getting more resources or by rethinking processes accomplishes that. If resources aren't the issue, work with them to help them rethink the problem (see the section, "Rethink your problems," earlier in this chapter).

3. **Then and only then talk privately to Joe.**

    Find out why he has been taking excess time away from the problem. If he has a legitimate reason, you can change his responsibilities — assign him to a different team or give him the time he needs to take care of his personal issues. If his reasons are not legitimate, you can still take whatever action you deem appropriate without harming the mission or the goals.

Concentrate on solving problems. Avoid assessing blame.

Your next question should be, "Is this an essential problem?" Many times, problems are brought to leadership solely because team members want to be assured that their problems — and they — have the leader's attention. The problem isn't really significant enough to warrant the leader's intervention, but if a team member or a group is feeling neglected, then the problem becomes magnified. This is where "leadership by walking around" comes in handy. If you make it a point to visit regularly with each group and ask about progress and problems, instead of waiting for trouble to come to you, you reassure people that you have their best interests and welfare at heart.

Your final question should be, "What will it take to get this problem fixed?" You should put that question back to the group and encourage the team members to come up with a solution, and then work with them to make the solution a reality. Often, groups will take the easy way out and answer, "Give us more resources." Your first response should be, "What have you done to solve the problem with the resources at hand?" and "Is there any guarantee that if I give you more resources, the problem will be resolved?" Make the team members prove their case, and if they cannot, sit down with them and go through a rethinking process.

# *Allowing Your Team to Find Its Own Path*

One of the most satisfying aspects of being a leader is giving your team the confidence necessary for it to solve its own problems. When that happens, you have achieved what every leader wants to achieve — leading a group of self-motivated people capable of selecting its own goals and implementing them. That group relies on the leader for vision, and sometimes for counsel, but it is capable of moving on its own. For a group to get to that point, a leader has to constantly ask the team

- Where do you want to go?
- What do you think of as legitimate goals?
- How do you assess your own strengths and weaknesses?

After you can answer these questions about your team, allow them increasing latitude in setting their goals and defining their mission. A leader with a team is much like a parent with teenagers. You know that you're not always going to be around to run their lives, so your responsibility is to equip them as well as possible with your values, test them by giving them responsibility, and allow them to test themselves by accepting it.

# Chapter 13

# Leading When You Aren't Really the Leader

●  ●  ●  ●  ●  ●  ●  ●  ●  ●  ●  ●  ●  ●  ●  ●  ●  ●  ●  ●  ●  ●  ●  ●  ●  ●  ●  ●  ●  ●  ●  ●

### In This Chapter

▶ Finding a way to lead when you're not an official leader

▶ Using your honorary title to enact positive change

▶ Leading when the cause is doomed to failure

●  ●  ●  ●  ●  ●  ●  ●  ●  ●  ●  ●  ●  ●  ●  ●  ●  ●  ●  ●  ●  ●  ●  ●  ●  ●  ●  ●  ●  ●  ●  ●

*Because of not daring to be ahead of the world, one becomes the leader of the world.*

—The Way of Lao-tzu

*L*ech Walesa — one of the founders of Poland's Solidarity movement, and its long-time leader — once said that "you become free by acting free." The same is true of leading. You become a leader by acting like a leader. You don't need the title or the authority. You only need to be willing to embrace responsibility, to be able to elicit cooperation from people, listen to their needs, and then place those needs above your own.

Making yourself a leader when you aren't one does not mean running around, as General Alexander Haig reputedly did after the assassination attempt on President Reagan, yelling, "I'm in charge. I'm in charge." It does mean acting on the moment and helping to pull your team together.

In Chapter 1, we talk about Situational Leaders, people who rise to leadership status because the time and circumstances are right for them. These are people who meet the opportunity when it arises. But every time is potentially right for leadership, and every circumstance holds within it the potential for leadership opportunity. Don't sit around waiting for someone to discover your leadership potential. Instead, begin making your reputation as a leader.

The way to become a leader is to view every situation as a leadership situation. Change takes place because people who are not leaders in any accepted sense take on the role of leadership in order to lead other like-minded people toward a desirable goal. This chapter looks at the notion that you can lead as a follower, that you can exert real leadership even when your title is honorary, and that you can succeed when others expect you to fail. In all three cases, you can demonstrate your leadership abilities in a way that draws positive attention to you.

# Leading as a Follower

Leading as a follower begins with a simple idea: No matter how little of your work responsibility is under your control, you always retain control of your dignity as an individual. Most Americans no longer work in extremely dangerous or hostile work environments, but many people still work on jobs where they have little control over their job content or their workplace. Most current workplace struggles, as a consequence, are no longer about the right to unionize or bargain collectively — although union organization is important when workers feel completely disenfranchised — but about the right to human dignity on the job.

If you read the papers or watch the news on television, you'll see a steady barrage of news about lawsuits — from sexual harassment and discrimination to repetitive motion injuries and work rules that prohibit placing personal objects around your workspace. All of these are human dignity issues. Many of these problems wind up as lawsuits because the company or organization did not recognize the fact that its workplace was changing, or there were entrenched interests that resented the changes.

## Improve even the simplest things

Often, the simplest thing you can do to add to the dignity of the workplace is to clean it up and make it more cheerful. Many people take the attitude that physical conditions in the workplace are solely the responsibility of management, and that they should not be spending their own time and money for the benefit of the company. But putting together a work detail one weekend to paint the walls of your office a brighter color, instead of waiting for maintenance to do it three years from now, can brighten everyone's attitude, both through the doing and through the end result. It will also make an impression on your group's leader and make him or her more receptive to your next suggestion about ways to improve work flow or profits.

## The Jaycee way of asking

Learning how to ask for change is probably the most important component of leading when you're not in a leadership position. The best way to approach a request is to act as if you are making a presentation as a leader. How do you do this? Look to the Jaycees for a model.

The Junior Chamber of Commerce of the United States, the Jaycees, encourage volunteerism among their members, but they use volunteering as a leadership training ground. The Jaycees expect every member to develop a project that they can complete on behalf of the community. Their model for how to go about that is excellent for learning to lead while you're still a follower.

The Jaycee model starts with a project statement, which defines the project and the benefits that it brings the community. This is equivalent to writing a statement of vision. "I want to build a new playground on the vacant lot on Main Street because it will provide a safer place for the kids in the nearby housing project to gather, and it will rid the neighborhood of a weed-infested, bottle strewn vacant lot" may be such a statement. Or, "I want to organize a group to redecorate the office on our own time, with the resulting benefit of improved workplace morale and productivity."

The next thing the Jaycees ask of their members is an action plan. What materials do you need? What is the cost? Who is doing the work? What required approvals, permits, and such do you need? Who is responsible for the project on an ongoing basis? What are its long-term benefits?

These are the same elements that go into any business plan. The Jaycees pick from many projects they receive on the basis of originality and resourcefulness: Who manages to do the most for the community at large with the lowest expenditure and the highest local and team involvement? The entire Jaycee experience is meant to replicate as closely as possible what a leader does in terms of eliciting cooperation from a diverse group and placing the needs of others above himself.

You don't have to join the Jaycees to be effective, though. You simply need to want to lead, no matter what your actual position. You have to want to improve the lives of the people around you, and you have to want to give something of yourself to others.

# Use information to build team spirit

As we note throughout this book, an effective leader is someone who pursues information so that he or she can make the best possible decisions. But often, information is valuable not for what it can do for you, but for what it can do for others.

For example, every person in your office or plant has a birthday. Take the responsibility of acknowledging those milestones, with a card and a brief ceremony. Everybody has important family moments. You should acknowledge these events also. If your company has a newsletter, take the responsibility for your group to supply it with information. If there isn't a newsletter, start one, even if it is just a photocopied single sheet of paper. You can contribute to the cohesiveness of the group by showing co-workers how much they have in common, and you can also help to build team spirit.

## Always ask on behalf of the group, never for yourself

Doing any of these things may ultimately improve your leverage with management when you want to ask for a bigger, more significant change. But when you do ask for a significant change, such as upgraded training, ask on behalf of the group, not yourself. If you couch your request in terms of how the group benefits, it may be taken more seriously. In order to demonstrate leadership in these situations, it has to be clear to whomever you're speaking that you represent the goal or needs of a group, not yourself alone. Group aspirations are why the need for leadership exists, after all.

## Get your group involved in the community

Companies and organizations exist within their larger communities, so take it upon yourself to improve your group's ties to the community as a whole. The public relations department or the head of the company may be making charitable grants, but that doesn't stop you from organizing a group to help in an area where you think you can do some good. A playground near your workplace may need some cleanup or improvement. You can organize it. If there is an accident or a local disaster, you can help with organizing a fund-raising effort. Is there a mentoring program or a literacy program to which you can contribute? All of these are opportunities to demonstrate leadership and involvement.

Most companies and organizations attempt to portray themselves as at least outwardly benevolent. So take advantage of that fact to gain volunteer time and access to company resources. It may get you noticed by higher levels of management.

## Get a logo

If you are indeed a team, get yourself a team logo. At NASA, every space mission has its own logo, and mission members wear their logo patches proudly, to let other people know what projects they are working on.

## Banning land mines

Jody Williams did volunteer work for the Vietnam Veterans of America, an organization that raises money for veterans programs. After talking to a large number of veterans who were victims of land mines, and after reading about the large number of children whose hands and feet were being blown off by land mines planted years before, Williams decided to find out more about the subject. She found dispirited support for a treaty banning mines, and took it upon herself to create something called the International Campaign to Ban Landmines. She became the coordinator of an effort that spans hundreds of organizations in more than 100 countries. Her leadership resulted in an international treaty banning such mines, which has been signed by more than 120 nations. For her efforts, she received the Nobel Peace Prize in 1997.

Back when one of your authors (Steve) was just a researcher at Newsweek International, he had 12-dozen shirts made up with the Newsweek logo, and the words "The International Newsmagazine" emblazoned across the front. He sent them out to reporters and correspondents around the world and to other selected friends, including a photographer who wound up doing a highly publicized model shoot with the magazine. The shirts promoted the separate identity of Newsweek International and helped turn a stepchild publication into a powerhouse of its own. The idea won him the attention of management so that when he proposed a new publication, they listened to his ideas.

## Don't pick fights with your bosses

Workplace dignity provides fertile ground for leadership opportunities. This *doesn't* mean actively seeking out confrontations with management. It means looking for ways to add to the value of the worker in the workplace.

# Leading When Your Position Is Honorary

Under any number of circumstances, someone may name you as a leader but you may have no real authority. Probably the most common form of honorary leadership, the one that nearly everyone experiences at one time or another during adult life, is serving on a jury. This responsibility is an awesome one, because you're being asked to decide the fate of another human being, one who has been accused of committing a wrongful act. Most people attempt to avoid serving on juries — it takes too much time away from their regular lives, the cases are often arcane and complex, and most jurors have little sympathy for the situations that put them in the jury box. But a leader embraces responsibility, and leadership in the jury room is critical if justice is going to be done.

Think about the basic leadership skills that we cover in Part I, and you recognize how critical they are to juries. Listening well means you have to pay attention to the proceedings. You can't doze off, and you must try to keep your personal feelings in check, because they may color what you hear and what you see. Eliciting the cooperation of others is critical because after you're inside the jury room, you're going to have to build a consensus for conviction or acquittal in a criminal trial, or find for the plaintiff or the defendant in a civil trial. Placing the needs of others above yourself means that you have to give careful consideration to all the evidence, because the future of a fellow human being is at stake.

As another example, you helped raise money for the local volunteer fire department and were so effective that the group names you "Honorary Chief." (See Chapter 14 for more on leading as a volunteer.) Aside from the plaque, what does that mean? If you really care about the fire department, it means that you now have an opportunity to add to its leadership. The real chief is responsible for running the department on a day-to-day basis, ensuring that the firefighters properly maintain equipment, and that the department is ready to meet all its responsibilities. But every chief has a wish list — a group of things he or she wishes to do if more time, money, or both are available. You can help the chief prioritize the list and then make the top item the focus of your next fund-raising effort, for example. Or, if the funds are available and the chief's time isn't, you can take charge of a project, such as organizing training seminars.

With any honorary title goes a *grant of opportunity.* Think of a grant of opportunity as a gift of money. How will you spend your new position? What will you do with it? Will you simply enjoy it until it's gone, or will you attempt to use it to improve your life and the lives of people around you?

To appreciate what a grant of opportunity means, think about Prince Charles and the late Princess Diana. Look past their stormy relationship and her tragic death to their roles as honorary leaders.

While Prince Charles waits to assume Britain's throne, he is severely constrained in what positions he can take by British law; Prince Charles has nevertheless managed to become an increasingly important force in late-1990s England. Charles has become an impassioned supporter of the arts and of good architecture, and favors all sorts of charitable organizations with his patronage. He proves that you can lead well even without a title.

Princess Diana proved to be an even more inspirational leader, with even less of a title. Following her acrimonious divorce from Charles, she was essentially cut off from the flow of opportunities that go with being royal in England. She took up the cause of eradicating land mines internationally and helped to mobilize world opinion to a treaty banning such weapons of destruction. Her death played a large role in gaining recognition for the work of the International Campaign to Ban Landmines and probably accelerated the Nobel Prize given to the group and Jody Williams. (See the "Banning land mines" sidebar, earlier in this chapter.)

Perhaps you think that it's easy to be a leader when you have public image advisors and all the mechanisms of the media at your disposal. But Princess Diana could as easily have chosen a more commercial path, like her sister-in-law Sarah Ferguson. She didn't, and you don't have to be a princess in the glare of the spotlight to do good when the opportunity presents itself.

Any time you're given an honorary title, take it as a grant of opportunity to do something besides stand on the dais beaming. Whatever you choose to do may be unexpected, and it may be more than anyone did before. It may also reinforce the good feeling that led the group to make you its honorary leader in the first place.

Keep in mind, however, that you're not really the leader, and you have to suggest and offer rather than plan and command. You have to prepare yourself for the real leader to say no, and you have to make certain that you in no way threaten the real leader of your group.

# Leading When You're Not Expected to Succeed

Welcome to the Department of Lost Causes. Because of the nature of organizations, even failing and dying organizations need leadership, lest they sell the furniture, close the offices, and let their workers go. An organization in its death throes is a sorry sight, especially if the organization has a proud history.

If it should come to pass that you're chosen to lead such an organization or group, what do you do? You could refuse, and allow the group to fail without you, or you can accept, even if you know that your chances of resurrecting the group are slim to none. If you choose to accept, you have to make sure that you won't get the blame for the group's failure, even if your turnaround efforts are unsuccessful.

## Homemakers for peace

In the early 1970s, two homemakers, one Protestant and one Catholic, were appalled by the sectarian violence in Northern Ireland. The pair, Betty Williams and Mairead Corrigan, formed an organization, Peace People, to begin a dialogue between women and children of the warring factions, reasoning that if hatred could be overcome in the home, it may be overcome in the streets. The pair's success led them to be recognized in 1976 with the Nobel Peace Prize.

## Rally the troops

It is important for you to meet with your group as soon as you have taken on the leadership role. Let the group members know that you are aware that things are grim, but that if they give you their support, even temporarily, you can at least attempt to find a workable course of action, which may include an orderly shutdown. People who work for a company often freeze up at the possibility that they may lose their jobs, for example, so it's your job to explain to them that even if that happens, you will do all you can on their behalf.

In this, you're much like a doctor who is attending a dying patient. On the one hand, you want to do everything possible to save the patient; on the other hand, you want to know when it is time to cease heroic intervention in favor of making the patient's last moments as comfortable as possible.

## Follow the money

Every organization depends on a flow of funds, so the very first thing you should do is have someone audit the books. This way you know how much money is really in the till and how it has been spent. Announce and publish your results to the entire membership. If you find that there has been no wrongdoing, your publication of the results may spur some members to increase their contributions. If there has been poor administration, you have given yourself and others valuable information about why things are going badly, and can begin to correct them.

## Pick a short-term goal

After you know the money and the people situations, develop a short-term goal. That goal will almost inevitably involve the funds of the organization. If there are problems that you can fix by spending money, spend it. If there are problems that you can fix by not spending, stop spending.

The second short-term goal is rebuilding trust. If you have a failing business, you have to rebuild trust with your customers. If you have a church with dwindling membership, you have to rebuild trust with the community. If you have a sports league whose membership is dwindling, you have to rebuild trust with the remaining members. They are your greatest allies in helping you to grow again.

## Know when events are beyond your control

Say your church is dwindling because of a demographic shift in your neighborhood. It used to be Baptist, and suddenly, there is a huge influx of new Indian immigrants, all Hindus, into the community. They may not want to pray at your church, but if you can, invite them to take part in the activities you sponsor. If you set up a group that helps them learn about the community or obtain assistance from the local social service agencies, you may help give your own church some new life.

But what happens when events are beyond your control? The demographic and lifestyle shifts that change so many communities, and the "creative destruction" of market forces almost inevitably mean that no group lasts forever. Under the circumstances, you have to be like the pilot of a plane that is crashing. Keep the wings level even as you crash, so that when somebody does the postmortem, he or she will say that you acted diligently and prudently and that nobody could have done more.

Failure can be a stepping stone to success at a later time — if you handle the failure well and learn from your mistakes.

# Part IV
# Leadership in Everyday Life

The 5th Wave          By Rich Tennant

"The first thing you need to know about coaching Little League is that it takes patience, understanding their limitations, and allowing them to feel like they're participating. And that's just the parents..."

## In this part . . .

*L*eadership is about embracing responsibility, but not only when it suits you. Some of the toughest leadership challenges are right in your own back yard: in your home and in the institutions that support your personal life, such as your community, your schools, your children's teams and your religious life. This part shows you how to recognize the needs of leadership in personal situations, and give you the tools to lead in "real life."

# Chapter 14

# Volunteering Your Time and Skills

• • • • • • • • • • • • • • • • • • • • • • • • • • • • • • • • • • • • • • • • • •

## In This Chapter

▶ Understanding the various types of volunteering

▶ Finding more time in your schedule for volunteer work

▶ Finding a good fit between your skills and a volunteer opportunity

▶ Contributing financially

• • • • • • • • • • • • • • • • • • • • • • • • • • • • • • • • • • • • • • • • • •

*You've got to prime the pump. You must have faith and believe. You've got to give of yourself before you're willing to receive.*
*—"The Ballad of Desert Pete"*

*V*olunteering, whether you are the leader of a volunteer activity or just a member of a group, is a form of leadership. Volunteering starts with the requirement that you place the needs of others above your own. To be an effective volunteer, you have to develop your listening skills so that you can give others what they really need rather than just what you think you're capable of giving. You definitely have to be able to elicit the cooperation of others because volunteering isn't mandatory. People who volunteer need all the encouragement you can give them, whether you are the recognized leader or not.

When someone asks you to volunteer your time, your first instinct may be to groan and mumble some excuse about how you're too busy. Maybe you should stop and think about it. The coach and her two assistants who are teaching your daughter how to play soccer are volunteers. The people who read to your grandfather in the nursing home every Tuesday and Thursday are volunteers. The Boy Scout who collects canned goods for the food drive is a volunteer. In fact, probably about half the activities you take part in rely wholly or partially on the efforts of volunteers. So you sigh, and say, "Okay, sign me up."

Just what are you getting yourself into? How do you make the most of the experience, and are there opportunities for you to display your leadership qualities?

In the United States probably more than any other country, volunteering is essential to maintaining the fabric of community. Volunteering got its start on the frontier. Back then, Americans had to shoulder burdens cooperatively so that the entire community could survive and thrive. Colonial-time volunteer activities such as quilting bees and barn raisings persist in some communities (particularly among the Amish) to this day. These activities still exist because small communities recognize that every person's efforts are vital to the group as a whole. Petty differences are put aside when someone's barn burns down or a tornado knocks it down, or when the community makes quilts to sell at the county fair to raise money for improved medical care.

Just because Americans are in the habit of volunteering doesn't make it a distinctly American tradition. Most tribal cultures have a cooperative tradition, one that is often displaced in the rapid move to urbanization but which finds itself in helping people find jobs and living quarters in a new city. This activity can be strengthened through community activism, as described in Chapter 18.

# Volunteers Come in Many Different Forms

You can volunteer for literally millions of activities, so choosing how you are going to give to the community can often be difficult. Basically, though, all volunteer activity can be classified in three ways:

- ✔ **Head volunteering:** Head volunteering is activity that engages the mind. Working on a political campaign, for an environmental cause, on almost any social issue that you can discuss in the abstract, in fact, is head activity. Here, the greater good is distant and somewhat removed, and the relationship between what you do and what ultimately happens is quite separate. If you deal easily with a lack of tangible rewards and if you care passionately about big picture events, you are likely to become a head volunteer.

- ✔ **Heart volunteering:** Heart volunteering is an activity that engages the emotions. Working on a literacy campaign or reading to senior citizens or children, building a house for Habitat for Humanity, becoming a Red Cross volunteer, feeding the homeless, taking food to shut-ins, or doing almost anything that benefits your immediate community is heart volunteering. Heart volunteers want to feel good about the contributions they make to the common cause, and they seek to raise the level of civility and cooperation within a community. If you want the visceral reward of seeing your efforts bear fruit in the improvement of others, you're likely to become a heart volunteer.

✔ **Hearth volunteering:** Hearth volunteering is based on the idea that if everybody spends some time improving his or her immediate surroundings, the world will become a better place. Hearth volunteers are Little League and soccer coaches, the people who volunteer to run the PTA bake sale to raise money to buy computers for their schools, as well as the people who spend their weekends doing carpentry and repair work at their churches or synagogues. If you live by your values and if you want to set an example for your family by giving of yourself, you are likely to become a hearth volunteer.

Despite the tens of thousands of organizations that seek to enlist the energy of volunteers, only a few, such as Habitat for Humanity, actually manage to capture the imagination and energy of large numbers of people. How does Habitat for Humanity do it? Two ways: First, the organization works on all three levels of head, heart, and hearth. Then, Habitat keeps it simple.

Large social policy implications attract head volunteers. The idea that everyone deserves decent housing is a powerful motivator for local organizers and fund-raisers. Such ideas are also motivators for the kind of people who are good at negotiating with zoning boards and government permit-issuing bodies, as well as negotiating with building supply companies for materials.

Heart volunteers enjoy the satisfaction of building a house side by side with the people who are going to occupy it. These volunteers can see the tangible rewards of their efforts as the house rises and takes shape, and they get the ultimate reward when the family they've helped moves in.

Hearth volunteers bring along their kids, and do all the support things for the work crews, such as making food and keeping the cold drinks flowing. These volunteers often work on the landscaping and painting and decorating in order to turn the newly built house into a home, thereby welcoming another family into their community.

The second part of the Habitat for Humanity success formula is keeping it simple. The national organization has a very small staff, whose job is to help organize branches in communities that need to build affordable housing for the poor. Though many of Habitat's branches have a church affiliation, that isn't a requirement. Government agencies, schools, and even prisons form Habitat groups. Additionally, the requirement that a family getting a Habitat house contribute significantly to its building is a powerful bonding element. You are helping a specific someone, not some abstract cause.

## Why volunteer? Networking!

When you ask yourself the question, "Why volunteer?" you are really asking "What's in it for me?" It's a fair question, given the strains that accompany everyday life. Aside from the emotional satisfaction that you get, volunteering helps to open up new channels in your life. Most people fall into a routine that tends to close them off from the world. Volunteering brings you back into contact with the larger community of humanity.

The new channels you open up can quickly pay off, especially for women. According to super headhunter Lester Korn, "Much high-level business in America is conducted outside the office, on golf courses, at black-tie affairs, at luncheons and dinners. Women are not yet a part of the working social fabric of corporate life —

the country clubs, the golf clubs, the social gatherings, the private luncheons."

The remedy for that at many large companies is high-profile volunteer work. Companies such as General Motors and IBM expect executives and managers to give a portion of their time and energy to the community. These companies often judge promotion as much by the leadership you display in volunteer work as on the job. If you are shut out from the deal making that takes place at the golf course, use your networking skills in the volunteer channel to meet the people who may do business with you later. They'll already know something about your accomplishments, and doors will open up as surely as if you can make the long putt.

# *Finding a Good Fit*

Doing volunteer work is like any other leadership activity. Before you can really be effective, you have to know your own strengths and weaknesses and the group's problems — that either can or cannot be solved through volunteer activity.

Before you think about volunteering, sit down and do a basic skills inventory. What are the things you do well? What are the things you like to do? What are the things you've always wanted to do but couldn't because you didn't have the wherewithal? We ask the last question because sometimes, volunteer activity can take unconventional forms. For example, thousands of people go to the Shrine's clown schools every year, just for the privilege of learning how to put on face paint so that they can dress up as clowns and entertain as volunteers in Shrine hospitals. It's not a run-of-the mill activity, but it must be one that is a secret longing of the people who do it.

After you inventory your skills, inventory your leadership skills in light of your proposed volunteer activity. Are you strong on listening but weak on cooperation, or vice versa? How easily can you sublimate your ego to the needs of a person or people who may be initially indifferent to your efforts on their behalf, and possibly, overtly hostile? How well do you respond to people who are different from you? Can you help them without moralizing or preaching or judging them? Only you can answer each of these questions, but after you do, you may have a pretty good idea of what you are capable of doing as a volunteer.

After you have a good idea of how your skill set matches up with what you want to do, look at the programs available to you. Your choices come in a wide range, including

- ✓ **Family-centered activities** such as coaching sports, teaching skills, and helping out with PTA activities.

- ✓ **Community-based activities** tied to your house of worship or your job, such as mentoring a group of disadvantaged students at a local school or organizing a youth basketball league to keep kids off the street.

- ✓ **Community-wide programs** such as becoming a Red Cross volunteer, a volunteer firefighter, or a Neighborhood Watch patrol person.

Assess the time demands, the skills necessary, and the relationship between the needs of the activity and your leadership skills.

Finally, make a decision. Is this an activity that you want to participate in, or do you feel strongly about it and see it as a potential forum for your leadership skills? If it is the latter, you should prepare yourself to give the activity the extra measure of time and attention that leading demands.

# Finding the Time

The major problem with volunteering is time. Many people commute long distances to and from work and have difficulty making enough time for their own families. According to the Department of Labor, more than 60 percent of all families are two-income families, and another 18 percent are households where a woman provides the sole support. With so much effort devoted to supporting families in so many homes, the opportunities for volunteering are limited to those who can afford the time.

Compounding the problem is the fact that parents want to spend more of what little time they do have with their children. That leads to an almost inevitable conclusion: Volunteer for activities that involve your children.

# The Clark Kent of volunteerism

Finding time, in fact is one of the first tests of your leadership skills. One of the things that leaders do well is improvise, and finding time in a busy schedule often calls for creativity in the extreme. Paul B. Brown, who chose to coach a Little League team more than 50 miles from where he worked, wrote about his experience in *My Season On The Brink* (St. Martin's Press):

"My choice was to keep working at a job that requires some travel and bizarre hours upon occasion, and to still try to coach at two games and a practice each week. If that's the route you take, you find yourself in some intriguing dilemmas. For starters you learn how to change your clothes in some interesting places. If you coach or manage at the big league level you wear a uniform, usually with a beer belly spilling over your belt. And since we at Little League do everything possible to emulate the big boys, it means our managers wear uniforms, too.

So, I learned to change my clothes on the train. It was sort of like being Clark Kent, but instead of rushing into a phone booth and donning my Superman cape at supersonic speed, I walked into the restroom of the 3:42 out of Manhattan, a room that measures four by four, and tried to take off my suit and put on my Little League outfit (T-shirt, sweatpants, sneakers), while the train hit every rut on the North Jersey Coast Line as it headed south toward Matawan, the station closest to my home.

There were other interesting changes in my daily outline as well. For one thing, non-mandatory meetings were moved to days when we didn't have a practice or a game. And I also fiddled with my travel schedule. Instead of looking for airlines that awarded the most frequent-flier miles, I now picked flights solely on whether they could get me back in time for the first pitch."

It is possible to make time for volunteer work, but you have to work on your schedule and become efficient in using time in other parts of your life. That means that you cannot procrastinate and allow things to build up. If you want to make room in your busy life for volunteer activities, you have to learn the meaning of now.

What if you don't have kids but still feel stressed by the needs of making a living and commuting? Even better, volunteer for an activity that is either close to work or close to home. The last thing you want to do is add more commuting time, so doing your volunteer time near where you work may actually take some commuting pressure off you. If you do your volunteer time right after work, by the time you are ready to go home, traffic may have thinned out, and your commuting hassle may be lower. You speed home instead of crawl, and you may feel better about yourself because you aren't concentrating on the tensions of the office.

## Gather extra time at lunch

How do you buy more time? Consider brown bagging your lunch on the days you are going to be volunteering. In addition to saving money, bringing your lunch saves you the time it takes to stand in line at the company cafeteria, or the time it takes to make a trip to the local restaurant or sandwich shop where you buy your lunch. With the extra free time, do something such as pay your bills, which is usually an activity that most people leave for the evening. By combining tasks, you pick up valuable time that you can use after work on volunteer activities.

## Volunteer at work

There are many potential volunteer activities at your place of business. Does your company have a day-care center? You may not feel like taking care of children, but you can come in and read them stories. Or, if you are handy with tools, volunteer to do maintenance and repair work at the center.

# Helping Lead Your Organization to Success

Often, when you volunteer at the head and heart level, you buy into an existing vision of a better world that excites you enough to make you want to commit your time and energy. But at the hearth level, the vision may often be yours. If you are a member of the committee planning a graduation party for sixth graders, one of you may come up with the party theme, and have to take the lead in the planning, figuring out how to cater the event, and getting the party favors. That requires vision. You have to know what kind of experience you want the kids to come away with.

### Following Dick Gregory's lead

If you can bring your lunch, you can forgo it altogether. Dick Gregory, the great 1960s comedian turned social activist, recommends that people at least partially fast three times a week. It makes people trimmer, he says, and allows them to use the time they normally spend eating doing something socially useful. If you can manage to skip a few meals, you should not only use the time but also allocate the money you save from not eating to your activity.

Likewise, if you are coaching, it's not enough to teach the kids and just concentrate on having a good time. You have to establish attainable goals and then help your team to achieve them. To do that, you have to inspire your team members to believe that they can do things they thought were impossible.

Vision works at the hearth level precisely because that is what is most lacking. Think of those old Judy Garland-Mickey Rooney movies about young Andy Hardy. Nothing happens until someone says, "Hey, let's put on a show!" Then there is a buzz of planning and a whirl of activity, until Judy sings the big closing number.

You have to do much the same thing. Put a bunch of people together in a room, and nothing much happens until someone takes the lead and says, in effect, let's put on a show. The show can be a bake sale, a car wash, a talent show, a food drive, or whatever you want it to be. The point is, the starting place for any activity at this level begins with your own desire to do something. (As you see in Chapter 15, sometimes the process of doing overtakes the outcome.)

## Why charitable organizations fail

When George Bush was the President of the United States, he tried to harness the volunteering tendencies of Americans to help remedy society's ills. He failed. Several years later, President Clinton enlisted the services of General Colin Powell to organize volunteer activity. With great fanfare, major companies such as Ford, Xerox, and IBM announced that they were pledging millions of hours of volunteer activity. Then the initiative promptly disappeared, never to be heard from again.

The sad fact is, every couple of years, somebody launches a blue-ribbon commission to figure out ways to get people to spend more time as volunteers, and they keep coming to the same conclusions:

- ✔ People lead busy lives.
- ✔ Most people are not well organized.
- ✔ Most organizations are not well prepared to use volunteers.
- ✔ Most organizations are more obsessed with internal matters than with effective outreach.

Though the first two problems — that people lead busy lives and that people are not well organized — are certainly deterrents, it is the organizational problems, we believe, that are the larger problems.

Most people already deal with several bureaucracies — the regimentation of their jobs, various governmental bodies, and the health care bureaucracy — in the course of their everyday lives. They have to put up with what they often regard as arbitrary authority and poor leadership because they have no choice. So why would they want to do the same thing when they do have a choice? Sadly, most volunteer organizations are poorly run, led by individuals who may be well-meaning, but who tend to be transitional or even hierarchical leaders. They are good people who are in the wrong place, or are there at the wrong time, and they often confuse the desire to do good with doing good itself.

How do you assess and fix a badly run organization? If you find a group whose cause you are committed to, begin with a review of the group's finances. If the group spends more than about 15 percent on administration, it is poorly run. When you join, ask the group's president what he or she is doing to reduce overhead.

After you are a member, ask for a statement of policies, goals, and objectives. Study it carefully. You are likely to find that the group is either attempting to do too many different things, in order to make itself appealing to the largest possible constituency — read this as *attract the most funding* — or it is trying to do one thing that is too grandiose for its capabilities. The mere fact that you are putting in the time to study the goals and objectives of the group and then making thoughtful recommendations can get you noticed.

Next, attempt to influence your organization's local chapter. Most organizations are broken into smaller units in order to be more responsive to local membership needs, but often, this causes an excessive duplication of overhead costs. Try to get several chapters to merge, or reorganize so that the chapters share certain items, such as stationery or fund-raising letters or mailing lists.

Develop a local chapter power base. Work on making your chapter more effective than others by helping to sharpen its focus and then tell your story up at the next level, with the recommendation that the state organization try out what has worked well in your chapter. If it works well at the state level, attempt to make it policy for the group as a whole.

In Yiddish, some leaders are called *machers,* which is a sarcastic word for people in charge. *Machers* are more concerned with the trappings of leadership, and with the title and power that comes with being in charge, than they are with leading itself. Such people are given that derisive name because in Judaism, charity and the doing of good works are supposed to be anonymous. People who intentionally attract attention to themselves for the good they do, according to tradition, do less good than people who toil without the expectation of praise or recognition.

# When Writing a Check Is the Best Way to Lead

A curious thing: Although less than half of all Americans volunteer, fully three quarters of them make regular charitable contributions.

What gives? Clearly, people find it easier to dig into their wallets than to share their time. And because many people believe that their efforts are lost in the inefficiencies of volunteer organizations, it's often easier to salve your conscience with a contribution than a commitment of time and energy.

Checkbook charity isn't all bad. Make the check large enough and regular enough, and you buy yourself a seat at the tables of power. How much is large enough? For many organizations, a regular donation of $500 a year gets you invited to all the fund-raising dinners and activities you want, and gives you plenty of networking opportunities. Raise the level to $1,000 a year, and you get to meet the elite of the organization, who make it their business to know more about you, because you may become an even larger contributor.

In fact, a simple rule for deciding whether to donate time or money is

✔ Work for visibility.

✔ Give for recognition.

When you are looking to use volunteer activity to help establish your leadership credentials in the eyes of others, your choice of work should always be keyed to the idea of putting your efforts in the best light. This does not mean attempting to become a *macher* or hogging the spotlight. It does mean that whatever you do, when you've done it, people recognize that it was your leadership skills that helped to make the event a transcendent success.

# Chapter 15

# Taking the Lead as a Volunteer

• • • • • • • • • • • • • • • • • • • • • • • • • • • • • • • • • • • • • • • • • • • • • • • • •

### In This Chapter

▶ Understanding why volunteers show up

▶ Mastering the ticklish art of volunteer diplomacy

▶ Building strong volunteer leadership eight ways

▶ Knowing when to hand off, bail out, and start over

• • • • • • • • • • • • • • • • • • • • • • • • • • • • • • • • • • • • • • • • • • • • • • • • •

*I would help others, out of a fellow-feeling.*
— Robert Burton

*W*hat better way to hone leadership than by helping others? As an aspiring leader, often you can observe firsthand how amazing people can be — in a wide range of ways — when they show up to help out.

Like most worthwhile activities, volunteerism has its star performers and its wannabes. Consider, for example, a gentleman named Bernie Wohl, profiled in the November 27, 1998, *New York Times.* Each year he presided over the turkey-carving activity for Thanksgiving dinner at Goddard Riverside Community Center, on Columbus Avenue near West 88th Street. Each year, Goddard Riverside serves more than a thousand turkey dinners to a small fraction of New York's homeless population. This particular Thanksgiving was special to Mr. Wohl — clearly a star performer — because he was retiring, and because droves of people came to help him. As the *Times* reported, "Dozens of would-be volunteers had to be turned away." Gives you a warm feeling about humanity, doesn't it? But the next sentence carried some November chill: "Sure, some may dismiss them as indulged yuppies out to feel better about themselves around the holiday. . . ." Say *what?*

In a time of a growing need for volunteers, why the apparent slam on people who want to put the needs of others above their own? Digging farther back into the *Times* archives reveals that volunteer work — especially cooking and serving meals at homeless shelters — had become one more way for upwardly-mobile young singles to meet others of their kind in New York. Ostensibly at the shelters to serve, some were really there to check out potential partners.

Mixed motives are nothing new. Other folks have had iffy notions of what constitutes a singles scene — as some leaders of codependents' support groups in the late 1980s could tell you. But the *Times* did make another interesting observation: "There was certainly no shortage of volunteers to cook and serve Thanksgiving dinner to the needy." Willing hands were there, for whatever reasons, and the work got done.

But is mixed motivation one of those "only-in-New York" issues? Or does everybody have it, at least potentially? What impact does it have on the work? And how do you deal with it as a leader?

# *Who Are We and Why Are We Here?*

Cosmic questions aside, imagine you're volunteering for a favorite cause, out of a genuine desire to do some good for humanity. We human beings have lots of reasons for doing what we do, sometimes without even knowing what they all are. The people with whom you voluntarily cast your lot can have quite a range of motives for volunteering. Here's a sample:

- It's a way for the lonely to fill time. (There are less useful ways — staring at a television, for example.)

- It's a way for people who lack self-esteem to feel better about themselves by reaching out to others who are "worse off." (That's only a problem if they do it badly or condescendingly. And anyone who's run afoul of a bully can tell you there are worse ways to build self-esteem than trying to help.)

- It's a way to meet potential mates without dating. (At best, maybe it beats founding a relationship on small talk in a noisy bar.)

- It's a way to have something interesting to put on a résumé. (We can't all be smokejumpers or paramedics, and often volunteer experience counts in skill development.)

- It's a way for newcomers to a neighborhood to expand their circle of acquaintances. (Not a problem if they do more working than schmoozing.)

In short, volunteering is a way to do a lot of things that have very little to do with helping others, or with leading. But as long as we're at it, consider: Are you also using the occasion for a secondary reason — to develop, exercise, and demonstrate your leadership abilities? (How could you be effective and *not* do that?)

These aren't bad reasons for volunteering, but no one of them by itself can sustain effective effort. Without flexible and savvy leadership, the goals of the group can get bogged down in the complex needs of the members. If you're seriously moved to help and you get involved with a group that seems to lean more toward social activity than social action, you may have a problem on your hands. That's why the upcoming sections of this chapter offer tips and tricks for leading a broad range of volunteers — star performers, wannabes, and tagalongs included.

## Draw your volunteers together with a group mission

However complex the organization or important the work, volunteering is not like working at a company. For one thing, leadership in companies is mostly top-down — when the higher-ups say "jump," everybody else grabs a pogo stick or risks getting fired. Of course, the really good corporate leaders give careful consideration to consensus among their team members — but most volunteer groups are run almost *entirely* by consensus. That's a whole different ballgame.

The first consensus that most volunteers reach is pretty easy: They want to feel good about themselves in what they are doing. There's nothing wrong with wanting to feel good, but it can obscure the purpose of what the group is trying to accomplish. What does the group exist for? What's its vision and mission? The need to feel good can often make group leaders fuzzy about mission. If you come charging in loaded for corporate bear — bristling with lofty goals, a mission statement, and an action plan — you can expect people to look at you like you're nuts for being gung ho or power mad for charging ahead without asking the rank and file.

Before you bring out the flip charts and laser pointers, get a feel for your group's consensus process. Start with what they agree on — feeling good — and solicit feedback that you can help them reshape into some nonthreatening, easy goals. The drafting of a mission statement can be one such goal. Gently (but firmly, and with good-natured humor) challenge them to use their imaginations to come up with a short statement that can instantly inform a total stranger of the group's purpose. Weave their ideas together, encouraging them to *feel good about acting as a team.* Then gradually raise the bar.

## Raise funds and hire professionals

Most folks don't have to be told to "get a life" because they already have one — and sometimes they suspect that *it's got them* instead. Most ordinary people don't have the same level of passion and commitment that professional, paid volunteers can bring to a task. How many, for example (besides immediate families), can really sit up for hours nursing a dying AIDS patient, or put themselves in harm's way to bring medical and relief supplies to starving children in Africa or victims of a hurricane in Central America? How many people really have what it takes — including the time and energy — to devotedly pursue a task that may risk life and limb but yield only psychological rewards?

Time may or may not *be* money, but like money, it's an indispensable resource — and securing it consistently often means paying for it. That's why so many larger volunteer groups hire salaried staff to do the actual day-to-day work of feeding the hungry, tending the sick, and clothing the needy. Some groups seem to exist (almost solely) as fund-raising vehicles to support the activities of salaried staff; the only contact between volunteers and the task at hand may be a pep talk from the executive director when the coffers are low. That's not all bad, but note how it changes the definition of what you can do as a leader. You may have to migrate from one activity — influencing policy — to another: fund-raising.

If you are relegated to a supporting role, you can still lead. You can take the initiative in finding new ways to bring in more money, new ways to inspire more people to take an interest in your cause, or new ways to educate people about the need for social or legislative action — all without taking part directly in the activity you're supporting.

## Great (modest) expectations

Superheroes are fictional for a reason; most people do no more than they can (and some not as much as they can), but can still contribute. The ultimate lesson in all activities that require you to lead volunteers is *Keep your expectations modest.*

- ✓ **Don't expect too much of the people you're leading.** If their livelihood doesn't depend on what you're trying to accomplish, they don't have to do as you say. If your volunteers are easily distracted, they could disappear — along with any chance of success — if you get them overly mired in tasks.

- ✓ **Don't set unrealistic expectations for your goals.** Most volunteer goals depend upon people who have limited resources. Inevitably the goals get diminished by a persistent reality: The need is often greater than the resources available to meet it. One reason is that often people feel able to give to no more than one competing cause. You may be launching a coat drive to aid the poor over the winter, for example, only to find that another group is launching a food drive to aid the poor at the same time. Many who donate a few cans of food to the Boy Scouts believe they have the legitimate right to refuse you, on the grounds that they already gave.

✔ **Remain flexible in your approach.** If you find that you're having difficulty achieving your goal, use the very process that gets in the way to
your advantage. Throw a party. Invite a bunch of people over to feel
good about themselves, with the understanding that donations at the
door are customary and expected, and then use the proceeds to boost
your contributions to the cause.

# The Sparkplug Sets the Wheels in Motion

Common wisdom counsels that *if you want to get something done, ask a
busy person* — but not just any busy-ness is evidence of a real doer.
Volunteer groups depend on their most competent, active members — their
*sparkplugs* — to get things done, more than they depend on those formally
identified as leaders. If your church or synagogue is having a rummage sale,
for example, the sparkplug (and real leader) is the woman who calls all her
friends and asks them to clean out their closets, drives to each house, personally picks up the clothing, and bags it — so the friends don't have to do
anything but have the goods in hand. If you're having a bake sale, the sparkplug (and real leader) is the person with the killer cookie recipe who is
willing to make hundreds of dozens of cookies, package them neatly into individual trays, and then drive them around to all the different sites where they
will be sold.

Behind-the-scenes leadership may also mean organizing and writing checks:
The person who provides the seed money or the matching funds for a fund-
raiser is such a leader. Or consider the person who organizes the phone
bank — and then makes sure it remains fully staffed throughout the drive,
even if it means personally occupying a phone position for five straight hours
or getting into a car to round up the people who pledged their time and then
forgot.

In many volunteer groups, leadership is not about who you are, but
about what you do — especially if you actually get it done (what a concept!).
A person who can connect with a legislator and coax a new bill into happening — or make the right contacts with the media to expand the influence of
the group — is the *de facto* leader, no matter who has the title. When a group
is in hot competition with other groups for the hearts and minds of a limited
number of possible members, consider who delivers the results. That's the
one to ask — the *effectively* busy person.

Better yet, become an effectively busy person, too. Or, if you already are one,
recruit.

## Whoever makes the best cupcakes is the leader

In an episode of his short-lived TV show, Gregory Hines plays a literary agent who is enlisted to help out with a fund-raiser for his son's school. He wants to just write a check and be done with it, but he is dragooned into leading the committee when he promises to deliver one of his clients, Kareem Abdul Jabbar, for a charity basketball game. While he is helping to organize the affair, he meets resistance from parents who have worked on previous fund-raisers, on the grounds that he hasn't "paid his dues." The most resistance comes from a group of mothers who have previously raised a lot of money through bake sales, who suddenly have no role in putting together the charity game. Eventually, everyone quits the committee, forcing Hines's character to withdraw in favor of a mother with a really terrific cupcake recipe. The lesson is threefold: (1) In volunteering, process often takes a back seat to goals, (2) a really effective process respects consistent results, and (3) sometimes the one who bakes the best cupcakes makes the rules.

# *Diplomacy Nurtures the Grass Roots*

Leading a volunteer organization is highly dependent on consensus, which involves all three leadership skills (see Chapter 1):

✔ Getting others to cooperate

✔ Listening actively to the ideas of others

✔ Putting the needs of others above your own

But to bring all those skills together and make them work, you need a fourth skill: diplomacy.

We're not talking here about the spy-movie diplomacy that sticks a knife in an enemy's back while shaking his hand. The diplomacy you need as a leader is an ability to harness the goodwill and energy of the individuals in your group, no matter how misguided they may be, and help the group members find an effective (or at least harmless) niche in the process of attaining the group's goals.

Suppose you're in a "Save the Whales" environmental group, and one of your members wants to organize a squadron of powerboats to go out and disrupt the tour boats that follow the whale migration, on the grounds that the tour boats disturb and exploit the whales. What do you do? Your first move would be to listen respectfully to the member's proposal, assess it, and then patiently explain that putting more boats into the area raises two problems:

(1) It disrupts the whales even more, and (2) it increases the chances of involving a whale calf in a propeller injury. If the person rejects these reasons and persists, you assign him or her to do some detailed research, find out everything possible about the best ways in which the group could improve its use of power boats (including how to avoid, prevent, or treat propeller injuries), and report back regularly. Keep your new expert-to-be going back for more research, reporting, and giving workshops on the responsible use of power boats until the whale migration season is over. Whatever you do, don't deride such enthusiasts, yell at them, or attempt to marginalize them within the group. They may be able to educate the whole group while you guide them toward new and appropriate niches for themselves.

## Effective diplomacy keeps everyone involved

The essence of diplomacy is keeping a group cohesive, even when it wants to pull apart — and that means keeping everyone involved. It's about the *process* of building consensus for the long run, rather than running roughshod over everybody to get to one specific, short-range outcome.

Leadership can be a balancing act between your group's strategic needs and tactics that may seem counterintuitive but get the job done. For example, if your group has had some success with a bake sale as a fund-raiser, but now needs more funds or a new approach, find a way for the bakers to bring in money in the course of the new fund-raiser, even if the new event is a black-tie dinner.

If you've chosen a new course of action for your fund-raiser, for example, it's because you wanted to take your group beyond the funds brought in by the bake sale. But why forego that income? If Mrs. Jones's chocolate brownies really are locally famous, make them the centerpiece of dessert, or have her make enough to put into tins and give out as a thank-you gift to all the people who attended your elegant dinner. People will be happy to get "for free" what they had previously paid for, and if you let Mrs. Jones in on the secret (her brownies will help lure guests to the dinner), she gets the pride of having contributed significantly to the new event.

Diplomacy in a volunteer leader is an art. People come to volunteer activities for all sorts of reasons, many of which have little direct bearing on attaining the group's goal. The diplomatic leader is faced with the task of constructing goals and missions in such a way that everyone gets to make an acknowledged contribution.

Everyone has a unique range of contributions to make; a totally objective measure of those gifts probably isn't possible. When you become a volunteer leader, do your own rough-and-ready rating of everyone on your "team."

To get a good working sense of your group members' abilities, skill levels, potentials, and interests, take some notes. Get yourself a bunch of index cards, and put down some information about each team member. Start with the basics: name, address, phone number (make that *numbers* — daytime, evening, home, office, cell phone, pager, fax), places where they're reachable, as well as their employers, staff assistants (if they've got them), and what hours and days they regard as free time. Next, assess them on their skills and note possible applications. Good speaking voice? Maybe a radio spot or a telethon would show it off. Good computer skills? That could fit in with planning and presentations, or with editing and graphics. After the skill assessment, consider personalities. Who is all talk and no action? Who is all activity and no plan? Who is the social butterfly? the empire builder? Finally, assess their reasons for being there. Is it activist or social? Does your group want to accomplish something or spend its time "planning" and feeling good about itself? Or is it somewhere in the middle? If so, what's the mix?

## I've got a little list

Take each of the categories — Skills, Personalities, and Reasons for Being Members — and a separate list for each of those categories, using data from your index cards. Those lists will tell you (1) what your group can and can't do, and (2) what your group probably *wants* to do. Knowing this information will help you (their fearless leader) to find a level of activity that is consistent with group members' needs and help you gain consensus much more quickly. The lists also serve to highlight the areas where your diplomatic skills will be needed. Because no group project can use every person's skills equally, you will know in advance where you have to work extra hard to find a place for a person who may be displaced by your new activity.

When you make up your lists, consider one more vital factor before you select a new project for your group: Have you identified and jotted down the skills of your group's sparkplugs? If you can find a way to channel them into a new activity, your undertaking will be a success.

# Eight Ways to Be a Great Volunteer Leader

If you're like most of the best leaders, you want to get two things out of volunteering: a chance to help out, and a chance to use your leadership capabilities. You don't want to make yourself angry or sick while you're doing it, and you want the satisfaction of having accomplished something worthwhile. Whether you're a volunteer leader or follower, remember some basic rules about the responsibilities of leaders and followers — transformed into eight highly legible headings (right before your eyes), and here they come!

# Be well informed

Knowledge is always power, but nowhere more so than among volunteer groups. The person who knows the zoning process and the home phone numbers of elected officials has power in community action programs. The person who knows where to find a substitute referee and knows the rules has power in a soccer league. The person who knows where to get all the party rental equipment and catering has the power when a fund-raiser is on the drawing board. Therefore, make it your business to learn the ins and outs of whatever your group is working on, and learn it better than anyone else.

# Be smart

It's not enough to know what you need to. Leaders are resourceful, and they can improvise when they have to. Having the best Rolodex is less important than knowing how to use it. When someone can't do you the critical favor your group needs, ask who may be able to help. Many people, especially if they are sympathetic to your cause, will pass you on to other people if they can't help you directly. Bobby Kotick, the CEO of Activision, has a motto that every volunteer leader should memorize and plaster on the wall: "You don't ask, you don't get."

# Be vocal

Leaders need to be able to communicate their thoughts well to their group, and that's not just a matter of buying a bullhorn. In volunteer groups, communicating also means getting the attention of indifferent nonmembers even while other groups are competing for time, money, and other resources. The best way to do that is to be vocal.

Don't be shy about putting your group's needs before the public eye. If you feel passionately about a cause (such as animal rights, for example), you have to recognize that although some other people may not feel as passionately about it, *they are still potential supporters*. Your job is to mobilize that group (common to every cause) that President Nixon once called "the Silent Majority." A PETA (People for the Ethical Treatment of Animals) demonstration against wearing fur may seem too dramatic, but when members doff their clothes in public, it does get attention — and for every person who laughs, at least one other makes a donation.

## Be determined

Volunteer activity takes third place in most people's lives, behind family and career, so in order to make things happen, you have to learn to not take "No" for an answer. In politics and in fund-raising, that means staffing the phones and getting the carpools organized so you can get your people where they need to be to help make something happen. In totalitarian societies, the ability of the ruling party to organize "spontaneous demonstrations" of tens of thousands of people seems impossible, but that's the model of organization and determination you have to muster. (Minus the secret police, of course.)

The key to bringing your supporters out in force is a *phone chain*. Get everyone's phone number, and give each member the responsibility for calling three other designated members. Make sure that at least two people call every other member, so that if your chain breaks down, a backup call will get the word out anyway.

## Be urgent

If your cause is important, then don't let it get bogged down by inaction. Volunteer activity needs to pay as much attention to deadlines as the most task-driven business organization. People tend to wander away from the group's work unless they're striving to meet firm schedules and hard deadlines. Your job as a leader is to keep your group moving toward its goals — and half the battle is communicating (consistently) the need to be at a certain place at a certain time. Remember the phrase, "Suppose they gave a party and nobody came?" That's what happens to the leader who is not urgent about group goals. Nobody shows.

## Be prudent

Leadership requires that you exercise good judgment. Volunteer leadership requires that you exercise prudence as well. So much of volunteer activity has a touchy-feely, feel-good quality that makes it easy to cross the line between leading a group and getting personally involved with its members. You may have joined a group to meet new people, and nobody is saying that you shouldn't socialize with your new friends. But if you take on a leadership role, your responsibilities change, and you have to make sure that *you* know it, as well as the people you lead. Separation between leaders and followers is vital to getting the job done. Sometimes that separation becomes personal. If you keep an appropriate emotional distance from the outset, no one gets hurt.

## Be consistent and dependable

If your group has a regular meeting place, be sure you're always the first one there to turn on the lights and the last one out who locks up and turns them off. Make sure your meetings start on time, that refreshments are always taken care of, and that the meeting doesn't dither when it should adjourn. If you're handling money, make sure you keep the accounts well and that you're prepared to give a full accounting to anyone on a second's notice. Hone your diplomatic skills by cultivating consistent behavior toward everyone in your group; keep their needs in mind as even more important than the stated goals and objectives of the group. Without them, the goals can't happen.

## Be trustworthy

Your responsibility as a leader is to inspire the trust of the people who have chosen you. Don't play favorites and don't get mired in the petty personality clashes that can afflict volunteer groups. Keep your goals simple, your mission and objectives direct, and the work you're doing out in front of everyone. As with the most complicated magic — *prestidigitation* (keeping the hand quicker than the eye, even under the audience's nose) — good volunteer leadership can be a delight: Everything happens out front, up close, and personal, but the end result leaves people *ooh*ing and *aah*ing and wondering how you *did* that.

# When to Get Out of the Way

Sometimes, no matter how good your leadership skills are, your volunteer group does not want to go where you want to lead them. Cohesion can break down; for example, suppose you've inadvertently offended one of the spark-plugs, who does not want to budge from what she or he has done in the past, because "it's always worked before." It may or may not be a danger sign, but when it happens, you have two choices (covered in the two following sections).

## Do what the group wants

In a 1999 episode of *Dharma and Greg,* an ABC sitcom, Dharma's mother wants to have her usual bake-sale fund-raiser for an environmental cause. In her conversation with her daughter's mother-in-law (who is a socialite), Dharma's mother says that she expects to raise a couple of hundred dollars. The mother-in-law laughs and says that by having a black-tie event and giving an award to a celebrity, they can raise thousands. The show is a funny culture-clash between do-good hippies and upscale San Francisco blue-bloods; the resulting event is a fund-raising success and a cultural disaster, as ducks invade the tent. The event raises a lot of money, but everyone goes home disgruntled. (How do you suppose they'll do *next* year?)

Sometimes, people in your group want to do what they've always done because that's what they feel good about or that's what they think they do well; you have little to gain (and much to lose) in trying to argue the group into accepting a major new initiative. Think of it as like trying to convince the Girl Scouts to abandon cookie sales as their major fund-raiser. Lots of girls dislike the old image of the girl with the cookies to raise funds for progressive activities (and lots of adult troop leaders aren't too happy about it, either). But the Girl Scouts without cookies just isn't the Girl Scouts.

A smart troop leader may turn the sale into a contest — the Girl Scouts of America already awards incentive prizes to girls and troops who do an outstanding job — and dig into her own pocket to enrich the incentives with CDs, concert tickets, and other things that the girls of the troop may want.

## Resign and form a new group

The more drastic alternative is to resign. Resigning from a group and forming your own is an old and honorable American tradition. (It goes back at least as far as Roger Williams, who resignied from the Puritan colony of Massachusetts and founded Rhode Island.) Many modern charitable groups are spin-offs of existing organizations, such as Greenpeace and Friends of the Earth from the Sierra Club. Activism inevitably breeds discontent: Some segment of a mainstream group feels that the group is moving too slowly in achieving its aims and wants more direct action. Far from thinking that resigning represents a retreat, if you're a leader looking for a cause, resigning from an existing group may put you closer to like-minded people who can help you achieve your ends.

Your new group may even have future opportunities to support joint efforts as an ally of your old group. After all, Rhode Island *did* become one of the United States — which itself "resigned" from the British Empire but helped its old affiliate as an ally in two world wars. Larger scale, same process.

If you're discontented, almost every group now has its own Web site, where members can discuss issues. Chances are, if you're unhappy, other people are unhappy as well. Use the group's Web site as a forum to determine the level of discontent and then use the e-mail addresses you've garnered to float the idea of a new group. You will quickly be able to determine how marginal — or how mainstream — your ideas for more direct action really are. The whole process can give you a clearer idea of when, how, or *whether* to leave your group to form a new one.

# Chapter 16

# Everyday Leadership: Training for Real Life

*Experience has shown that every man is the architect of his own fortune.*

—Gaius Sallustius Crispus

It's worth repeating: Everyone has the potential to be a leader, and leadership is common in everyday life, even if you don't always recognize it. Whenever you take the initiative in getting something done in your own life, you're practicing leadership at its most basic level, even if you're only leading yourself.

If the idea of leading yourself sounds silly, consider this: How can you lead others effectively until you're on friendly, well-practiced terms with your own brand of self-discipline and emotional maturity? Articulating goals and visions for other people goes much more smoothly when you've practiced that skill effectively enough to take care of your own needs.

Even the most altruistic person has personal wants and needs, desires and ambitions — some of them altruistic, some simply human. By the time you've identified yours and organized them into a framework that allows you to accomplish more, you're already developing skills any good leader needs. (Besides, if you have a bone to pick with your "leader" at this stage, you know right where to find yourself. Now, as later, *no matter where you lead, there you are.*)

# Size Yourself Up — Fairly

As experienced leaders can tell you, leading others begins with taking a personal inventory of your own strengths and weaknesses and then assessing the opportunities and threats that are likely to present themselves as you lead. Leading *yourself* begins the same way; think of it as having one promising follower who deserves your best guidance. Sit down with a piece of paper and list all the things you're good at, including what you're *good enough* at to get by.

If you don't consider yourself world-class at anything, then start with a list of all the things you've accomplished. Be imaginative and give yourself realistic credit where it's due. Nobody *has* to be world-class to have real accomplishments — and who says this list has to be the last word?

## I did that?

If you're like most folks, you may have been taught not to brag, not to take credit (even if it belongs to you), always to choose skillful, competent people as role models, and almost never to assume you can equal their feats. The social upside of such modesty is to reduce the amount of bragging everybody has to listen to. The personal downside is that you may have some difficulty thinking of anything as your own accomplishment. If that's the case, you're not alone — but you don't have to stay there.

It's easier to recognize accomplishments if you start basic. *Really* basic. For example, you have learned

- How to read (or you wouldn't be reading this book now)
- How to do arithmetic (or you wouldn't know how to buy things)
- How to express yourself in words (Okay, so you're not Shakespeare — he's dead and nobody *else* is Shakespeare either.)

Well, regardless of how easy or hard it was to learn all those things, they're all *information-processing and learning skills*. Put them down, along with a grade for each skill. If you were a good student, give yourself a higher grade, say a B+ or an A. If you were a not-so-good student and got through the course anyway (or got something out of it), give yourself a B. Really. After all, if you're still using some of what you learned, then you got the real point anyway.

How hard or easy you are on yourself is a reflection of how tough and compassionate you're likely to be as a leader; both qualities can inspire trust. Therefore grade yourself as fairly and realistically as you can.

Now go through some other things you learned. Did you learn how to ride a bike? Shoot baskets? Repair clothes? Drive a car (or, for that matter, a nail)? Those are *physical and coordination skills;* you can grade yourself on those as well.

Do you have a job, credit cards, some money in the bank? Did you earn money mowing lawns or raise funds selling Girl Scout cookies? Were you treasurer of a club? Did you ever change currency or take out a loan? Those are *financial skills,* and they should go on your list as well.

Do you form relationships — and treat the people in them — reasonably well (or better)? Whether you're highly social isn't as important as what you *do* with your relationships after you have them. These actions reflect your *social skills.* Do you have close friends? Give yourself a grade that reflects the closeness and commitments of your relationships.

A grade is an *estimate of ability,* not a hammer to bash yourself with. If you gave yourself a D on anything, acknowledge that you've identified an area that needs more work, but don't flunk yourself out. If you ever flunked in school, write down what the *experience* taught you — and whether it's still a sore spot. Such information is worth more than any letter grade — especially if you jot down one or two realistic ways you could improve.

## Thinking in the box (es)

After you develop your personal report card (which, for once, you *don't* have to take home to your parents), take stock: Where and how can cultivating your leadership skills make an impact on each of these aspects of your life? Make your assessment in terms of the following leadership skills:

- **Willingness to embrace responsibility:** Can you identify your responsibilities, take them on, and carry them out good-naturedly?

- **Ability to elicit cooperation from others:** *(Elicit* is a delicate word for *draw out without having to use a two-by-four.)* Can you get other folks to play along, play nice, and get the job done?

- **Ability to listen:** Can you pick up on the details as well as the broad outline of what someone is telling you and give appropriate feedback?

- **Ability to place the needs of others above your own needs:** Can you help out when needed, even if it costs you?

To get the clearest picture of your leadership skills, lay them out as an inventory table. Go back to your list of skills — learning skills, physical skills, financial skills, social skills — and put them into a column down the left side of a big piece of paper, giving yourself some room to write. Now, take the four leadership skills just listed and write them separately across the top, as column headings. Table 16-1 shows you what the resulting inventory table looks like.

| Table 16-1 | Personal Inventory of Skills | | | |
|---|---|---|---|---|
| | *Take Responsibility* | *Elicit Cooperation* | *Listen* | *Others' Needs* |
| **Learning** | 1 | 2 | 3 | 4 |
| **Physical** | 5 | 6 | 7 | 8 |
| **Financial** | 9 | 10 | 11 | 12 |
| **Social** | 13 | 14 | 15 | 16 |

You now have 16 boxes to fill in. Number the boxes across the table: 1-4 for learning skills, 5-8 for physical skills, 9-12 for financial skills, and 13-16 for social skills. Then (after noticing that you're also pretty good at following directions) fill in the boxes. In each case, remember two or three instances from your life, evaluate each one with a number between 1 *(I blew it that time)* and 5 *(I did all right or better),* average the numbers to make a rough-but-fair estimate, put that number in the box, and go on to the next one. We've included some examples of the questions you may ask; you may be surprised at what you find.

Yep, this is another exercise in evaluating yourself. Nothing scientific about it, but it's a handy skill for a leader to practice. Honesty (ahem) is another.

✔ **Box 1:** Box 1 is about learning skills and being willing to take on personal responsibility. Did you ever do projects for extra credit in school? Did you take it upon yourself to find out about career or college opportunities after high school? Did you fill in the applications and get them in on time, without being hassled by your parents? If you did, give yourself a 5 for the willingness to embrace responsibility. If you find that, in going back over your life, you had to be pushed and prodded a bit, take off a point. If you gave your parents a hard time about your future (without creating a workable alternative for yourself), take off two points. If you were completely lethargic about the whole process, wake up and take off three points.

✔ **Box 2:** Box 2 is about learning and the ability to elicit cooperation from others. Do you ever ask for extra help without being prodded? Have you ever worked on a paper with another student and taken the lead in making sure it was done on time? Do you ever go up to somebody — a parent, teacher, or friend — and ask to be taught something new? Do you go to the library to check out books on subjects that spark your curiosity, and get the librarian to help you ferret them out? Did you remember to express appreciation for what you learned (with a card, return favor, or a simple "Thank you")? If you can answer Yes to all of these questions (or reasonable facsimiles), give yourself a 5. If not, take off about a point for each No — drop *two* points if you neglected to say thanks.

✔ **Box 3:** Box 3 is about learning and the ability to listen. Did you attend classes regularly, or did you cut class more than normal? Did you pay attention in class or on the playing field, or was your mind somewhere else? Were you an active participant in class lectures? Were you well-behaved in class or do you remember every detail of the principal's office from frequent involuntary visits? If you were attentive, well-behaved, and took part in class activity, give yourself a 5. Take off a point for cutting class, and drop two points for disruptive behavior during class. (Sorry, that *does* include smart aleck remarks, passing notes, or flinging spitwads. If you did more than one, more than once, you may want to drop *three* points.) If you are back in school, what's the difference between your habits then and now? If they've improved, you've obviously learned something along the way. If so, add two points.

✔ **Box 4:** Box 4 is about learning and the ability to place the needs of others above your own. Have you ever tutored or mentored anybody, or given extra help to a friend who didn't understand the classwork? Have you ever organized a study group? Did you ever accumulate a data resource that could be used by several fellow students, family members, or coworkers? If so, give yourself a 5 if you've done all of the above (or equivalent). If not, subtract one point for each activity you haven't done. (If your score is lower than a 3, then you've been missing some great opportunities.)

✔ **Box 5:** Box 5 is about physical skills and the ability to embrace responsibility. Are you a gym rat? Have you ever stood out in the rain shooting hoops so that you could perfect your jump shot? Have you spent countless hours working on your figure-skating moves, even though you never expected to make the Nationals? Did you ever approach any physical activity with enough passion that you went out of your way to get better? If you were a member of a team, did you attend practices regularly and play to the best of your ability whenever you had the chance? And have a look at the present day. If you have a regular workout, do you do it at (or near) your scheduled time, no matter what? If so, give yourself a 5. If not, put down a smaller number (*and* the remote control).

✔ **Box 6:** Box 6 is about physical skills and the ability to elicit the cooperation of others. If you had to struggle as an athlete, did you find somebody to help you improve? Were you able to get a coach or a skillful player to stay after regular practice to go over a new play or a particular skill? Did you express appreciation for getting the benefit of the person's time and knowledge? Did you follow through by practicing on your own? If you can answer Yes to these (and similar) questions, give yourself a 5. If not, drop about one point per No.

✔ **Box 7:** Box 7 is about physical skills and the ability to listen. Were you "coachable," able to accept constructive criticism and act on it? Or were you the Loose Cannon Kid, addicted to grandstanding and allergic to advice? (*Hint:* Did you spend a lot of time on the bench, even though you had a pretty hefty talent for a sport?) Did you get better enough at the activity to stick with it for more than a year (or, say, your chosen sport for more than two seasons), even if you didn't make first team? If not, did you find a physical activity that fit you better, and stay with it long enough to get pretty good? Coaches appreciate hard-working players who listen well; if that describes you, give yourself a 5. If not, drop about one point per No.

✔ **Box 8:** Box 8 is about physical skills and the ability to place the needs of others above your own needs. Have you ever spent time coaching kids, or helping a klutzier kid on your team get some practice? Did you ever sacrifice the spotlight to help your team win? Did you ever pass to an open teammate instead of keeping the ball (or, if you're a musician, keep a steady rhythm going so someone else could solo), even though you had more advanced physical skills? If you've done things like those, give yourself a 5. If not, shave some points off your estimate.

✔ **Box 9:** Box 9 is about financial skills and the willingness to embrace responsibility. Do you pay your bills on time? Do you keep your checkbook balanced? Do you make it a point to make regular deposits into your savings, go easy on the credit cards, and keep your spending habits in check? If you do these things well, give yourself a 5. If not, drop some points and stop wondering why your cousin beats you at Monopoly.

✔ **Box 10:** Box 10 is about financial skills and the ability to elicit the cooperation of others. Have you ever taken part in a fund-raising drive or made a generous contribution that depends on the willingness of others to contribute as well? Have you been able to persuade a bank to give you a loan (or a store to give you credit), even when your credit rating was less than perfect? If so, give yourself a 5. If you haven't, knock off some points, but don't give yourself less than a 3. Many young people have only a limited credit history, and little experience with charitable giving, though they may have donated time and handled money responsibly. Gauge your estimate according to how much experience you've had in this realm.

✔ **Box 11:** Box 11 is about financial skills and the ability to listen. Do you cut back your spending when you have a large expense coming up, such as a vacation or a car purchase? In this area, *listening* means responding to your inner voice and regulating your own behavior. Score yourself on your ability to adjust your spending to meet your needs, while staying safely within the limits of your ability to pay. Score a 5 if you do this well; if you do it less well, scratch off some points and think about cutting down on those lottery tickets.

✔ **Box 12:** Box 12 is about financial skill and the ability to place the needs of others above your own needs. Do you have an elderly parent whom you assist? A sibling who needs a little extra monetary help occasionally? A charitable organization to which you give time, money, and your skills? If you do many of these things, give yourself a 5. If you do a few, score a 4. If none, score a 3.

✔ **Box 13:** Box 13 is about social skill and the willingness to embrace responsibility. If you're single, do you make the first call to arrange a date? Do you have a range of activities to offer before you call? In the workplace, do you respect other people's time (or are you the one who always drags into meetings late and ill-prepared)? In social life, do you respect others' rights to privacy and dignity? Are you willing to call a halt to a relationship that isn't going anywhere? Are you the one who makes the plans for your group and makes certain that everyone is included? Do you go out of your way to help a friend find a job, a date, or a babysitter if asked? If you can answer yes to these or related questions, give yourself a 5. If not, knock off some points; if your estimate is lower than 3, consider starting group therapy or becoming a hermit (just kidding).

✔ **Box 14:** Box 14 is about social skill and the ability to elicit the cooperation of others. Have you ever planned a party for someone else? Arranged a no-pressure occasion for shy people who may like each other? Ever mediated a dispute to reach a compromise, change a contract, or prevent violence? Have you worked as a volunteer for a crisis line? If so, give yourself a 5. If this isn't a regular part of your life, it's worth exploring — it's an especially vital area of leadership.

✔ **Box 15:** Box 15 is about social skills and listening. Do you listen well to your friends? Are you a sympathetic listener? Do you call your parents and friends regularly, so they don't have to wonder whether you've been snagged by a UFO? Do you pay attention in group situations such as a bus tour, outing, or strategy meeting, so that you don't have to ask anyone to repeat the instructions or where you have to rendezvous? Can you accurately hear someone's feelings in his or her tone of voice, as well as the actual words, especially if they don't match? These are all social listening skills; if you do them well, give yourself a 5. If you don't, erase some points and don't go anywhere without a roadmap (just kidding).

✔ **Box 16:** Box 16 is about social skills and the ability to place the needs of others above your own needs. Have you ever helped a friend in trouble? Have you ever intervened to make sure that a friend or family member didn't get into a serious jam? Have you cared for a chronically or terminally ill person without letting heartache or frustration stop you? If so, give yourself a 5. If you haven't, look at this area as a major opportunity for growth — and if you've ever gone the extra mile for a stranger, give yourself a bonus of 20 points.

Now, add up the scores in all the boxes.

- ✔ Think of a total of 80 to 100 as a pretty good indication of strong personal leadership skills. If you score that high, then you are probably "the captain of your soul." Take a look in the mirror, snap off a crisp salute, and then get out there and *lead* something.

- ✔ If your score lands between 60 and 80, then you have a very good chance of becoming a leader, You're in pretty good control of your personal life, and it's probably time to extend your abilities into the larger world.

- ✔ If you score between 40 and 60, you've still got good potential to be a leader, provided you work hard to bring up the areas where your score didn't blow the top off. If you score below a 40, don't worry — as we said, this exercise is an estimate, not an indictment. You aren't out of the game yet, but you do have some work to do in your own life before your leadership skills are ready to take on a larger field of action. Maybe all you've been waiting for is the right person to lead you into leadership; maybe that person is you.

    Granted, some people who score well below 40 may nevertheless be considered strong *situational* leaders. Dynamic, charismatic — and often self-centered — they step in to provide emergency leadership in response to special circumstances. Often they are in the right position to deliver the goods when the chips are down, but leadership isn't their forte, and when the crisis is over, they're glad to vacate the driver's seat. Becoming a charismatic situational leader is like winning the lottery. It can happen, but you can't build your life around the possibility that it will, and it may not be all you hoped for if it does. Developing and maintaining leadership for the long haul is a *choice*.

# But What Do You Really Want?

Now that you've gone to the trouble of assessing your personal leadership skills, it's time to ask *What do I want to accomplish?* Well, for openers, how about accomplishing a clear definition of what you want to accomplish? Get yourself another piece of paper and write three headings across the top:

- ✔ Where I am now
- ✔ What it takes to get there
- ✔ Where I want to be

For each column, you fill in your evaluations and dreams, as follows:

1. **Start with the last column first, "Where I want to be."**

This is fantasy time, so aim high and don't worry if the goal seems silly or childish; it will evolve along with you. If you want to have millions of dollars, a castle in Scotland, a purple Lamborghini, and a personal Space Shuttle, put them down on your wish list. If you want to conquer a disease, address the United Nations, or study with the Dalai Lama, put them down. Think of your dreams as visions to which you can aspire.

2. **Now go to the first column, "Where I am now," and list your current situation for each vision.**

   If your vision is to have millions, list your current assets and your current work position. If it's travel, list the last three places you've been to, and how you felt about each trip. If it's education or enlightenment, start listing what you want to find out.

   If you look at the list at the left and the list on the far right, you may get discouraged. Don't get discouraged. Every goal and desire has a pathway that leads to it, provided you're willing to find it, put in the hard work necessary to get there, and learn all that going there has to teach you.

3. **In the "What it takes to get there" column, begin formulating a mission with a set of near-term goals.**

   For example, you may write *Achieve financial independence by paying off all my credit card debts*. The same process goes for each of the other visions on your list. Figure out a strategy that will increase your chances of allowing you to achieve what you want to achieve. For example, if you want to land a major recording contract or get a play produced on Broadway, you pretty much have to move to Los Angeles, New York, or wherever the people you need to know congregate. If that's what you really want, then you have to begin to figure out what you're going to do for a living in any one of those cities first, and then go on from there. (Hey, we didn't *say* it was easy.)

   Is it travel, adventure, enlightenment, or service to humanity? You may want to consider a stint in the Peace Corps, or one of the volunteer groups that aid people in trouble in far off lands — such as Oxfam, Habitat for Humanity, or Save the Children — or (if your goal is to attain a specific kind of protective and patriotic honor) you may want to consider joining one of the branches of military service. Our point here isn't to provide career guidance, but to suggest that a legitimate pathway exists to almost any dream or vision. If your first thought is that you're "being unrealistic," consider: "Realistic" is relative. You have a right to *find out* what is realistic *for you*.

F. Scott Fitzgerald is supposed to have said, "There are no second acts in American life." Maybe he just forgot to come back in after intermission. People change themselves for the better all the time. They change jobs, improve their education at night and on weekends, change where they live, change how they live (and with whom), all at the drop of a hat. If you make those changes with some method, the chances are that you'll improve your life each time you make a change.

## The millionaire and the battery

In America, the richest nation on earth, one popular obsession is getting enough money to bankroll the good life. Thomas J. Stanley and William D. Danko, two professors who wrote a brilliant book called *The Millionaire Next Door*, point out, "Many people who live in expensive homes and drive luxury cars do not actually have much wealth. Many people who have a great deal of wealth do not even live in upscale neighborhoods."

After more than 20 years of research, the two professors discovered that seven factors separated wealthy people from people who merely had high incomes, but not much residual wealth. Consider these seven factors as a list of areas to investigate if you pursue this goal:

✔ Wealthy people live well below their means.

✔ Wealthy people allocate their time, energy, and money efficiently, in ways conducive to building wealth.

✔ Wealthy people believe that financial independence is more important than displaying high social status.

✔ The parents of wealthy people did not assist them in building their fortunes.

✔ The children of wealthy people are economically self-sufficient.

✔ Wealthy people are proficient at targeting market opportunities.

✔ Wealthy people are proficient at choosing the right occupation.

If you look at all those factors, they boil down to a couple of simple points. If you want to be wealthy, you have to be disciplined about accumulating money — living below your means — and you have to be alert for ways to maximize the opportunity to make your money grow. Anyone who knows the seven principles and deeply wants to get there can do it.

If you look at the seven factors of accumulating wealth, however, you can see that many of them require the same skills as leadership, just orchestrated a little differently. For example, living below your means and allocating your time to building wealth efficiently both reflect a *willingness to embrace responsibility*. Making your children economically self-sufficient is one way to *place the needs of others above your own needs*. Becoming proficient in targeting market opportunities involves the *ability to listen*, as does choosing the right occupation. In effect, you can look at money as just one more form of energy, no less so than electricity. Leadership is about how you manage your own energy to manage that of other people. A big battery holds a lot of electricity. But how you use it makes all the difference.

# Training Kids, and Yourself, for Real Life

One of the most interesting questions about leadership is, "When do I get started, and how?" The answer is that if you're old enough to understand the words in this book, you're old enough to begin to apply its lessons to become a leader! To prepare yourself, you have to do three things:

✔ Figure out how to ask for and listen to explanations.

✔ Purge the word *tomorrow* from your vocabulary as anything to put next to the word *do*.

✔ Never say "I can't." Say "I'll keep trying and see what I learn."

# For Parents: Teach Your Children Well

As you probably know, leadership qualities can be amazingly durable when they're cultivated young and developed (through frequent use) over a period of years. It's a fortunate child who learns these skills early enough to be comfortable with them by the time he or she is grown up. What can you teach your child about leadership, even if you don't consider yourself a leader? As a parent, you're a leader. In having a child, you have assumed responsibility for another human being. To teach your children to be leaders, show them how to be responsible, cooperate with others, listen, and put the needs of others above their own. This section shows you how.

✔ **Help your child embrace responsibility.** If you're going to embrace the responsibility of being a parent, start by teaching your children to embrace responsibility for their own lives. Help to make them self-sufficient at an early age. Teach them how to make choices and then let them live with their choices. If you believe their choices are dangerous, or will have long-term negative consequences that you can foresee but they can't, it is your responsibility to make those choices for them.

Too many people use the idea of making their children self-sufficient as an excuse for abdicating their responsibility towards their kids. There is often a fine line between letting your kids do whatever they please and controlling a situation too much, so here are a few questions you should ask yourself:

- Is the behavior of your children annoying or dangerous to others? If so, you have to step in.

- Is the behavior of your children dangerous to them? If so, you have to intervene.

- Is your children's behavior likely to compromise their future? If so, you have to intervene.

- Can you afford your children's mistakes? If not, then step in early with an eye toward preventing them.

For all other instances, the answer to your children, if they want to do something, should be, "If it doesn't hurt you or anyone else, and it doesn't materially contribute to disorder or a lack of harmony in the house, be my guest."

✔ **Show your child how to elicit cooperation.** You have to teach your children to cooperate with others and to elicit cooperation from others. The easiest way to teach the ability to elicit cooperation is to ask your kids to provide a rationale each time they want to do something they haven't done before. If your child wants to cross the street, make her tell you why she wants to do it, how she's going to do it, and where she's going, and make her speak about the potential dangers that come with crossing the street. Ask specific questions of little children, because they aren't capable of stringing together complex thoughts.

If you make asking permission and explaining habits with your children, they will quickly learn that they need your cooperation in order to progress in their lives, and they will learn to provide the context within their answers that make you feel comfortable.

✔ **Teach your child to listen.** The best way to do this is to constantly ask your children questions. Get them into the habit of reading a newspaper at an early age, and ask them to tell you about articles that they read. Get your children used to the idea of "reporting," by not punishing them for telling you when things have gone wrong, even when they are the culprits. For you to maintain household harmony, you need to put right any problems that arise, not punish the guilty parties. Getting your children into the habit of reporting takes the need to lie out of their lives.

How is reporting related to listening? Your children will have to learn how to listen to themselves first in order to provide you with the information you need to make an informed decision, and they will get into the habit of taking in information so that they can give you an accurate report. For example, if your child wants to go over to a friend's house to play, you need to know if there is going to be a parent in the house. You have to ask your child this question enough times so that when the child wants to go over, he or she will automatically tell you if there isn't going to be a parent present, even if that means that they may have to forego their play.

✔ **Teach your child about the need to put the needs of others above their own needs.** Being a child is all about immediate gratification, and it's often hard for kids to think of anyone other than themselves. Start them out by giving them an allowance, but requiring that they bank part of the money. This will not only help them develop a savings habit, but it will help them understand the idea of delayed gratification. After they've saved some money and want to spend it on a toy, make it a rule that they spend a third on a charitable cause, for example, Toys for Tots at Christmas time. If your kids know that they have broader social commitments than their own needs from an early age, they will begin to think about charitable giving as a natural component of their lives, and they will have broadened their horizons on humanity from an early age.

# What to Do about Why

Learning how to learn is the hardest lesson. It's not about taking notes and being well-organized, though such things help. Learning how to learn starts when you assume that life's lessons are all around you, and then seek to know what they have to teach you. When your boss tells you to do something, for example, learn to ask for an explanation *after* you've complied with her request.

Suppose your boss asks you to prepare a marketing plan, something you were not prepared to do. You struggle through it, and after the task is completed, you may ask her (gently and politely) to explain to you why the marketing plan couldn't have been done by the head of marketing, instead of by you, an administrative assistant. If you've done the task without argument or complaint, your boss should be willing to share her reasons for telling you to do something you thought wasn't in your responsibilities. She may say that she wanted to see if you could do it, or she may want a fresh perspective from someone who is probably going to be the target audience of the product. Or perhaps the marketing executive was busy and she was evaluating your potential to become his assistant. If you learn to do as you're asked and *then* ask why, you quickly accumulate a valuable storehouse of knowledge about what your leaders want from you. Just as important, you'll be building trust. All the privileges and responsibilities that come with moving up in the ranks are based on trust.

If you never learned how to ask why-type questions as a child, it isn't too late to start asking them now. You no longer care why the sky is blue, or why you can't see air. Your questions now will have a more practical bent. Why does the bumper you are installing on the assembly line need to be made of so many pieces, when it could be injection molded? Why do hot dog rolls come in packages of eight, and hot dogs in packages of six? (That's a question you might want to ask in a letter to either your roll supplier or your hot dog vendor.) Why does your HMO insist that you accept a physician who has a substandard record of conduct? If you learn to ask why questions, and learn to listen to the answers, you will be arming yourself with information and the ability to take on the responsibility to initiate change.

## There's no tomorrow like today

Getting rid of "tomorrow" from your vocabulary is all about embracing responsibility. In order for there to be harmony in your home, you have to learn to do things when they need to be done or sooner. Getting the basics in your life done quickly, especially where pets or your own children are concerned, without constantly feeling harassed for time, or short-tempered by having to make yet another lunch for your kid, is a sign that you can place the needs of others — in this case your entire family — above your own immediate needs.

Learning to do things before you have to will help you make decisions and manage your time so that you can keep from getting rushed or buried under homework. You will have to learn how to "keep the decks clear" in case there is a sudden change in plans. If you're up on your chores, you don't have to worry about getting nagged when you want to go out. If you're up on your schoolwork, you'll nail that "pop quiz" better. Do that often enough, and your grades improve. Better grades are another sign that you can be trusted. And later, if you're always just a little bit ahead of the game, you'll know things a day before your competition does, which is another quality that people look for in leaders.

## Keep trying

Stick-to-itiveness is one of the most desirable traits in a potential leader. Few important skills are mastered easily; most take patience, repetition, and learning from endless mistakes. As the Danish mathematician Piet Hein put it, you have to be willing to "err and err and err again, but less and less and less."

This one is for both parents and children: If you set out to build a reputation as someone who isn't stymied by mistakes, you build *credibility,* which means people can believe you and trust you. If you back up your credibility with honesty, you start to think of yourself as a leader: one who can handle responsibility, is worthy of trust, and can be counted on to listen. If you make these practices into habits, you can become the kind of strong, determined character who makes a good leader at any age.

# Chapter 17

# Leading When You Coach

● ● ● ● ● ● ● ● ● ● ● ● ● ● ● ● ● ● ● ● ● ● ● ● ● ● ● ● ● ● ● ● ● ● ● ● ● ● ● ● ● ●

## In This Chapter

▶ Discovering four reasons why parents become coaches

▶ Understanding why sports exist

▶ Keeping your distance from overbearing parents

▶ Finding a way to make sports enjoyable

▶ Reviewing ten ways to become a successful coach

● ● ● ● ● ● ● ● ● ● ● ● ● ● ● ● ● ● ● ● ● ● ● ● ● ● ● ● ● ● ● ● ● ● ● ● ● ● ● ● ● ●

> *In life, as in a football game, the principle to follow is: Hit the line hard.*
> — Theodore Roosevelt

*O*ne of the most common volunteer leadership activities is the coaching of children in organized sports such as Little League, soccer, and football. Probably no other country rivals America when it comes to organized play for children. Whereas kids in most parts of the world are content to make do with a soccer ball and a bare patch of ground, or a rusting hoop and a lumpy basketball, Americans coach and send their children to sports clinics, sports camps, and even sports schools, hoping to transform their young children into superstar athletes.

Although thousands of parents willingly give their time and energy to coaching, few parents are really good at it. All too many parents bring along their own emotional baggage when they are coaching children. This extra baggage results in the coaches becoming unhappy and quitting, the children becoming unhappy and quitting, or the parents of the children becoming angry or offended and pulling their kids from organized sports.

Although the number of children who play in instructional leagues numbers in the millions up through the third grade, participation falls off dramatically among kids in organized sports after real competition begins. We believe that if coaching and leadership were better at the lower levels — when kids are first mastering their skills — then more children would continue to participate in organized sports. This chapter deals with the reasons why coaches fail the kids they are supposed to be teaching, how parental expectations drive a wedge between coaches and their teams, and finally, what you need to know if you want to become a good coach at any level.

# Why Parents Become Coaches

Basically, people of four personality types — some that bring emotional baggage — take up coaching. The following sections can help you decide which one you are.

## Faded glory

Far too many people go into coaching children to recapture something that they thought they once had when they were young. There are plenty of small towns where people never leave, and where high school football, basketball, or wrestling — depending upon the part of the country you happen to live in — are metaphors for the social order of the town. In towns like these, team sports are a way, at best, to recapture your own youth. At worst, they are a chance for redemption or settling old scores. Parents who go into coaching to recapture their youth can be charismatic leaders, or they can be deriding bullies, who constantly tell their kids that "when I was a kid, we tried harder." If you're a parent and hear your child's coach say things like that, move your kid to another team. If you're a coach who is attempting to revive the heroics of yesteryear, you should rethink your motivation.

## Getting even

For every coach who used to be a star, there are a dozen coaches who were never any good at sports as kids. These people are the kids who were always picked last, or not at all. Such parents bring a strong redemptive wish to their coaching efforts, even if they don't bring a lot of skill. They think they're going to make it up to the kids they coach, and give the kids an experience they never had. It rarely works. Such coaches become more obsessed with winning than with coaching, and because they lack the basic athletic and coaching skills, are constantly irritated by their failures. If your child has a coach like that, don't expect your kid to have a very good time. If you're a coach who is getting even, take some lessons and find out about the game you're going to coach.

---

## The long march

One of the challenges of organized sports at the beginning levels is that parents, rather than professional coaches, are asked to contribute their talents and energies. Some people are good at it, many people are only adequate, and some are terrible. Like any other leadership activity, becoming a good coach is something you can pick up. Just as there are very few natural athletes, there are very few naturally gifted coaches. If you look at the ranks of professional coaches, you will see that coaches such as John Madden and Jimmy Johnson put in long, often painful apprenticeships at the junior high and high school level, first as assistants and then as head coaches. They then started over as assistants at the college level, and then after moving up to head coaching responsibilities, starting the process yet again as assistants in the pro ranks. Becoming a head coach in the pros generally represents a more than 20-year "long march" in which failure at any point along the way can be enough to wipe out a career. Most corporate chief executives do not work nearly as hard as the average coach to reach a comparable level of responsibility, nor do corporate chief executives have as short a tenure in office after they arrive at the top job.

With this in mind, it's almost silly to imagine that you can easily coach children just because you're a parent. Coaching well is hard work.

---

## Having a good time

There is also the parent who wants to use coaching as an excuse for social activity. This is the parent who "just wants the kids to have a good time out there" and whose concern isn't with whether the team wins or loses. In lower age instructional leagues, this is often viewed as a good thing; but in fact, failing to teach kids basic skills at a young age does them a disservice, because it leaves them unprepared for real competition when they get older. Your kids should have fun while they're playing, because learning about the joy of the game is one of the things that keeps them involved with their activity. But having fun isn't a substitute for not learning, and good-time coaches are often poor teachers. Such coaches are often popular with kids, because all of the parents pitch in to help, bringing oranges for half time and ices or ice cream for after the game. The camaraderie is great, even if it doesn't usually translate into skills that are usable down the line. If your coach is a Good-Time Charlie, your kids may have a lot of fun, but they may drop their sport as soon as they reach a competitive level, usually around the fourth grade.

## Being the teacher

Finally, there are a few coaches — figure one per league, pick your sport — who are real teachers. They are in the sport because they have some skills and want to pass them on. They can lead young people by being fair and winning their trust and confidence, and they prepare their teams well enough so that, although they may not always win, they are at least competitive. Such coaches don't need to yell at the kids they coach or bully them into learning. They lead by example and are not afraid to get sweaty with their team by leading them in a lap around the field or a skills drill.

# What Every Coach Should Work On

If you decide to become a coach, you have to begin to do the things that make you effective even if you don't have good teaching skills, or if your primary concern is that you want your kids to have a good time. The following sections discuss four coaching skills you have to know.

## Sports are about mastering skills

Your team can't successfully play any sport unless they master the basic skills. So no matter whether you want your team to be fiercely competitive or laid back, you still have to prepare them in the basic skills and in the rules of the game. No kid likes to be embarrassed, or hear about what fools they were out on the field at school the following day. Therefore, you have an absolute responsibility to become completely familiar with the rulebook, and with the fundamental plays that make up any game. If it's baseball, you have to teach your team not only how to throw, but who to throw to under different situations. If it's football, you have to teach your team to block properly, both to prevent injuries and to keep the other team from running through the holes in your line. If it's hockey, you have to teach your team skating fundamentals — how to skate backwards effectively, for example — and how to anticipate where the puck is going so that they can be there when it arrives.

ANECDOTE

## The uncoachable kid

How do you deal with kids who don't want to be coached? Follow the Justin Marconi rule, says Paul B. Brown, author of *My Season On The Brink*. The rule says that "coaches must take advantage of a player's weakness, rather than [his] strength." Justin was a right-handed hitter on Paul's Little League team, and he always moved his left foot backward just before he swung. Instead of trying to correct the flaw,

Paul found that by pitching inside, Justin could hit the ball consistently to left field. "At some point — when the kids got bigger and more coordinated — coaches would be able to correct the flaws in those swings fairly easily. But for the time being, the Justin Marconi rule would help build my players' confidence and keep them from striking out."

Each sport has its own special nuances that you have to master before you can effectively teach your team, so give serious consideration to taking some coaching theory courses at your local college before you decide to invest a lot of time in becoming a coach. Investing time in learning is even more important if you decide to teach in an instructional league. Also, if your league give rules clinics, attend them religiously. The better you understand the differences between the rules of the sport as it's played at the professional level and the way it's played at a junior level, the better you can prepare your players.

## *Sports are about mastering weaknesses*

Teams function best when you teach them discipline, but remember: The children you have under your tutelage are there voluntarily, so you have to figure out how to elicit their cooperation. You also have to teach them how to cooperate with each other. It also means that you have to help children master their own personalities — not an easy thing when the kids on your team come from widely disparate backgrounds. You may have many kids who don't know how to pay attention when you're coaching at the fundamentals level. There will always be at least one kid who wanders off and plays on the swings instead of in his or her position and another who seems to constantly hear voices besides yours. You may have a lot of kids who don't like the idea of being coached after you get up to a more competitive level, especially in sports like basketball, where schoolyard play without coaches is still the norm. Imagine what it's like to have a kid who has been practicing from three-point range when you want her to learn to drive to the basket. Well, you get the idea.

Wherever possible, drills should be done in pairs, and you should change the pairs frequently so that each team member learns the strengths and weaknesses of every other team member. You want your team members to concentrate on mastering their own skills, but you also want them to learn how to help their teammates without calling them names or stalking off the field in anger. You, on the other hand, have to master your own frustrations. If you're a good athlete, you have to remember that you once struggled to master basic skills, and that only with the patience of your parents and coaches, and a lot of practice, did you become much better.

Whatever sport you coach, have your team play another sport from time to time. Many coaches believe that the limited amount of time they have available for coaching means that they have to impose rigid discipline on the kids that they coach. Often, it's better to watch them play a different sport (maybe basketball) to see what their coordination and cooperation skills are really like. Do they hog the ball or pass off? Do they have good judgment, or do they take shots they can't make? Are they afraid to shoot when they're in position, or do they drive to the basket? By watching your team play something besides the sport they're supposed to be playing, you can find out a lot about their strengths and weaknesses, and make adjustments in your coaching based on what you see.

Sometimes, it pays to have your kids simply *think* about the game. If you remember *The Music Man,* Professor Harold Hill, who sells the town a load of band instruments and is then pressed into service to teach the kids how to play them, tells the kids, "If you think Mozart, you can play Mozart." Visualization is a technique that professional coaches often employ to help their athletes do better, and it works for kids as well. Most kids are playing a sport because they've seen it played professionally. Have them visualize their favorite pro and ask them to describe what the athlete is doing. Then have them try to do the same thing; often, their performance improves markedly.

## Sports are about competition

Although many parents think that kids have plenty of time to compete when they are adults, children are naturally competitive, and they keep score. If one of the girls on your soccer team, for example, is the fastest kid on the field, every other kid may be pointing at her when she comes out to play, because word gets around. If your team has been running up big wins over your opponents, your kids may get the kind of schoolyard adulation that's usually reserved for professional athletes, at least on the school bus the morning after a game. And if your team loses a close one, they may be crushed, and they won't need you to tell them all the things they did wrong.

Don't attempt to discourage the competitive nature of children, because you may only wind up frustrating them. Instead, find out how to harness it. If your team has won a game, don't turn it into a huge celebration. Instead, ask your team what they know about the next team they're going to face, and what they think they need to do to get ready for them. If they lose a game, take them out for some ice cream and ask them why they think they lost, and what they may think about doing better the next time.

Make your first practice after a win harder than normal, to prevent overconfidence, and make your first practice after a loss a little easier, to improve morale. Most kids get praise and punishment for the wrong reasons, so if you reverse the usual pattern, you do them a big favor.

## Sports are about preparation

Branch Rickey, one-time President of baseball's National League, once said that success is the residue of preparation. If you're going to coach children, you owe it to them to prepare them fully for each game. Your team should know what equipment is mandatory and what field they are going to play on. They should also know who their opponent is and what the opponent's current record is. Your team needs know who the opponent's best players are and what positions they play, and what changes you're going to make in your lineup or play selection to help prepare them for the game. You should also instill as much confidence in your young charges as you can muster through solid preparation.

# Beware of the Crazed Parent

You don't have to have a child playing a sport to be a crazed parent. You know these people: The ubiquitous parents who drag their kids around to every game, who know every sub-paragraph and interpretation of the rules, the parents who harass the coach to give playing time to little Johnny or Jane. These are parents who scream at their kids from the sidelines, and scream at every contact between their kids and another kid ("She fouled him. C'mon, ref. Are you blind?").

Writes Paul B. Brown, in *My Season On The Brink,* "As I quickly found out, parents could be vicious. Especially the mothers. . . . In a lot of ways, Holmdel is a throwback to *The Donna Reed Show* and *Father Knows Best* suburbs of the 1950s and '60s. A surprisingly high percentage — well over half, I'd guess — of the mothers don't work outside the home. In that kind of environment, some women tend to live their lives, and derive their sense of self-worth, through their husbands and children. Therefore they saw any slight to their kid, real or imagined, as an attack against them. And lack of quality playing time, or losing a Little League game that involved her son — her son who was clearly destined to become a Rhodes scholar and professional athlete — definitely qualified as a slight."

The "crazed parent" phenomenon is one of the most irritating things about coaching children. Years ago, John Klingl, one of the founders of "Gifted Children's Newsletter," and now a successful magazine consultant, said that the success of his newsletter was due entirely to its name. "What parent does not believe that his or her child is gifted?" he asked. Or, as Paul B. Brown describes it, in his tale of Stevie Moreno:

Here was the kid I was most worried about. On the surface, you wouldn't think that would be the case. Stevie lived in a house nearby, is a good friend of Peter's (Paul's son), and is the nicest kid you'd ever meet. He was quiet, had wonderful manners, and got along with absolutely everyone.

So what was the problem? In three words: Steve Moreno, Sr.

Steve Moreno, a salesman's salesman, had a great sense of humor and was levelheaded about everything except his son. Where everybody saw Stevie as a nice little kid, an average ballplayer who had just turned seven and was on the small side, his father saw him as a combination of Mickey Mantle and Ozzie Smith. To hear his father tell it, there had never been a better athlete.

Oh, joy!

There are basically only two ways that you can deal with parents who act out their own fantasies through their children. You can't ignore them because that may magnify the slight, shifting it from their children to them directly. To avoid harassing phone calls in the middle of the night, it pays to follow the tips in the next two sections.

## Give the kid more playing time for a game or two

There comes a pivotal moment in every game where it's either out of reach or your team is cruising comfortably with a big lead. Situations like those are a good time to experiment with new players and new plays. Don't wait too long, though. If it looks like you're putting in somebody's darling in a last-minute bench-clearing, everybody-gets-in-the-game exercise, then you may only reinforce the parent's notion that you're discriminating against his or her kid. Opt for situations where the game is still close enough that it seems like the other team can rally, but you know in your heart of hearts that they can't. If little Johnny or Jane does well, that is even better. You may have built their confidence in a noncritical situation, and may be able to use them earlier in the next game.

## Change your lineup

Whether you're coaching kids or adults, there is always the question, "Do I put my best players in first and try to break for a large early lead, or do I save my best players for later when the other team is tiring?" Most professional coaches choose the former strategy, which we can best characterize as "There's no tomorrow." Either you crush your opponent early, or you're out of the game, attempting to play catch-up.

But little kids are different. Their skills aren't well honed, so big leads don't stand up. If you want to get a parent or parents off your back, hold your best kids back for a couple of innings, or the first quarter in football, and let your bench play. Again, they may surprise you, in which case you can really crush an opponent. Or, they may play true to form, which is to say, not very well, and you may have to work a little harder to pull out a win.

If you're going to use the lineup-change strategy, scouting becomes critical. Never force kids to prove themselves when they are playing their toughest opponent. A lineup change may cause hard feelings all around if you lose. Pick an opponent near the bottom of the pack, somewhere in mid- to late-season, where the playing tendencies are fairly well known. You may know that little is at stake, but your parents may appreciate the face-saving gesture you make toward them.

# Keeping Sports Fun

No matter what level you're coaching, try to instill in your kids a love for their sport that endures beyond a single season as much as you are attempting to win. To do that, you have to figure out how to make coming to practice and putting in the time to hone skills a fun activity.

## What's the question?

Most games are more complicated in reality than they seem when you start them, so you have to find a way to master the nuances. Instead of handing your kids a thick playbook for football, or putting them through endless drills in baseball, basketball, or soccer, you have to find ways to draw knowledge out of them. One tactic is "Jeopardy!." Like the game show of the same name, this exercise involves your describing a situation to your team and having someone frame it as a question. For example, you're coaching baseball and you say, "A batter hits the ball into the hole between first and second close to the first baseman and someone covers first base." The answer is, "Who is the pitcher?" Make up a bunch of play descriptions and play a round of "Jeopardy!" before every practice — give prizes to the winners. It takes you some extra time to come up with the situations, but your kids may retain the information faster and better.

## Change positions

In business, one of the best ways to learn to respect someone else is to do his or her job for a day or two. You should spend part of each practice with your players rotating positions. If you're coaching football, for example, you should have everybody take a try at field goal kicking, playing the line, or even playing the glamour position — quarterback. Finding out that the quarterback's job depends on the ability of the line to hold is a useful lesson to linebackers, just as learning that running pass routes properly is critical to a quarterback's success is equally important.

## Practice improbable drills

Every soccer player knows that it's important to kick the ball with the side of his or her foot, but can you do it while you're hopping on that foot as well? Think of a summer company picnic and the inevitable sack races and carrying eggs in spoons and you may understand what this activity is all about. People concentrate better when they have to slow down, and finding a fun way to slow your team down may make them concentrate on their coordination. It doesn't matter what the sport is, you should make it a practice to put in more concentration drills, so that your players focus.

## K.I.S.S. me

Remember the K.I.S.S. rule? Keep It Simple, Silly. If you're coaching kids, their ability to master a lot of complicated plays goes down with their age. If you give a kid too many plays to remember, being on the team becomes more like work and less like play, and that's no fun at all. In addition, kids may not be up to the tasks you give them. When kids can barely throw the ball, it makes no sense to try to get them to throw from center field to home plate on a fly. Set up relay teams. Sure, the probability that someone is going to miss the ball is going to increase, but Little League kids are a lot slower than a thrown ball, so you can still catch them at home. If you're coaching football, forget about multiple option plays. There may only be one good runner and one good receiver on your team anyway. Look for ways to get them open, and then allow them to do their thing. The same thing goes for hockey or basketball.

## One thing at a time

It was once said of former President Gerald Ford that he couldn't walk and chew gum at the same time. Neither can most kids. When they run on a rutted field, they fall, and all too often, they don't get up. So have a falling drill at the beginning of the season, where everyone deliberately runs and falls and learns how to roll to get back up quickly. After they get the hang of learning to get up quickly, try another absurd drill, like having kids intentionally throw or shoot wide.

In basketball, for example, rebounding is a critical skill, but most kids spend too much time watching to see whether the ball is going to go into the hoop, so they are late trying to get the rebound. Take the hoop off the backboard and just throw the ball up against the backboard so that they have to do nothing more than jump for the rebound.

In most sports, it's better to master one skill than to unsuccessfully attempt multiple skills. When kids are younger, helping them to become "role players" builds their confidence and gives them the assurance that they can do at least one thing right, and perhaps even well.

## Do you feel lucky?

Kids are incredibly susceptible to superstition, so why not take advantage of it? If you win a game, look for a talisman that they can all focus on. Pick something like the fact that the center's towel was a particular color, or that the first baseman forgot to wear his official league pants and wore sweats instead, and have that player do the same thing next time. We both know that superstition has nothing to do with the outcome of a game, but when you're coaching young kids, luck does have something to do with the way things turn out, so why not allow your team members to feel lucky? It's no substitute for learning the right skills, but it takes your kids' minds off of the pressures of winning, and as the joke about the dead man and chicken soup goes, it couldn't hurt.

# Ten Rules for Being a Successful Coach

Coaching well is not easy, but you can do things for players and parents alike that can ensure that your coaching tenure is fun for you, and ultimately, successful for your kids.

First, we don't define success as compiling a winning record. Winning is an ultimate success, but real success in coaching comes from two things only:

✔ **Your kids stick with the game.** You're coaching to help your kids develop skills that they can use throughout their lives, not just this season. You're attempting to instill enough desire into the kids as possible so that they want to go out and shoot baskets for ten hours in the rain, spend three hours throwing a football through a hanging automobile tire, or spend a couple of hours a day in a batting cage working on their swing. The inner ambition to do these things does not come from the possibility of being a star, but from a kid's knowing that he or she has a future in the sport that he or she chooses. If your team members spend all their time sitting on the bench and learn nothing, what's the point of going on? There are many paths to success and happiness, and the kids under your charge may just take another path.

> ✔ **Other coaches may want to recruit your kids.** Whether you win or lose, you want people to have respect for what your team accomplishes. The greatest respect you can attain is having a coach at the next level up call you to ask you to intercede on his behalf to get "your kid" on his team. Well-coached kids are valuable commodities in youth sports. If you can develop a commitment to preparation, you can enjoy yourself, and you can serve your kids in the right way.

There are dozens of things that go into the making of a good coach; the following sections highlight ten of them.

## Never presume

Here, a lesson from *My Season On The Brink:*

"I always start practice by numbering the bases."

That statement, from a neighbor who had been coaching for ten years, had been rattling around in my head ever since I got the phone call telling me that I was going to be in charge of a team.

"What are you talking about?" I had asked him.

"It's simple," said Tom, the father of three, who coached everything from soccer to track as his kids grew up. "The first year I was coaching Little League, I laid out the bases. Then I had the kids line up and said, 'To warm up, let's have everybody jog around the base paths.' The first four kids took off toward third. Ever since, I've numbered the bases and explained that you have to run them in order. You'd be amazed at the number of kids who go from first to third by cutting across the pitcher's mound."

**The lesson:** No matter what level you're coaching, never presume that your kids know something that you know. You have to explain everything.

## Delegate

Coaching and managing even a small team of kids is a big job simply because there are so many things for the kids to find out. It helps in two ways if you have some assistants. First, you at least have another adult to talk to when you start to go crazy because you can't get your point across. Second, there is strength in numbers. Kids may not like your coaching style, but they may gravitate to someone else's, who can teach them a particular skill a bit better. Having a couple of assistant coaches ensures that every kid gets enough attention, and that nobody is excluded.

## Involve all the parents

Most kid leagues have a rule that every parent has to take a turn at some activity, whether it's coaching, refereeing, or bringing the ice pops for after the game. It pays off for you to obsess a little before the start of the season in lining up these activities, and then call parents to remind them of what they have to do and when they have to do it. For one thing, you involve the parents with the call, and this keeps them off your back. For another thing, the call is a way to transition into other things, such as how each child feels about their team experience, and what potential problems the parents may see. Involving the parents is a pre-emptive strike against the "crazed parent" syndrome because it addresses the concerns of parents early and often.

## Accentuate the positive

More words of wisdom from *My Season On The Brink:*

> "While general managerial instructions such as, 'Come on, guys, show more hustle,' were fine, comments like 'Michael, keep your body in front of the ball' as another one went zipping by Michael G. into left field, were not. After being glared at by the Goodmans, you only heard positive things ('Nice try, Michael, but maybe next time you should think about. . . .') coming out of my mouth for the rest of the season."

It doesn't do you, your team members, or their parents any good to criticize a player directly. If a player has done wrong, pull him from the game between plays and talk to him privately, never in front of the entire team. Never, never, never make one player the scapegoat for a team's failure. In sports such as soccer and lacrosse, where the goalie may be giving up lots of goals, remember that scored goals happen because of the breakdown of the entire defense, which is your fault, rather than the poor play of the goalie.

Instead, work on keeping your words encouraging and positive. As their leader, you're attempting to elicit cooperation from your team members, not turn your team into an adversarial pressure cooker.

## Coach to win

Every game is independent of every other game, no matter what the league standings say. So you should go in with the desire to win every game and you should encourage your team members, no matter how badly they have played in the past. Remember the motto of the National Football League: "On any given Sunday, any team is capable of beating any other team." Upsets do happen, and sometimes everything falls into place for your team or everything falls apart for your opponent.

But you can't win if you don't coach to win. Although you have to make some compromises in the players you use in order to keep every parent happy, and all of your kids interested, in general you should use your best kids in their strongest combination, and use less talented kids as role players.

## Be opportunistic

When you're coaching small children, there is no such thing as well-executed plays, no matter what the sport. Things happen, and you should teach your kids from the beginning to take advantage of unusual situations. If one of your players hits the ball to the outfield, have the child keep running until she actually sees the ball being picked up and thrown. If you have kids playing basketball, teach them ball-hawking skills from the outset.

There are two reasons for doing this. First, your kids may play better if they know that they can control the tempo and pace of a game by being slightly aggressive. The game becomes more fun in the process. Second, good play creates mistakes on the part of your opponent, and your kids may quickly gain a reputation as being more skilled than they really are.

Finally, as you're teaching them the skills that they need, their confidence may increase.

## Don't favor your own kid

Most adults who coach do so because their own child is playing the sport. In fact, in many leagues, there is an unwritten rule that you get to choose your own child for your team, so that some other coach doesn't take advantage of you at a critical moment by benching your talented young superstar. But then the opposite happens. If you give your own son or daughter too much playing time or coaching time, the other parents may begin to accuse you of favoritism.

If you want to give your child extra coaching, do it on your own time.

## Don't cheat

There is a tendency, however minor it may appear to be, to want to bend the rules a little when you're behind, or to want to be too literal about the rules of a game when you're ahead. In some sports, where there are no umpires and the coaches make the calls, there is always one coach who gives all the disputed calls to his or her own players. Resist the temptation — even though about half the time you're going to make calls that go against your own team, that's better than developing a reputation as a coach who cheats in order to win.

The same thing goes for unnecessary violence. In sports like soccer, basketball, and football, there is always one player on the field who is demonstrably weaker, slower, or not as skilled as the other kids. Resist the temptation to "headhunt," to focus your action on that kid in order to score off him, or to show him up. You only end up embarrassing yourself and you may find out that the kid has a parent who is a lot bigger — and a lot more belligerent — than you, after the game.

## *Remember that it's only a game*

More wisdom from *My Season On The Brink:*

> "It started innocently enough. I had to go out of town for a couple of days and while I was gone, we were scheduled to play a game. No problem. That's why they have assistant coaches. However, one of the reasons assistant coaches are often assistants is that they don't want the grief and aggravation that comes from being in charge. They don't want to have to deal with the parents, make all the phone calls, and worry about working with [other head coaches, who may be obnoxious].
>
> Frank Roman, who served as my primary assistant, was pretty aggressive when it came to dealing with his son, but he took a different approach with everyone else. He didn't want the hassle of telling anyone "no." Frank asked if I could fill out the lineup before I left. That way he could blame everything on me if somebody was unhappy.
>
> No problem, I said. I'll make up the lineup before I go. But I got backed up at work, and then they moved my flight up so I didn't have a chance to drop off the lineup before I left.
>
> Where I ran into trouble was the way I made out the lineup. I did as I always did — with a myriad of options. After all, you never know which kids would show up or who would play where. So, I prepared not one lineup but seven, and not one defensive configuration but four. I was just covering every possibility. The result was that the fax I sent Frank wound up being eleven pages long."

You should strive to keep the game simple not only for your kids, but for yourself as well. If you find yourself spending too much of your free time obsessing about your team, it's time to take a break from coaching.

## *Remember that it's only a game, Part II*

One of the joys of being a coach is that you get to teach, but you also get to serve. As a leader, you are expected to put yourself out for others so that they can become better at something they think they want to become better at. You may get lucky and have a kid who makes it to the pros one day, and who gives a speech attributing all his potential to you, but don't expect it to happen. Less than one thousandth of one percent of all children who play in Little League or other sports leagues make it to the professional ranks, so keep that in mind when you have parents on your back or when your kids are getting dispirited. You're there to teach them to love the game the way that you do, or to teach them to have fun, and maybe, along the way, prepare them with some skills so that they have a chance of winning. But it's only a game, and it's how you play it that counts, not whether you win or lose.

# Chapter 18

# Organizing Your Community: Lessons from Saul Alinsky

*Conscience is the guardian of the individual of the rules which the community has evolved for its own preservation.*

—W. Somerset Maugham

There comes a time in your life when you don't like what's going on in the community around you. It doesn't matter what sets you off. It could be the neighbor's dog — or more likely the neighbor who walks the dog and doesn't clean up after it — it could be kids smoking on the corner, the fact that the local community has neglected its parks, or the upsurge in graffiti on the buildings around you.

All that matters is that you are angry, and after you talk to your neighbors, you find out that they're angry, too. You pick up the phone and call City Hall, and you get the bureaucratic runaround. Or maybe you don't, and a sympathetic official tells you that she wishes they could do something, but there isn't a law or there isn't money in the budget to help you.

Or maybe there is a situation that isn't exactly a matter of law, but is more a matter of social justice. A gay man is beaten in a local park, and even though the police are investigating, no one has been arrested, even after several weeks. Or someone robs a homeless person, but the community views homeless people more as an eyesore than as a problem that needs solving.

What do you do when someone who could take corrective action won't lift a finger to help? You go to Saul Alinsky's playbook and organize your community for action.

Saul Alinsky was to community action what Henry Ford was to building cars. Alinsky, born in Chicago in 1909, "wrote the book" on grass-roots community action. He stimulated the creation of numerous activist citizen and community groups. Alinsky didn't set out to become a community organizer. He studied and worked as a criminologist in Illinois for eight years, and he came to realize that one of the major root causes of crime was poverty. In 1938, he started his first community organizing campaign, the Back of the Yards Council. Its aim was nothing less than ridding the impoverished area around the Chicago stockyards of crime and civic neglect.

As it began to succeed, Alinsky began to shift his emphasis from organizing to training other people how to replicate his work in other neighborhoods. In 1940, he founded the Industrial Areas Foundation (IAF) to train community organizers. For more than 30 years after the creation of the IAF, he ran what was essentially a school for people who wanted to extend democracy at the civic level. In addition to the IAF, Alinsky founded the Community Service Organization of California, which served as a training ground for people such as Cesar Chavez, who organized the United Farm Workers and ran several successful national boycotts of table grapes during the 1960s and '70s.

Alinsky's legacy lives on, not only in the IAF and the Community Service Organization of California, but in literally thousands of groups in communities around the world.

# Why Organize Your Community

The first response when people think about community organization is, "That's what I have elected officials for." But one of the things that Alinsky discovered after he first began organizing was that elected officials work off a patronage system. Rather than do things to benefit the community at large, they spend much of their time gathering money for the next election and dispensing favors only to those likely to help them get re-elected. Occasionally, money for projects would trickle down to the people of a neighborhood, but if the neighborhood didn't have sufficient political clout, it was left to its own devices.

In Alinsky's day, that meant that poor neighborhoods remained poor in resources. But nowadays, there are fewer poor neighborhoods, and the cause of poverty is really one of lack of access and marginalization. Government still tends to dispense most of its favors on the core of people who stress the resources of government the least — middle class, tax-paying, quiescent citizens who don't have "issues."

The problem is, there are many problems that conventional government organizations were never designed to handle. Teen pregnancy, racial conflict, illiter- acy, lack of affordable day care, and other problems do not tend to have well-funded, ready-made institutions and solutions to handle them. To take on prob- lems like these, and many others, you need to begin to reinvent citizenship.

Active citizenship is practiced and developed by people coming together to organize for a cause. Active citizenship begins when you decide that the line between public life and your own private life is arbitrary, and that if you don't take some action, nobody will. It is one thing to watch television and com- plain about how unfair things are. It is something quite different to pick up your phone and call a friend to discuss what you heard on TV, and it is yet another step forward to begin to think about organizing.

But organizing is necessary. We live in a world where power is growing increasingly distant from local roots. Despite the growth of a service eco- nomy that preaches the "act locally" doctrine, decisions are made farther and farther from the sources of problems. Hans Morganthau, a political science professor at the Massachusetts Institute of Technology, who was a prominent figure nearly 50 years ago, described this problem as being akin to how you feel pain. If you stick your hand in a fire, Morganthau taught, you feel the pain almost immediately, and scream out in anguish. If somebody sticks your hand in the fire, it takes that person a little while longer to react to and register your pain, and pull your hand away. If there is somebody in a distant place who is giving the order for someone to stick your hand in the fire, that person won't hear your pain at all, and may not listen until the cries of thousands have been heard.

Flash forward to the Reverend Al Sharpton, who has taken Morganthau's mes- sage to heart. In late January 1999, an African immigrant named Amidou Diallo was shot to death in the Bronx by a quartet of New York City police. Sharpton, who is one of New York's more confrontational civic leaders, has been attempting, unsuccessfully, for more than two decades, to force New York City to make substantial reforms in the way it polices black communities.

The Diallo shooting has provided a civics lesson for the city, as disgusted people have shown up day after day at police headquarters to demonstrate and to be arrested, in order to generate the kind of political heat that may eventually lead to substantive change. Whether you agree with Sharpton or not is unimportant. His success at getting other people to demonstrate by their own arrest that they feel Diallo's loss, however, is important.

# Mobilizing Issues

Civic responsibility begins with a set of decision-making steps. These are the basic steps in Alinsky-style community organizing, and if you follow them, you may notice that they bear a remarkable resemblance to the activities of leadership. The following steps are based loosely on *Coalitions for Building Community Understanding,* published by George L. Stevens of the Cooperative Extension Institute of Agriculture and Natural Resources, University of Nebraska-Lincoln.

## Express concern about the problem

Expressing concern about a problem is the equivalent of recognizing and reacting to a problem. Often, it's a problem that affects you directly. Do you need affordable day care and you can't find any? How would you go about determining if the problem is with you or the community? First, you may make some phone calls to your local church or synagogue, to your city or town's Department of Social Services, or to the local YMCA, to see what is available. You may talk to other parents, because you are not the first parent who has this problem and are not likely to be the last. Has someone found a realistic solution to the problem? If so, you can probably stop right here because by expressing enough concern about your problem to look into it, you find a solution. But what if there is no day care in town?

At this stage, it's important to document everything you are doing. Do not rely on hearsay or opinions. Write down what each group says about the day-care problem, interview as many parents with children who need day care as possible, and turn their comments into documentary evidence. What price ranges do people consider to be "affordable"? What do people find wrong with existing day care? What about the relationships between providers and users? The more you know, the easier it is to define the problem later on.

## Become involved and identify all players

In the course of calling around, you may talk to people about your problem and get some reactions of concern. While you talk, ask people if they can think of anyone else in your town who may have grappled with the problem of day care at one time or another. While you are doing this, begin to extend your thinking. Talk to people who may not think that affordable day care is a community need and listen to why they don't think it is. In their answers may be the beginnings of an argument that may convert an opponent later.

This is the point where you want to begin to develop a network of people who can help you. Because other issues may be contending for time, energy, volunteer commitment, and money, you need to gain support from people who may not necessarily be day-care users. So you have to do the following:

1. Gain support from other groups in the community.

2. Develop a list of groups or individuals who may be interested in knowing more about your problem.

3. Arrange an open meeting for discussion among interested parties.

4. Publicize the problem through newspapers, radio and television, and through a series of meetings.

## Clarify the issue

Is the issue day care, or affordable day care? What does "affordable" mean and to whom? Is the issue tangled up with questions about welfare, or is there opposition to mothers who work? You may find, in talking with many different people, that what appears to be a straightforward issue to you is really a much more entangled issue to others. You have to figure out how to pull the central problem — quality day care that is not costly — out of the morass of politics, morality, and other social concerns that may cloud your issue.

## Consider alternative solutions

If you have been able to get enough people to come up with an acceptable definition of the problem, this is the time when you begin to think of ways to solve it. There are many ways to solve problems. Day care requires space, care givers, toys, furnishings, food, and drinks, but it must also be located near to where parents can conveniently drop off and pick up their children. The best day-care center put in the wrong place is as bad as no day-care center at all. As you consider alternatives, you have to consider solutions that work for a large number of people. This may mean that you have to compromise on a facility in order to reach another goal — participation.

Considering alternate paths involves a lot of listening and a tremendous amount of eliciting the cooperation of others. You are probably going to have to persuade people to make donations of time and equipment in order to keep down costs. You may have to raise money for an operating budget or create a volunteer schedule that people will be happy with. All of this calls for you, as the organizer, to constantly put the needs of others above your own needs.

At the moment when you decide that research needs to yield to action, you need lots of outside input. Invite human resources people from your town's major employers, as well as politicians, school board members, and other influential people to your meeting. Present them with the evidence of your problem and some alternative solutions. Ask them to involve themselves and help come up with other solutions. Go to the local university and find out whether any experts on the day-care problem are available for you to enlist. In short, leave no stone unturned in trying to find ways to solve this problem.

# Consider the consequences of each alternative

Just as you would do a SWOT analysis (Strengths and Weaknesses, Opportunities and Threats) on a job (see Chapter 12 for more information on SWOT charts), you have to do the same when you are mobilizing a community to action. For each proposed alternative, you have to be very deliberate in figuring out what can go wrong, as well as what can go right. Do you need more permits for one site over another? Is a less expensive site in a higher crime neighborhood, requiring more expensive security? Is one site more accessible to public transportation than another? No solution can be perfect, but if you analyze each possible solution equally and fairly — looking for the unintended consequences of your decisionmaking — you won't go too far wrong.

# Inform others of your choice

After coming up with a solution, you need to get as much group support as possible. It becomes your role to explain your decision to all the other parents and community groups that you have gotten involved in helping to make this project work. At this point, you can expect that your choice is going to alienate someone and maybe even a few people. If you have been applying the rules of leadership to this project, you may have already been building coalitions within your group, so that friction is minimal. The one thing you don't want is for people to be taken completely by surprise by your decision. If you have been keeping everyone in the loop, you shouldn't have much trouble moving ahead.

# Activate the decision

After a decision is clear, it's time to take action. Draw up a list of resources that you need and ask for follow-through from those who make commitments to help you. Create a detailed plan with a mission statement that every interested party signs (see Chapter 6 for more on mission statements). The mission statement should be a compact, much like the old Mayflower Compact, where a group of individuals and organizations mutually commit themselves toward a course of action. At this point, you should divide responsibilities and begin appropriate activities, such as incorporating, opening bank accounts, finding space, and so on.

## Evaluate the choice

Very early in the process of activating your decision, you should begin evaluating it. You need to look at the depth and honesty of commitment by various groups and individuals. Look at the actual execution of your plan and the needs you may not have anticipated, no matter how well-planned your activity was. If all is going well, you may begin looking at other community needs and start the process of evaluation all over again.

While you are organizing your community, remember the words of William H. Hastie, the first black Federal judge in the United States, who described democracy in this way: "Democracy is a process, not a static condition. It is becoming, rather than being. It can be easily lost, but it is never finally won."

That brings us to Alinsky's "Iron Rule," which is that decisions are made by the people, not by organizers. If you become a civic organizer, it's up to you to allow the people who may be affected by your efforts to make as many of the decisions as possible. Your job is to educate them, gain their trust and cooperation, and mobilize their energy. It is not to tell them what to do.

# Making Things Happen

There is the theory of community action, and then there is the practice of community organization. The following sections are four short case studies that cover a broad range of activities. Each uses a process similar to what we describe earlier in the chapter, and each is successful in creating dynamic change.

## Communities Organized for Public Service

Perhaps the most important single success of Alinsky-style organizing is the transformation of San Antonio from a bitterly divided community into a model of race and community relations. Like many cities, San Antonio did not lack for attempts at civic improvement. There was a well-established "Good Government League" that was a chamber of commerce-style organization whose members — the property-owning, wealthy Anglos of the town — set the civic agenda without consulting the town's disenfranchised Mexican-American majority.

As Henry Cisneros, who would later become mayor of San Antonio, noted in a 1988 article in *Commonweal*, the city's barrios were "so poor that Peace Corps volunteers were trained in the barrios to simulate the conditions they would face in Latin America. Thousands of Hispanic and black families lived in *colonias*, with common-wall, shotgun houses built around public sanitation facilities and outdoor toilets. The barrios had no sidewalks or paved streets; no drainage system of flood control. Every spring brought flooding: families were driven from their homes and children walked to school through mud sloughs. In the shadow of downtown San Antonio, lurked a stateside 'third world' country."

Into this swamp came Ernesto Cortes, a San Antonio native, who learned about community organizing from Alinsky and the Industrial Areas Foundation. In 1974, Cortes founded the Communities Organized for Public Service (COPS), an umbrella group for all the small groups in San Antonio's barrios. From the outset, the group set a goal to reorganize the city's government to transfer power from the Anglo minority.

With a bit of help from the Federal government, COPS pushed through a referendum that changed the governing City Council from a city-at-large election to representation by district, a measure that virtually guaranteed a Hispanic majority. The city elected a liberal female mayor, then a Hispanic (Cisneros), and began to spread the civic goodies. They paved streets, built firehouses, put in sewer and water lines, and increased police protection to the entire city, not just to the Anglo north end.

San Antonio, through the efforts of COPS and the Metro Alliance, a civic group founded in the Anglo north end, has changed radically. It is now considered one of the most civil places to live in the United States, and its slums are almost entirely gone. Most importantly, the COPS and Metro Alliance organizing staffs have remained minuscule, with a total staff of only five and a budget of about $300,000 a year. According to Cisneros, "I can say unequivocally, COPS has fundamentally altered the moral tone and the political and physical face of San Antonio."

# Hartford Food System

The Hartford Food System was founded in 1978 after a comprehensive study of local hunger and poverty in Connecticut's capital found that, although the city was rich in self-help food activities, they were not very effective in getting food to people. At first, the organization tried to create an umbrella group to coordinate activity, but many of the groups and charities that helped the poor refused to give up authority or cooperate. After three years of struggling, the Hartford Food System reorganized itself, began to focus on identifying gaps in the system, and began to provide some programs to fill those gaps.

✔ Among its successes are Holcomb Farm, a 16-acre facility that produces fresh vegetables for the city's poor. The farm has 100 shares that are sold to middle-class people for $375 per share. This entitles the shareholders to an estimated 400 pounds of food over the farm's 22-week growing season, and provides the farm's operating income. Ten social service agencies pay the farm an additional $850 per organization in return for more than 4,000 pounds of food each that they distribute among each organization's clients.

✔ Main Street Market is another activity of the Hartford Food System. It brings the neighborhood farmer's market, increasingly a fixture of upscale urban neighborhoods, into Hartford's poorest areas. In addition, the Main Street Market built a semipermanent market in Hartford's downtown on a piece of vacant real estate. Besides selling food and earning money by renting space to local farmers, the market also has a stage that provides a venue for local musicians during the spring and summer. Musicians donate these concerts, and the money they raise is used to support programs for children and senior citizens.

## Madison Park Development Corporation

Madison Park was a rundown local park in Boston's Lower Roxbury neighborhood. It has become the focal point for the redevelopment of the neighborhood that was devastated in the 1960s by the most destructive kind of urban renewal. The renewal included the wholesale tearing down of buildings and the city's running a superhighway through the middle of the neighborhood.

Beginning in the late 1960s, the Lower Roxbury Community Corporation, later renamed the Madison Park Development Corporation after the park, began to reclaim what was left of the neighborhood. They started by first building senior citizen housing in 1973, and then building low-income housing for the area's poorer residents. The key to the group's success has been its ability to find ways to work within Boston's intensely political city government structure, and to leverage both public and private money to rehabilitate existing housing and to build new units where the community needs them. To ensure that the housing doesn't become warehousing, Madison Park Development Corporation brought job training into the neighborhood, enlisted the poor in managing their complexes, and built a large industrial kitchen adjacent to the senior citizen apartments, to augment the local Meals on Wheels program.

## El Centro de la Raza

Seattle, Washington, never had much of a Hispanic community, so it was easy to ignore the community's needs. That all changed after mechanization overtook the farms of the Yakima Valley and the displaced migrant farm workers began migrating to Seattle and other Puget Sound cities.

In 1972, after being denied the right to set up an English as a Second Language (ESL) program in an abandoned elementary school, Roberto Maestas, a Latino community organizer, occupied the school building and stayed there for four months until the City Council agreed to lease it for $1 a year. With the building in his possession, Maestas created El Centro de la Raza to become a resource center for the Latino community.

The following are two of El Centro's projects:

- ✔ The Frances Martinez Community Service Center offers employment counseling and placement, and assists newly arrived Latinos with housing, food, clothing, and transportation.

- ✔ La Cocina Popular is a soup kitchen that is set up to look like a quality Mexican restaurant. It not only provides meals for the poor, but operates a money-making catering service as well.

El Centro aims all its projects at smoothing the integration of Latinos into the larger Seattle community, while helping them to maintain their culture in what they consider to be a strange and often inhospitable environment (just think of Seattle's weather compared to, say, Mexico's).

# Part V
# Leadership and Vision

The 5th Wave          By Rich Tennant

"I think Dick Foster should head up that new project. He's got the vision, the drive, and let's face it, that big white hat doesn't hurt either."

# In this part . . .

*1* f you think of leadership as the point of an arrow, then the vision is the target to be hit! This part explains what vision is, why vision is necessary, how to develop a vision, and how to implement your vision.

# Chapter 19

# What's a Vision?

*Your old men shall dream dreams, your young men shall see visions.*
—Joel 2:28

With just a little training, people can learn to operate in a cooperative manner, without the imposition of leaders. A group can be trained to set its own goals, implement its own mission, and move to action just as if it had a leader, but with responsibilities shared among all members of the group. So why bother with leaders at all? Why not just train people in their tasks, integrate those tasks with other jobs and roles, and set a whole group in motion?

Invariably, situations arise that require something more than group thinking and collective action. A challenging problem may arise that requires a totally new direction, or a group may have been successful in its mission but reached a kind of dead end. In both cases, the group needs something that it can't supply: *vision*.

# Where Do Visions Come From?

Successful leaders provide vision to a group. Leaders communicate to their followers the overarching, doable dream that's somehow different from the present reality. That vision is what keeps everyone on track and is the touchstone against which the mission and goals of the group are judged.

As long as the circumstances facing a group remain constant, a group can operate pretty well without a leader. Even if circumstances change somewhat, if the change is gradual enough, the entire group can adjust to the change. But when people are confronted by the potential of radical or dramatic changes in their future, or when they feel that they need a dramatic change, they need the quality of vision that is offered by a strong leader. Vision is what defines a future and allows groups to seek continued growth and challenge.

A vision comes from three places:

- ✔ Experience
- ✔ Knowledge
- ✔ Imagination

All three are related, but each is different. The following sections explain how these factors combine to create a vision.

## Experience lets you visualize from the way you live

If you're working on an assembly line in an uncomfortable position, a lot of formal education isn't necessary to figure out that standing rather than bending over all the time would reduce the pain in your back at the end of every work shift. That's exactly what workers at Volvo figured out on their own about two decades ago, and when they asked the company to improve the ergonomics of their jobs, the company complied by building a new factory at Uddevala. In the new factory, the assembly line raised and lowered cars so that the part that was being worked upon was always at mid-arm height, eliminating work fatigue. When women began working on the line a few years after the plant was opened, the company redesigned all its assembly tools, so that they would fit into a woman's hands, and multiplied a woman's mechanical advantage to equal a man's.

## Knowledge lets you visualize from what you've learned

Knowledge is the reason you go to school. A large body of knowledge cannot be taught by experience alone. Sometimes, acquiring knowledge from books is the best way to do it. Reinventing the wheel isn't necessary when you can learn the process by which the wheel was first invented. After you have acquired knowledge, you see the world in a different light.

When Wilbur and Orville Wright were young, they were great kite flyers, and they were fascinated with the flight of birds and the rush of air currents. But it wasn't until they had some physics in school that they discovered Bernoulli's Principle, which taught them that the differential between air flowing over a curved surface and air flowing over a flat surface would cause lift. It was Bernoulli's Principle, not experience, that allowed them to design a wing that would support heavier-than-air flight.

## Imagination helps turn randomness into a vision

Imagination springs from the randomness of life, because it synthesizes knowledge and experience, but it's also connected to desire. By taking your life experience and factoring in all the possibilities and all the ways that you can see yourself and the world, your imagination allows you to grasp the possibility that waits just over the horizon. Think of the Jay and the Americans song "Only in America." They sing, "Only in America can a kid without a cent/Get a break and maybe grow up to be President."

Luck and possibility are intertwined, because a change in luck can determine your possibilities. And possibility is the stuff of visions. Think of the Horatio Alger stories that were popular in turn-of-the-century America. Young Horatio is a plucky lad who does everything right — he sells newspapers to support his poor mother, he studies hard and always looks for opportunity — but it isn't until he saves a rich man's daughter that his fortune turns.

Is Horatio Alger just the stuff of myth? Consider David Sarnoff, a young boy who worked his way up from the ghettos of New York's Lower East Side, and studied what was then the newly discovered invention called radio, until he landed a job as a radio operator at the station atop New York's John Wanamaker department store. In 1912, while he was manning his post, the distress signal from the sinking *Titanic* came over his receiver in Morse code. Sarnoff stayed awake for more than two days, coordinating rescue efforts and relaying news to the nation's newspapers. The head of General Electric, who was aboard the ship and survived, told young Sarnoff that if he ever had an idea for a business, GE would finance it. That idea came a decade later, when companies began to broadcast sound over radio waves. Sarnoff went to GE and, with its financial resources, founded the Radio Corporation of America (RCA), the pioneer in the coast-to-coast presentation of radio programming and the Microsoft of the pre-Depression Roaring Twenties.

# Supplying the Human Element

The philosopher Pierre Teilhard de Chardin once wrote that the greatest force for the advancement of the human species is "a great hope held in common." That's what a vision is. It's what moves people to action, and, because of their action, it's what allows an organization to make progress.

Almost by definition, people are believers. They may not be religious — they may, in fact, be atheists — but almost everyone believes in something. To lack belief is to lack the will to live, and when people lack the will to live, they often turn to a charismatic leader who gives them something — anything — to believe in. When people feel sufficiently hopeless and threatened, they turn to an individual who promises that they can have a better life, even if it means at the expense of someone else's life. That is at once the great weakness and the great strength of belief. After you believe, you're willing to go to great lengths to protect your belief.

Vision supplies people with something in which to believe. Martin Luther King's "I Have a Dream" speech crystallized in the minds of millions of Americans the vision of racial peace and diversity and gave momentum to the civil rights movement. King had both the vision and the courage to express his vision. King paid the ultimate price for his vision, but his words and dreams continue to provide a positive goal to race relations in the United States.

Leadership often focuses on seemingly mundane tasks — raising profitability, fixing a problem, expanding the membership of a group, or winning a championship. Any of these things can be done without belief. They are, after all, just tasks that can be mastered by hard work and discipline. And people will often decide that it's in their own best interest to provide the hard work needed to accomplish a task, without the pushing and prodding of a leader, if only to see something through to completion. But for a group to truly move forward — to achieve a higher purpose — takes a commitment by the group to the leader's vision.

## A vision is a reminder of why you joined the group

You can't gain the commitment of followers for long without a vision. Inevitably, things go wrong.

- A star player is injured and the team's season looks like it's going down the drain.

✔ A competitor comes out with an improved product, and your carefully thought-out sales plan goes up in smoke.

✔ Your group is beset by illness and fatigue, and the things you want to accomplish become ever more distant goals.

A vision reminds everyone why they are members of your group, and why they are struggling. A vision tells people that no matter what happens, their struggle is worthwhile. By supplying a vision, a leader can hold a group together, even when things go wrong. The group accepts that whatever setbacks it may be suffering, the object of the vision means that they can achieve ultimate success.

When George Washington spent the winter of 1777–1778 in Valley Forge, Pennsylvania, his troops were starving and his desertion rate was high. The Continental Congress had not appropriated money to pay the army, provisioning of the army had been mismanaged, and the soldiers could see across to English-held areas, where people were well fed. One day, near Christmas in 1777, Washington told his army that every man had the right to decide for himself whether to return home, but that, if they did, the dream of liberty and freedom from England would be lost forever. Almost no one left Valley Forge, even though staying meant enduring one of the worst winters on record, and nearly starving to death. The common belief in liberty, coupled with improved training, turned Washington's army of 11,000 men from a ragtag bunch of rebels into an efficient fighting force when they left their encampment the following June. Their belief in Washington's vision had seen them through.

Whether your group is an entrepreneurial company, a volunteer group, a team, or a large, established company, if it does not have a clearly articulated vision, maintaining the group's cohesiveness for very long will be difficult. Before joining a group, learn as much as you can about its vision for the future. If you don't subscribe to this vision, remaining true to the group's mission as a follower or member will be close to impossible.

Remember, whether you're a leader or a follower, you should gain as complete a knowledge of the group's vision as possible.

## A vision attracts commitment and energizes people

People need a significant challenge, something they can commit to that is worthy of their best efforts. Getting people to make an emotional investment in the pursuit of an incremental gain in quarterly profits is never easy, but people are willing, even eager, to commit voluntarily and completely to something they perceive as truly worthwhile. Every enterprise faces obstacles in its development and growth, but without a shared vision, people will not willingly endure what is necessary to turn an idea into a successful enterprise. A shared vision makes them more than willing to sacrifice time, effort, and energy on behalf of the enterprise.

In that context, a vision is a rallying point for people. Often, a vision that can be crafted into a well-articulated story attracts followers to a movement all by itself, even without a leader having to actively recruit members. For example, when Charles and Maurice Saachi started their advertising agency, Saachi & Saachi, in the late 1980s, they were considered to be so much in the forefront of their business that résumés flooded through the door. Not only that, but companies in related fields, such as market research and public relations, begged to be acquired by the brothers, so that they could be part of the Saachi's vision, as it changed the face of advertising in the United Kingdom, and then around the world.

# Establishing a Standard of Excellence

Most people want to be thought of as doing a good job, to have the feeling that they are effectively advancing the organization's purposes, and to be recognized for their contributions. To do so, they have to be clear on what those purposes are and when an action is likely to advance them. A vision spells out what the purposes of the organization are. It tells employees, suppliers, customers, and competitors what you stand for, and where you see yourself going now and in the future. A vision establishes a standard for everyone to live up to, and lets people benchmark their own progress within an organization.

At salary review time within your company, write a memo that may loosely be titled, "What I Have Done for You Lately." In that memo, outline your achievements in helping the organization reach its current goals. This kind of memo will help your superiors see why you deserve a raise. But if you really want to be promoted, you should include a section in your memo addressing the ways in which you have helped the organization advance its vision even further.

# Helping You Stay ahead of the Game

A good leader, while managing in the present, is always looking ahead to see what threats are just over the horizon, and what opportunities are there, as well. Vision is a kind of distant, early-warning radar that is set two steps into the future, like a chess player anticipating his response to all the possible moves an opponent may make, and knowing the outcome of the move after that as well. Good leaders train themselves to keep looking toward the horizon and beyond it, while maintaining a firm linkage to the present and to reality.

# Becoming a visionary

A vision requires a visionary, someone who can see what may become possible if only one or two things fall into place. The visionary, who is usually — but not always — the leader, has to look at existing events for his or her group and be able to say, "We can do a lot better and a lot different if X and Y can be made to happen."

Here's a look at two visionaries:

✔ Gordon Moore, Robert Noyce, and Andrew Grove had the vision to create a computer on a chip — the microprocessor. But they were able to have that vision only because an entire sequence of events had already taken place that suggested to them that their vision was doable.

First, the transistor had to be invented. Then, the integrated circuit, which placed a number of transistors together onto a single piece of silicon, came along. Then, a number of integrated circuits, each with their own logic, or software, had to be put together. During this time, from 1948, when the transistor was invented, until 1971, when Intel, the company they created, introduced the 4004 microprocessor, thousands of engineers at many companies had to work out the processes of continually shrinking the size of each transistor, so that more and more of them could be placed into an ever smaller space. Fulfilling the vision of creating a microprocessor was impossible until all the previous steps had taken place.

But Moore, who was the visionary in the group, saw that it could be done. He had plotted the density of transistors onto silicon chips and had developed something that is now known as "Moore's Law," which states that the number of transistors on a chip doubles every 18 months. Moore figured, rightly, that at a certain point in the doubling, the number of circuits that could be made would be large enough to duplicate the functions of a hard-wired computer memory. He was right, of course.

✔ Mel Farr, a running back for the Detroit Lions during the 1980s, had a vision of becoming a successful black businessman after he retired from football. Because the Lions are owned by William Clay Ford, a descendant of Henry Ford and an executive of the Ford Motor Company, and because Detroit is the Motor City, Farr thought that the best way to success was through a car dealership. But he discovered that there were few African-American–owned dealerships at the time. A combination of lack of capital and a general reluctance to sell cars in black neighborhoods had made it difficult for African-American entrepreneurs to move into auto retailing. Farr examined the problem and determined that the poor credit histories of his customers, perhaps more than anything, were the greatest deterrent to their owning new cars. So he began with used cars, and instituted a tough repossession policy on people who missed their car payments. At the same time, he designed programs to help customers budget their money better, so that there would be less likelihood that they would actually miss a payment. Over the past decade, Farr's business has grown steadily, so that he now is in the new car business, and at $400 million in sales, is the largest African-American dealer group owner in the nation.

Farr's vision from the beginning was not simply to become successful, but to become involved in auto sales. His connections and star status with the Detroit Lions ensured that he would get the chance, and then he made the most of the opportunity after he had it.

## Benchmarking everything

Keeping ahead of the competition also entails keeping up with them. Don't be afraid to admit that someone else is doing something better than you are and to take advantage of their example.

ANECDOTE

### When vision fails

A good example of what happens when vision fails are the sky-high stock market valuations of Internet companies. In 1989, right after the U.S. government decided that it would allow its ARPANET computer communications system to be opened to general use by the public, large companies could have taken over the Net and its communications protocols (which make up the World Wide Web), for next to nothing. But nobody wanted to make even the small investment required, because companies realized that the Net was slow and fragmentary, and that there were still only a couple of million personal computers in homes. The argument was, "How many people wanted to spend their lives scurrying around the Web looking for things?"

But a group of small start-ups, led chiefly by America Online, reasoned that they had little to lose (except some investor money) and much to gain, if Web use caught on. Scores of other small entrepreneurs had the same idea, and before long, the Internet was flooded with services, tens of millions of people had hooked up, and companies began using e-mail in place of the telephone for intercompany communications. Internet use skyrocketed, and large

companies began to realize that if they wanted to survive into the future, that they would have to buy into the burgeoning Net economy. In the meantime, however, the price of entry had risen dramatically. Companies like America Online and Amazon.com had developed huge customer bases, which larger, better established companies were willing to pay billions of dollars to have access to. That access price is reflected in the stock prices of e-business companies. If established companies had had some vision of the Internet's potentials, they would have bought in early, made the necessary investments, and reaped the benefits of growth themselves.

That's what vision is all about. It's the ability to see what isn't there in terms of what is. Any established company could have seen that the Internet would grow to become very large at some point, but because leaders of large enterprises become averse to taking risks, they couldn't see far enough over the horizon to know at what point they should make their investment, and so they missed out on a once-in-a-century opportunity.

As a leader, you're responsible for having a complete knowledge not only of your own group's resources, but of the widest possible resources available. Gordon Moore, from Intel, was building upon the work of thousands of others, and so should you. If you're running a community group, you should make it your business to find out which other groups — anywhere — are running programs similar to yours, and you should learn from the best. If your Sunday school attendance is down, for example, and you have taken on the role of principal of the school, contact your synod or diocese or synagogue council and find out where Sunday school attendance is up, and then go off and learn what they're doing that you're not.

This process is called benchmarking, because it comes from the idea that the best practices are a benchmark for everyone to emulate. But when you benchmark, don't confine your imagination just to Sunday schools. Think about other kinds of programs where attendance is vital, and where people have worked hard to improve it, for example. You may come up with something like a computer user group, or you may even want to take a look at a company whose sales have suddenly begun to improve by double-digit amounts. What are they doing right? Can you use their methods? These questions are the ones you should be asking yourself.

# A Vision Links the Present to the Future

There is an old saying, "The future is now," and whoever first said it probably had vision in mind. A vision is a bridge between the present and the future. Because enterprises are increasingly complex, you can easily lose focus while you're caught up in the pressures of simply getting the job done. A vision moves an organization and its people beyond the status quo and keeps everyone sharply focused on why they are doing what they're doing in the first place. The vision sustains and constantly renews their commitment, keeping the organization moving toward the future, focused on new ideas and services, and keeps them contributing not only to the operation of the organization but to its progress as well.

## Building on the present

We're reminded of some old advice about telling jokes: You can't go over the head of the audience. That's a simple way of saying that people have to understand a joke's frame of reference before they can find a joke funny. The same thing is true for visions. If you're in the clothing business, and you assemble your workers and tell them you've decided to turn your company into an Internet Service Provider, they're going to look at you as though you've just gone bonkers. Nobody in the room knows how to do that, and so your vision for a new enterprise probably means that they are all going to get fired so that you can hire an entirely new team.

Because visions are doable dreams, they have to be able to take advantage of the resources you have on hand, or those you may logically be able to get. You can have the best idea and easy access to venture capital, but if you don't have the experience, persuading others to let you do what you think you want to do is going to be difficult. The best business plan in the world, and the ablest people, are not enough if no linkage exists between what those people are doing in the present and what they propose to do in the future.

Steve Kindel (one of your authors) found this out himself in 1998, when he and his business partner came up with an idea to distribute supermarket coupons over the Internet. They wrote a vision statement that clearly articulated their goals as well as the benefits to consumers, and then they followed that with a detailed business plan. They had ample access to venture capital sources, all of whom agreed that the plan would likely work, and every venture capitalist they spoke to was willing to commit to putting in money if they could hire a group of executives with operating experience either in brand management, coupons, or selling to supermarkets. After dozens of interviews, they could not put together the right team and had to forgo the opportunity.

## Envisioning the future

Most people have difficulty seeing tomorrow, let alone next week or ten years from now. But successful leadership requires you to envision the future and persuade other people that your dream is both realizable and worth pursuing. This is a two-step process. First, your vision must be realistic and doable. We're not talking about get-rich-quick schemes here. Many people have interesting visions that are immediately dismissed by their friends, family, or coworkers as "pie-in-the-sky," or unrealistic, or beyond the scope of their resources. Listen carefully to what people are telling you and see if you can connect the dots in your mind to create the vision that you see.

The second part of the process is your ability to convince others that your vision is worth pursuing. Often, a person who has a vision isn't a leader at the time the vision appears. He or she has to articulate the vision, and by doing so attract followers who believe in the vision strongly enough to help make it a reality. In articulating a vision, the person emerges as a leader. In other cases, a group has a goal that it can't reach and needs someone to help get them there, and so a leader comes on board. Then the vision does not belong to the leader alone, but to the group as a whole, and cooperation is generally easier to come by.

# Chapter 20

# Developing a Vision

· · · · · · · · · · · · · · · · · · · · · · · · · · · · · · · · · · · · · · · · · · ·

· · · · · · · · · · · · · · · · · · · · · · · · · · · · · · · · · · · · · · · · · · ·

*Where is the love, beauty, truth we seek, But in our mind?*
—Percy Bysshe Shelley

**C**hapter 19 discusses the need for a vision, which is often the dream of a single individual who sees an opportunity to create change, or sees a need for a product or service, an application of a technology, an opportunity to create a more effective organization, or an opportunity to right a wrong.

But the transformation of a vision into reality can often be a complex process. Many visions, though doable in theory, require tremendous technological or social changes in order to become reality. This chapter shows you how to do that.

## A Vision Is a Doable Dream

Of all the elements that a leader must successfully execute, a clear vision is perhaps the most important. Remember *Man of La Mancha* and Don Quixote's "Impossible Dream," in which he was trying to right the unrightable wrong, beat the unbeatable foe? A vision is just the opposite. A vision is a doable dream based upon the realities of a group's strengths and resources. Far from being wide-eyed and dreamy, a leader's vision is sober and reflective.

## Heigh-ho, heigh-ho!

Consider Walt Disney's vision for Disneyland. Here is how he wrote it: "The idea of Disneyland is a simple one. It will be a place for people to find happiness and knowledge. It will be a place for parents and children to spend pleasant times in one another's company: a place for teachers and pupils to discover greater ways of understanding and education. Here the older generation can recapture the nostalgia of days gone by, and the younger generation can savor the challenges of the future. Here will be the wonders of Nature and Man for all to see and understand." That is a clearly articulated vision, and it has carried Disneyland and Walt Disney World along for decades.

# *Understanding what is doable*

What is doable? The physicist Isidor I. Rabi, who worked on the Manhattan Project and later won a Nobel Prize, once said, "With enough money, you can even suspend the laws of Nature. Temporarily!" What he meant was that if a thing could be imagined, it could be done. You have to figure out the cause, whether the price is too great to pay for the result, and, finally, whether the result is sufficiently permanent to justify the effort. Those are often hard to know in the short term, but what makes certain leaders great is the persistence of their vision. For example:

- ✔ Carbon paper was invented in the late 1800s, shortly after the invention of the typewriter. Carbon paper had been in use for about 50 years, and was the accepted form of duplicating, when Chester Carlson decided in the 1930s that a better way to produce copies quickly had to exist. Carlson's idea, a process that he initially called electrophotography, slowly evolved over a decade into a process called xerography (Greek for "dry writing"). By the time electrophotography became xerography, in the late 1940s, Carlson's original work had been supplemented by the work of hundreds of engineers and scientists from the Batelle Memorial Institute in Columbus, Ohio. It then took the Haloid Company, which bought the process from Batelle and Carlson, another two years to create a machine that could actually make copies, but the resulting company, renamed Xerox, began with Chester Carlson's vision.

- ✔ In the case of McDonald's restaurants, the initial vision of a good hamburger restaurant belonged to Dick and Mac McDonald, the two brothers who opened the first "Golden Arches" hamburger stand in San Bernardino, California, in 1948. But it was Ray Kroc, a man who sold malted milk machines, who was so impressed by the constant traffic around the McDonald brothers' hamburger stand that he kept coming back, trying to figure out why it attracted so much more business than other hamburger stands in town. Kroc finally figured out that it was not quality alone, but consistency — the ability to become efficient and profitable by doing the same things the same way over and over — that was making the McDonalds wealthy. With this in mind, he went to the McDonald brothers in 1954 and persuaded them to let him sell franchises that would exactly duplicate their methods. A year later, Kroc opened his first McDonald's in Des Plaines, Illinois, and built the concept of repeatable consistency into a multibillion-dollar company. The McDonald brothers were doing what came naturally, but it was Kroc who had the inspirational vision to figure out exactly what made McDonald's, and not some other hamburger chain, worth replicating.

✔ In 1905, Sarah Breedlove, a black washerwoman, had an idea for a product that would straighten the curly hair of African-American people, and began to sell it locally in St. Louis, where she lived. It was a modest success until she hit upon the idea of hiring other people to sell her product as agents. By 1910, she had nearly 3,000 agents selling her hair straightener and other beauty products developed for African Americans. Having married Charles J. Walker in 1906, she named her company the Madame C.J. Walker Company and moved its headquarters to Indianapolis, where she became America's first African-American millionaire.

What all of these visions share in common is that they began with ideas, usually for products. But it was not the idea that attracted followers; it was the *outcome* of the idea. People weren't attracted to the way McDonald's made and sold hamburgers, but to the hamburgers themselves. People were attracted to the idea that black women could gain more freedom in their hairstyles rather than to a sales device.

## Keeping the vision simple

A vision should be both simple and straightforward. People who are asked to help turn a vision into reality should be able to understand what the vision is, without a lot of additional explanation, and should have an innate sense that the vision is doable even before they begin to explore what's necessary to actually make it so. In a sense, a vision represents an interesting paradox: Visions are not obvious before they are articulated, or they would already exist. But after they are spoken, or put down on paper, they should inspire an "Aha!" or "But, of course!" from whomever is asked to help make the vision a reality. One obvious indicator of whether you want someone on your team to help make your vision a reality is how quickly he or she can grasp both the uniqueness and the obviousness of your vision.

# A Vision Is Not Just an Idea

Although many visions begin as ideas, a vision is different from an idea. Ideas are abundant. Almost everybody has them at one time or another. An idea that becomes a vision begins with the desire to bring the idea to reality. Many people's ideas never get beyond the "What if . . ." or "I wish I could . . ." stage, because they don't have the energy, the will, or the ability to carry their idea forward. To turn a vision into reality requires leadership, the willingness to embrace the responsibility for getting the job done.

Many more ideas are abandoned after a bit of research, when people discover that a reasonable approximation of what they want to do, or what they wish, already exists. But a few ideas become fully fledged visions when, with a little help from other people, a leader manages to translate an idea into reality. A vision depends on the ability to create a plan, the ability to create a team, and the ability to meld the two into an organization that can bring success to the marketplace. By marketplace, we don't mean only the world of business. We mean a marketplace of ideas and a marketplace of social responsibility.

The following sections examine the components of vision.

## A vision depends on your ability to create a team

Most ideas come from the knowledge, experience, or imagination of a single individual. Edwin Land of Polaroid, Chester Carlson of Xerox, Fred Smith of FedEx, and many others are singular individuals who had a defining idea of a product or service. But shaping a vision from an idea is seldom the work of a single individual. Every single personal vision that has been translated into a successful and sustainable enterprise has been done by bringing together a group of forward-looking, knowledgeable people who understand the nature of the idea, its implications for the future, and the knowledge, resources, and leadership needed to make it work.

Perhaps the single best example of the kind of team it takes to turn a vision into a successful enterprise is the saga of Apple Computer. The idea for a cheap, affordable personal "computer for the rest of us" was not new. Companies such as Altair had been selling kit computers almost from the moment the microprocessor was invented in 1978, even though they didn't do very much and were lacking in the features we think of as typical of personal computers. But Steve Jobs and Steve Wozniak, two kit-computer builders, thought that they could mass-produce a low-cost computer that did more. Their early effort, the Apple I, was a hand-built machine, but their second device, the Apple II, incorporated major changes gleaned from a visit to Xerox's famed Palo Alto Research Center (PARC). Xerox had developed an advanced computer called the Star nearly a decade earlier that incorporated all the features we expect to see in a personal computer — a graphical user interface, a mouse, a large screen, WYSIWYG (what you see is what you get) word processing, and more.

When they went out looking for money to finance their vision, their venture capitalists put together a team and really went to work. With Jobs in command of the vision, they teamed the new company with Regis McKenna, a public relations specialist, who designed the company's logo, and Mike Markkula, a savvy finance man who helped keep expenses under control. With additional team members handling software, and Frog Design providing hardware design integration, the first product, the Apple II, was a hit almost from the beginning. As the product was introduced, other members, such as Jay Chiat, who created the company's innovative advertising, were brought on to the team. Without the total team effort, the personal computer would have remained an artifact in a garage, and Silicon Valley would not be the driving force it is today.

One of the best ways to learn about team building is to play Fantasy Baseball, in which you join a baseball league that exists on paper only. Each person in the league is a manager, and each person is given a certain amount of money to "spend" on personnel. Managers "buy" players until their roster is filled and their money exhausted. The players are actual major leaguers. As each day's major league scores and batting averages are recorded, you get the production of the roster members of your team. So if you were smart enough to put both Mark McGwire and Sammy Sosa on your team at the start of the 1998 season, you would have gotten all their home runs, and all their strike-outs as well. The object of fantasy baseball is to force you to think about real players in real situations, and to force you to put those players together in optimal conditions.

When you're attempting to translate an idea into a vision, you have to do the same thing. You begin with a clean sheet of paper and a question: "If there were no restrictions on resources, where could I go and what could I do?" Such questions eliminate, for the moment, all the arguments from potential naysayers about why your idea can't possibly work, and why your vision should be discarded, or reduced in scope. By asking a no-limits question, you confront physicist Isidor I. Rabi's statement that there are no limits, except the laws of nature, and that even those can be overcome for a while if you want to spend the money.

After you put your vision down on paper, over weeks and months, if you investigate your idea, research it, and learn as much as possible about what it may take to bring it to fruition, a vision may emerge that has a chance of succeeding. As you're doing your research, you're beginning to know what types of knowledge you don't have, and what knowledge and experience will be essential to making your vision into a reality. As the leader, it's your job to begin building a team.

## Checklist for launching an enterprise

Perhaps your vision involves launching a new business. Before doing so, double-check that you have the knowledge, expertise, and experience to successfully launch a new enterprise.

✔ **Do you know your market?** Nothing happens without sales. And sales come only with good marketing. Who are your customers going to be? Where are they located? Do you know what quantities they will buy? At what prices? Through what channels? Remember, this applies to non-profit organizations as well as to products and services that are going to be sold for a profit.

✔ **Do you have an essential expertise?** If you open a restaurant, for example, do you know how to cook or manage a dining room? If you want to launch a high-tech business, can you be the technical whiz? Remember that "if wishes were horses, then beggars would ride." It's not enough to have the desire to do something. You have to have some practical expertise, or the chance of acquiring it, before you can hope to turn a vision into reality.

✔ **Do you know how to run an enterprise?** If you've never been a leader at any level, it's hard to start at the top. You need to acquire some experience leading and turning visions into reality at some level, and then continue acquiring experience. This is what is known as the *scale problem.* If your only experience is in running a ten-person enterprise, leading a thousand people will be substantially more difficult for you. You should beg off, and take on a hundred-person task first.

If you have a great idea for an enterprise, but not enough skills, consider finding a partner who shares your values and your enthusiasm for the idea, and who complements your skills and knowledge. Many successful businesses, including Apple, Intel, Hewlett-Packard, and Microsoft, started that way. *Remember:* It takes a team to turn a vision into reality. Very few people can do it by themselves.

You have to pencil in a name and responsibilities to fill in each gap in your knowledge. If you're intent on providing shelter for the homeless, you have to get someone who knows about permits for homeless shelters, an architect, a banker or some type of money person, someone who has worked with the homeless and knows their needs, and someone who can be an advocate of your project to people who can help you, for example. Each one of those people will be able to help you make your vision a reality, and each will help you shape your original vision and give it the limitations and scope that will make the project doable.

Because the process of building a vision generally involves the people who have to carry it out, team building helps you achieve a consensus and a common commitment at the early stages of a project that are needed to take a vision from a dream to a reality.

# A vision depends on the ability to create a plan

As you go from an idea or a dream to a vision, you will slowly begin the process known as *planning*. The purpose of planning is to answer this question: "What should we be doing and how should we do it?" William Ouchi, a consultant who wrote *Theory Z: How American Business Can Meet the Japanese Challenge* (published by Perseus Books), has observed that Japanese firms spend about 80 percent of the time required to launch a new business in planning, and only 20 percent in execution, whereas most American firms spend 20 percent of their time in planning and the rest of the time floundering around, struggling to execute properly. To give any organization its best possible chance of success, you must develop an idea, within the knowledge and experience of the team, and within the context of its marketplace — where it is now and where it's likely to be five years from now. That plan will determine whether your vision is doable, and whether it can become a reality.

## Information — we want information!

Good planning begins with collecting information. Information is not a set of half-baked hunches, nor is it the personal opinions of the members of the team. It's composed of what Harold Geneen, the former chief executive of ITT, called unshakable facts. Said Geneen, "No matter what you think, try shaking it to be sure."

In addition to the facts, planning rests on an agreed-upon set of assumptions about the marketplace, your resources, and your knowledge and skills. If you don't have agreement on these areas, your planning will never have a firm foundation, and you will constantly be shifting emphasis.

## Planning is everybody's business

Planning requires the participation of every member of your team. If people don't participate, you'll never know whether they have wholly bought into the assumptions inherent in the vision or not. Spend time with all the team members so that you know their point of view going into the creation of an enterprise. You're likely to find, when you're turning a vision into a business, that there are many things you haven't anticipated. One of them should not be sudden and late opposition from members of your own team.

Proper planning involves finding out what your resources are, and aligning those resources with your vision. Proper planning is also the opposite. If you're bent on your vision, then you must make a list of the resources you're going to need to make your vision a reality, and couple that with a list of where to find the resources you need. If you need money, you need to develop a comprehensive list of venture capitalists and bankers. If you need experts, you should be talking to the best and the brightest in your field, asking them for recommendations.

# A Vision Is Based on Reality

Having a vision when you have little or no hope of bringing it to reality doesn't do you much good. All successful visions begin with a sober assessment of the strengths and resources of the group. Those strengths are people, capital, location, intellectual property, desire, market share, and previous success, no matter what kind of enterprise you're leading. (This may require a little analogizing on your part.) If you're coaching a team, you may ask yourself what that has to do with market share. Your winning record is your market share. Your playbook is your intellectual property, your recruiting ability is your capital, and your players are your people. Your desire to win, of course, is desire.

✔ The belief that Robert Noyce, one of the founders of Intel, had in his ability to create a microprocessor was based on the fact that he had already co-invented the integrated circuit in 1958. He was one of those thousands of engineers who had worked out the problems of cramming transistors into a small space. Noyce and his partners, Gordon Moore and Andy Grove, had all worked together for another semiconductor company, and they had not only gained experience in running a business enterprise, they had gained an understanding of each other's skills, strengths, and weaknesses, and they had learned to trust each other. Each had specific experience to contribute to the new enterprise — Noyce's technical skill, Moore's long-range planning abilities, and Grove's knowledge of manufacturing. Without those strengths and resources, the company they created, Intel, may not have turned their vision of creating a microprocessor into a reality.

✔ By the time Mel Farr, the former Detroit Lion professional-football-player-turned-car-dealer, had opened his first new car dealership in lower-income neighborhoods, he had already proved to skeptical automobile companies that he could sell used cars in Detroit successfully, and that he had developed practices to ensure that his customers had credit records similar to those in suburban neighborhoods. Each new step that Farr takes in widening his vision is based on his prior experience and on the growing resources of his company.

A vision is not short-term. A vision is something that will carry you through the achievement of several short-term goals, to achieve some sort of enduring greatness or distinction, something for which your group or enterprise will be known and remembered. It can be as simple as the desire to open and operate the best French restaurant in the neighborhood, the restaurant that everybody talks about and that will cause people to line up for reservations. Or it could be the goal of establishing an employment agency that helps large companies effectively recruit minorities. Every vision is different because it's based on the experiences, strengths, and resources of the person having the vision. But all visions should be the same in that they are a challenge — a call to action — to the people who will formulate a plan to execute the vision.

# Thinking beyond available resources

In addition to recognizing the abilities of existing resources, a good leader thinks beyond the available resources. If you're running a company that makes toothpaste, you have to consider resources from all over the world. You have to consider your intellectual property to be your formula, but also the work that researchers may be doing elsewhere that may cause you to consider changing your formula. The point is, you can't look only at what you have, but at what you may have if you were a little bigger or a little richer. A good leader is always a little covetous of what is just over the hill and wants to take his group there.

# Responding to diminishing resources

The best vision in the world, coupled with the savviest knowledge and the deepest experience, can't help you if your resource base is cut or diminished. What happens, for example, when a rival company comes in and hires away your most knowledgeable workers? What happens when you're running a soccer league and a group of parents set up a rival league that is better-funded than yours? What happens when you own the best restaurant in town and decide to open another branch, but the community won't okay your zoning request?

Mocha Mike's is a drive-up espresso and cappuccino emporium located in Bethlehem Township, Pennsylvania. When it first opened in 1996, its single, tiny, drive-up booth was located in the parking lot of a local Italian restaurant along a moderately traveled road. As word of the quality of its coffee drinks spread, people began to come from miles around for coffee, bagels, and biscotti. But in late 1998, the owner of the Italian restaurant decided that he wanted to expand his parking lot and that he wanted to serve espresso and cappuccino also. So he told Mocha Mike's to vacate its premises. What to do? Mike took on a business partner, who invested enough capital so that Mike could open several new stands. Each one is in a less desirable location than the original, but with additional investment and good word-of-mouth, the business continues to thrive.

The lesson of Mocha Mike's is that any good leader has to respond to diminishing resources — or any new situation. Leaders have to be resourceful, which means that they have to find new ways to do the things they were doing before, or new ways to do new things, if they want to put a vision into practice.

You should never be hindered by the word "no" if there is something that you really want to do — assuming, of course, that what you want to do is legal, moral, and ethical (if not, then you should always be deterred by the word "no"). A way to turn a vision into a reality always exists.

# A Vision Helps You Harness Opportunities

Don't think that opportunities are rare — they are abundant and have always been in every age. The magazine *Business Week,* for example, started in 1929, at the beginning of the Great Depression. The great failure of companies and individuals is not that they lack for ideas, but that so few ideas are well thought out and planned. We live in a society of abundance, but that abundance still rests on a product failure rate of greater than 90 percent.

Forget the phrase "Opportunity knocks only once." The reality is that opportunity is a steady hammer on your windows and doors, a constant noise that you spend most of your time attempting to block out by stuffing cotton in your ears. The reality is that opportunities abound. Opportunities are everywhere, if you can learn to recognize them for what they are.

Most opportunities arise in one of three ways, covered in the following sections.

## Spotting an opportunity

In 1980, IBM was looking for a way to respond to the growing strength of Apple Computer, Inc., but did not want to invest the resources to invent a personal computer of its own. Bill Gates told IBM that he could do it to a very tight deadline at a very low cost. Gates bought the rights to QDOS (short for "quick and dirty operating system") for $50,000 from Seattle programmer Tim Paterson, renamed it the Microsoft Disk Operating System (MS-DOS), and resold the rights to use it to IBM. Gates spotted an opportunity and created a giant company out of it.

Opportunities are out in the world all the time. All you need to do is open your eyes. Deborah Fields was walking through a mall with her husband and suddenly had a hankering for a chocolate chip cookie. She couldn't get one anywhere at the mall, so she said, "If I have a hankering, maybe other people will, too. And if I can fresh bake them, the smell will attract customers." Out of that idea came a vision for Mrs. Field's Cookies, one of the great franchise hits of the 1980s. It wasn't a giant leap for mankind, but it satisfied a genuine need.

If you want to get an idea of what kind of opportunity exists, take a trip to a big city and walk the streets for a couple of days. Look at the great number and variety of the shops, and every time you see a store that looks like nothing you've ever seen before in your own hometown or your local mall, go in and look at the merchandise. Take along a notebook and make notes. We guarantee that you'll come back home with at least a hundred ideas.

# Searching out an opportunity

If a business is making money for one firm, it means that at least enough of a market exists for one, but it probably means that untapped market potential is available for a competitor. Never be deterred by someone else's success. In fact, that ought to spur you to try to emulate it, and then beat it. Some of the most successful businesses began as me-too operations that one-upped existing companies.

The same thing goes for social organizations. Just because a successful charity exists in town doesn't mean that it's immune from competition. If you don't like the way the organization goes about its work, join it, and learn as much as you can about how the organization works (and doesn't work) and where and how the money is spent. You'll find the organization's weaknesses, and doing so will help you develop a plan for your own charity that will allow you to offer the same or better service at a lower cost, which ultimately will help you attract sponsorship. Your overhead and effectiveness will be your selling point.

# Creating an atmosphere in which ideas flourish

In 1944, Minnesota Mining and Manufacturing Company chief executive William McKnight decided that the company could not rely solely on Scotch tape for its future. So he created a policy that encourages innovation, saying, "Management that is destructively critical when mistakes are made kills initiative, and it is essential that we have many people with initiative if we're to continue to grow." Today 3M expects its engineers and technical people to spend up to 15 percent of their time tinkering with new products. This time, called *bootleg time,* has been responsible for the creation of thousands of successful new products, such as Post-it notes and reflective, glow-in-the-dark tape.

Employees deep within every organization often have ideas about new products or services — and about possible new directions for your enterprise — but they simply haven't been asked to contribute. As a leader, your job is to ask them. You have to find a way — beyond the typical suggestion box — to get your people to come up with new ideas that move your enterprise's vision forward.

Many firms pay employees for money-saving or moneymaking suggestions. But firms should also get into the habit of developing vision quest competitions. If leadership can articulate its vision — and it should if it's effective leadership — then it should hold a competition every few years in which employees are encouraged to write about how they would extend the vision over a succeeding five- or ten-year period. Ask people what challenges they think the firm is going to face and how the firm may deal with those challenges. You'll get a lot of expected answers, but you may find a future leader deep in the pack. If you find such a visionary, put him or her in charge of developing the vision into a plan.

During the 1970s, Corning Glass Works actually hired Robert Christopher, formerly an editor at *Time* and *Newsweek,* to become its house visionary. Christopher spent some time learning about the glass business, and then he spent time exploring the American political, economic, and social structure. One of his ideas — that Corning develop solar heat exchangers — was considered good enough for the company to turn it into a business. Although the idea ultimately did not prove workable — the price of oil plummeted by the time the heat exchanger was developed, so that solar power diminished as a viable, marketable product — the company proved that it could generate new visions and turn them into reality.

## Moving from an idea to a plan

Good planning begins with collecting information and testing assumptions. Unfortunately, many enterprises fail because leaders, in their enthusiasm for an idea, fail to plan or test. To succeed, the idea that underlies a vision should be able to answer the following questions:

- ✔ **Why should customers buy your product or service?** What is the significant difference between your product and its competition? Why should they buy from you rather than from someone else? A product or service does not have to be limited to a company. If you're starting a new church or synagogue, or contemplating starting up a charter school, you will be offering a vision of the delivery of a service. Why is yours different from — and better than — what people can already get. Until you can answer that question convincingly, not to your satisfaction, but to the satisfaction of a potential member or customer, you haven't got an enterprise.

- ✔ **Will it last? Is it enduring or a fad?** You'd be surprised at how many things fit this phrase: "It seemed like a good idea at the time." Before you invest a lot of time and effort, take the trouble to investigate whether conditions are likely to change in the near future that will make your product or service obsolete. Keep in mind all those people who invested in solar energy. They all thought that the price of oil had nowhere to go but up, and never considered that Americans could develop conservation technology or that they may simply drive less or turn down their thermostats. They certainly never considered that the greed of OPEC nations for money would be as great as Western greed for oil.

- ✔ **Will competition let you survive?** What is the experience of others in your chosen competitive field? Who are the big players? Will they ignore you, try to force you out of business, or offer to buy you out? These questions are not ones to be answered lightly. Many excellent ideas never make it to the marketplace simply because their developers did not have the resources to see their idea through to victory and were squeezed out by better-financed competition. When you're contemplating starting a new enterprise — whether it's a business or a charitable organization — you have to ask yourself what the barriers to entry are. If they are low enough for you to enter, will they be low enough to attract additional competitors? And what about resources? If your major resource is people, your competitor may simply be able to outspend you and lure your best people away.

✔ **Can it be profitable?** Good enterprises require good profits. If you're starting a business, will it provide you with enough profit margin to allow you to maintain a steady pace of growth in the face of rising competition? If you're running a nonprofit, are you running it efficiently enough so that you can increase your levels of service without taxing the membership? Can you generate enough social profit to attract additional donations for your good work? That should be your goal, and if your enterprise is going to operate on a shoestring, you should rethink how you're doing your work.

✔ **Can it be implemented?** Are you using the right technology? Can you find the right people? Can you repeat what you're doing consistently? Can your enterprise be financed adequately? Turning a vision into reality requires resources. You should be able to design into your planning document a large margin for error, on the assumption that things are going to go wrong along the way. If you rely on a key person, what happens if a car hits him or her? Can you replace the person quickly? Make a depth chart so that you'll know whom to turn to in the event of the unforeseen.

Likewise, what happens when you're working furiously on a technology and a new technology turns out to work better than yours? Can you shift gears fast enough, or will you be dead in the water even before you start? You should make it your business not to be taken by surprise by events.

✔ **Can the enterprise grow?** Most enterprises, except specialty retail businesses and local social service agencies, ultimately fail if they don't grow. Does your enterprise have the potential to continue growing? Will your success lead to other products and to leadership in its field? Do you have a plan to move your enterprise from a local to a regional to a national level? You should be thinking of the next stage even while you're busy planning the current stage of your enterprise.

✔ **Will being in this enterprise satisfy your needs?** Start by asking yourself the question, "What would I do if I had no limits?" Then, after you've finished the planning process — but before you begin to implement your vision — ask yourself, "Do I really want to do this?" Implementing a vision takes time, energy, and commitment. It may require you to spend countless hours away from your family and friends. It may put you in contact with a lot of stubborn, tiresome people. If you're not prepared to "live the vision," think seriously about whether you should be leading the charge, or whether you need to find someone else to be the leader, while you take on the role of *consigliere* — the behind-the-scenes advisor.

In turn, ask yourself whether your idea-turned-vision really inspires you to do your best. Does it fit your lifestyle? Will it meet your long-term goals? Is it worth the effort? Whatever you decide to undertake, remember that executing a vision takes maximum, unswerving commitment. Other people will be counting on you and pinning their hopes on your leadership. If you can't embrace that responsibility, rethink your position.

# A Vision Is Dynamic

In many organizations, because leaders know that their tenure is limited, a tendency to not want to make plans too far into the future is common. "After all," the leader reasons, "I'm not going to be here to see my plans carried out, and I don't want my vision to become a burden and an imposition on the person who succeeds me." This idea is wrong-headed. Because you don't know much about the quality of the people who may succeed you, giving your group or organization a very strong vision is always important so that they have a constant sense of mission and an expanding sense of possibility.

In fact, one of the jobs of a good leader is to spread a sense of vision throughout the organization. It's not enough for the leader alone to have a vision. That vision must be integral to everything that every member of the group does, so that when new challenges or opportunities arise, somebody — not necessarily the leader of the moment — will recognize that the time has arrived for an expansion or a change of vision.

Many leaders are reactive or hierarchical, which is to say that they are in the wrong place or are there at the wrong time. (See Chapter 2 for more information on situational, reactive, and hierarchical leaders.) Such leaders often lack vision, but they can be effective nonetheless — if the situational leader before them provided them with a solid vision.

Because visions change, you should review the driving forces of your group on a regular basis. Say, for example, that you're trying to open the best day-care center in the area, and after a lot of hard work, you have done exactly that. Now what do you do? Do you improve the existing facilities to the point where they are "gold-plated" — that is, filled with expensive and unnecessary luxuries — or do you attempt to expand your day-care vision to new sites so that other parents can have access to the same high-quality facilities?

# Part VI
# Team Building

The 5th Wave                    By Rich Tennant

@RICHTENNANT

Excuse me, Hannibal, but would crossing the Alps on, ohh let's say— MOUNTAIN GOATS severely compromise your vision?

# In this part . . .

*B*uilding effective teams is one of the most important aspects of leadership, because after all, it's your team that's going to do the heavy lifting. In this part, we show you how to create teams that can get the job done, how to pass on team knowledge, and how to how support and encourage your team.

On the other hand, sometimes things go awry between the leader and the team, and this part also gives you instruction on what to do when things get out of kilter.

Finally, we give you some pointers on how to create and profit from ethnic and gender diversity in your team.

# Chapter 21

# Why Depend on Teams?

................................................................

................................................................

*Before a group can enter the open society, it must first close ranks.*
—Charles Vernon Hamilton

The concept of leadership that relies on teamwork and consensus building — which is really what this book is all about — is substantially different from the concept of teamwork that was taught a generation ago. In order to be a team leader, you have to be able to get people to *want* to do what you *need* them to do rather than simply ordering them to do what you want. Your skills have to take into account their needs rather than yours, and your mission (see Chapter 6) has to be inclusive rather than simply goal-driven.

Admittedly, leading teams is more difficult than giving orders. But a well-formed and well-led team is capable of great things. This chapter explains why teamwork is important, and what its benefits are to the team. In subsequent chapters in this part, we tell you how to shape and manage teams, and what you have to do to make your teams want to excel.

## Teams Create Many More Hands and Heads

The primary reason that teams are worthwhile — and superior to a command system where the top-down leader is responsible for everything — is that many hands, and heads, are better than one. Most projects are very complicated, and no one person can hope to master all the details of a single undertaking, no matter how smart and how talented he or she is. A leader

## Putting the US in U.S.A.

Not so long ago, joining an organization or a company meant becoming a cog in a large machine. You had your desk or your place on the assembly line, you learned to take orders, and you didn't ask questions.

For a long time, American organizations had no incentives to change and used the same kind of organizational command structure that had gotten us through World War II.

But competition emerged, first from Japan, and then from other Asian nations. Asians began to out-produce Americans without using a command economy. Instead, the Japanese relied upon *consensus management,* in which workers and managers acted in partnership. The emphasis was on harmony as much as it was on productivity.

By the late 1970s, a number of American organizations had begun to reshape themselves around the same concepts of teamwork that had driven the Japanese. The results, after some initial stumbling and poor planning, were generally beneficial, and teamwork has now become the norm rather than the exception in most American organizations.

may retain ultimate responsibility for a project, but a team leader knows that it's best for each team member to "lead" the portion of the work in which he is most expert. The team member, then, takes the responsibility for that portion of the work, and the leader's role becomes one of tying together the work of all the members of the team.

Here is how teamwork is different from command work:

| Roles of leader | Command work | Teamwork |
|---|---|---|
| Vision | Inspirational | Shared |
| Planning | Done by chief of staff | Done by team activity |
| Mission definition | Defined by leader | Created by team |
| Responsibility | Leader's | Shared among team members |
| Glory | Leader's | Team's |

Significant differences exist between command work and teamwork. These include the following:

✔ **Vision:** A command leader, as Moses did himself, goes up the mountain and comes down with a vision, and then announces this vision to the group. The group accepts it, or the leader casts out nonbelievers, or the group casts out the leader. With teams, the leader asks many questions, gathers information, listens to numerous people, and then crafts a vision that everyone can understand. The leader then works to develop a consensus among the group's members to accept the vision, modifying it and reshaping it so that it's as inclusive as possible.

✔ **Planning:** In command work, planning is a leadership task, reserved for the leader and his or her most trusted allies. Planning is often done in secret, and it's presented as a take-it-or-leave-it finished product.

In teamwork, planning is a shared task. Each member of the team is there because he or she has a specific skill, and the skills of all of the team members are needed to make the plan come together. The leader's role is first to draw the maximum amount of information and insight out of each team member, and then to act as the systems integrator, putting the various components of the plan together into a workable whole. At this point, the leader has to sell the workability of the plan to the team before taking it to a larger group.

✔ **Mission definition:** Mission definition in command work is the leader's sole responsibility. One of the reasons the leader is "in charge" is the idea that people will not accomplish a mission without being told when, where, and how to do it. An axiom in economics applies to battles. Basically, it says that, if each soldier has to decide individually whether to fight or flee, all soldiers will choose to flee, because no one trusts the next soldier to fight on his behalf. The purpose of command is to ensure that no one flees, by providing a penalty for desertion.

In teamwork, because everyone is in it together, team members define their own mission and buy in with their willingness to work on its behalf. The leader acts as a coach, suggesting strategies that help the team shape its mission, and then providing tactics to help the team overcome obstacles. The team does not flee in the face of danger, because everyone knows that their future depends on their ability to stick together.

✔ **Responsibility and glory:** Responsibility and glory in a command situation belong to the leader, and the penalty for failure is that the leader falls on her sword. That is the story of much of history. We know who the leaders were in the major battles, but not the names of the people whose lives were sacrificed for the leader's glory. With teamwork, because everyone shares responsibility, everyone shares the glory — or the failure.

# Teams Create Benefits for Team Members

Team members, by accepting the responsibilities that go along with being a part of a team, gain certain rights that don't exist within command structures.

## Team members gain ownership

When you're a team member, you gain ownership of your work. Ownership can be literal — you and your team are the sole beneficiaries of the output of your work — or it can be figurative, in that you wind up taking great pride in your accomplishments, even though your larger organization benefits. Ownership is another way of describing acceptance of responsibility, and with it go both the benefits of success and the penalties of failure. When you own your work as a team member, you are, by definition, becoming a leader, even if nobody gives you the marshal's baton or the white hat.

You can see what happens when teams are successful. Just take a look at the following examples:

- ✔ In a World Series winning baseball team, everybody's salary jumps and every member of the team is in demand in the marketplace.

- ✔ On Wall Street, a winning team may be recruited in its totality by another firm — not just the manager, but the entire team.

- ✔ The soul of entrepreneurial activity is teamwork. People who have been successful working on a project for a company are far more likely to join together and collectively go out on their own, because they know that they can trust one another and that they have a record of accomplishment under their belts.

## Team members gain accountability

In addition to ownership, team members gain other rights that used to be routinely denied to them. They gain accountability. If team members are accountable to the leader, then leaders become accountable to the team. Think of the old black-and-white chain-gang movies, where two people are running for their lives, chained to each other. When one person jerks on the chain, the other person lurches. In a similar manner, your team and its leader are chained together. If the leader jerks the chain, making peremptory changes in the business plan, constantly forcing people to shift positions, then it becomes more difficult to accomplish the mission. Likewise, when a team decides to retaliate by slowing down, the project deadlines don't get met, and the leader looks bad. So you really are accountable to each other.

## Team members gain permission

Team members also gain permission. In a command organization, orders are given from the top down, and people are expected to obey. But in a teamwork organization, a good portion of the decisions flow from the team members upward to the leader, who has ultimate authority. So the leader grants permission instead of giving orders. This instance is another one in which a

TIP

## Who's the leader is less important than who the followers are

If you're trying to decide whether to become involved with a group, don't ask who is in charge. Instead, find out from members of the group how much they really know about the group's aims. The fuller the disclosure of the leader, and the more tolerant the leader is of dissent during the planning phase of any mission or goal that the group undertakes, the greater the likelihood that people within the group are going to be willing participants in their own future, and the greater the certainty that you will be joining a group that is not torn apart by unhappiness.

leader has to be a good listener, because often, people are not asking for straightforward permission but rather for encouragement. A good team leader has to be able to understand the difference. When team members come to the leader with a proposal, the leader is responsible for giving them a thorough hearing and asking a lot of questions. This process gives the group confidence in its knowledge and in its choice of tasks. Then, when the leader gives permission, he or she is encouraging team members to go forward and do what they think they can do.

## Team members gain acceptance

Team members also gain acceptance. To become a member of a team means to become part of a larger whole. A prospective team member has the right to feel that he or she is accepted into the team not only for the specific talents to be contributed but also as an individual whose personality traits will also amplify and strengthen the team's abilities. One problem of managing in a cross-cultural situation is that it magnifies the need for acceptance (see Chapter 29 for more information on the problems of accepting leadership from people who are culturally different from you). The team leader's job is to make certain that all team members accept new members of the team by bridging any gaps that may arise.

## Team members gain forgiveness

There is nothing more destructive to team management than the human need to blame someone when things go wrong. In a command structure, when someone makes a mistake, the leader can fire the person, or worse. In the old Roman army, if a legionnaire was cowardly in battle, every tenth man in his unit was killed as a reminder to all. (The word *decimation* comes from that practice.) In modern armies, when people fail to carry out their mission, they are court-martialed, reduced in rank, or sent to prison.

In most groups, the penalty for failure is being fired or ostracized. But with a team, it's different. Think of any sports team, if you don't have experience with being on a team yourself. Does the manager kill Mark McGwire when he strikes out three times? Was Sammy Sosa fired because he couldn't lift the Chicago Cubs to a pennant? Of course not. Winning and losing in sports is a team effort. One great lacrosse coach once said, "Defense is a team activity. If someone gets as far as the crease (the semi-circle in front of the goal) and has an opportunity to score, it's because the entire defense has broken down, not that the goalie has failed." Accepting the idea of collective failure accentuates the need to forgive.

In work situations, most people assume that if they've made a mistake, it's their fault. But mistakes are an opportunity for a quick review of a situation. A leader who is faced with a team member who has botched an assignment should ask the following questions:

- ✔ Why did this happen?
- ✔ Were the instructions clear?
- ✔ Did the mission make sense?
- ✔ Was the person given adequate tools and motivation?
- ✔ Was I leading effectively?

If the leader can answer yes to those questions, then, and only then, should the leader take action, and the action taken should be corrective rather than disciplinary, especially the first time a mistake is made. If the same mistake is repeated, clearly there is something wrong, and not necessarily with the person making the mistake, but maybe with how the task is designed to be handled.

# Chapter 22

# Creating a Winning Team

• • • • • • • • • • • • • • • • • • • • • • • • • • • • • • • • • • • • •

• • • • • • • • • • • • • • • • • • • • • • • • • • • • • • • • • • • • •

*Work is love made visible. And if you cannot work with love but only with distaste, it is better that you should leave your work and sit at the gate of the temple and take alms of those who work with joy.*

—Kahlil Gibran

*W*inning and success are wonderful, so they ought to provide a natural incentive to leaders to create the best possible teams. But that's easier said than done. Building good teams requires a lot of insight into human nature and the ability to carefully align skills and personalities. A leader's success depends on an ability to get the maximum amount of effort out of the team in reaching a goal. In this chapter, we show you how to put together winning teams.

## Select Your Team Carefully

As with schoolyard games, it is often the leader who chooses the team. Even when a new leader inherits an existing team, the leader has the right to reshuffle assignments to get the maximum value out of the people on the team.

So, how do you choose? The first thing is to talk to potential team members. Tell them about the mission, and listen to how they react. Do they think that the mission is worthwhile? Do they think it can be accomplished? Are they interested enough in accomplishing it that they are willing to commit their energies? All of these are fair questions for a leader who is choosing a team.

Next, make a reasonable assessment of the intelligence of the team members. You don't need highly educated people — often, an education that is too specialized can narrow a potential team member's thinking — but you do need signs of resourcefulness. Ask potential team members to describe a difficult problem that they once had to solve and the solution they came up with. Tell them that the example can be from any facet of their lives, because often, the most innovative thinking comes in the solution of personal problems. (Think *National Lampoon's Vacation* and what Chevy Chase did with the deceased Aunt Edna.)

Next, select for skills. As the leader, you should have a good idea of what technical and personal skills are needed for your team to fulfill its mission. Select people who have the best possible matchup of skills to needs, although resourcefulness, intelligence, and experience can sometimes overcome a lack of skills.

## Making your team diverse

Diversity is one of those words that means different things to different people. Mostly, diversity nowadays means incorporating people who are culturally different from the heterosexual white male norm of American business. We talk more about that definition of diversity in Chapter 29, but for now, we'd like to talk about a narrower meaning of the word. When you're putting together a team, you want a range of points of view, and of skill levels. Yes, you'd ideally like to be Joe Torres and be managing the 1998 Yankees, but the workplace doesn't generally provide you with enough resources to hire nothing but the best and the brightest.

Although you may want to lead a team of seasoned experts, you can generally get more out of a team that is just coming up. You may be sacrificing somewhat in professionalism with a group of rookies, but you may well be gaining in a fresh perspective and attitude. Part of the problem with elite professionals is that they've seen it all before — or at least they think they have. Someone who is a veteran player probably believes that every play is a routine grounder, until the ball takes a funny hop. This situation is part of the game of baseball, and it's part of life as well. As much as we plan against it, unexpected things do happen. And when they do, a veteran may react in a completely predictable way, which may very well be the wrong way. The benefit of diversity is that if you take your responsibilities as a team leader seriously, and are able to give time to your team — having a wider array of perspectives is a positive benefit.

Just remember to not make your team too diverse! Diversity can also work against you. If you dip too deeply into the talent pool and come up with nothing but newcomers, you run the risk of having to put out too many fires. Your role is not to become either a drill sergeant or a mother hen to the members of your team, and if you have too many inexperienced people, you will wind up taking a disproportionate amount of your time solving their problems instead of working on the team's goals. One of your first acts as team leader should be to assess your team's skill levels and to then form partnerships within the team, a kind of buddy system that pairs up the more experienced people with the less experienced, even if their skills are not alike. For example, you may want to pair an older finance person with a younger quality-control person, because the older finance person will force the younger quality-control person to remember that everything comes at a certain price.

Also remember that one team's castoff may be another team's gem. Someone who may not work well with one team may be perfect in another situation, because of your leadership or because the mission was better suited to their talents.

## Limiting team size

In sports, team sizes are fixed by roster limitations. In command models, team sizes are fixed by the decision of the head of command. In real life, take your example from sports, from the army, and from Zen.

### The least way

When you're putting together your team, start with a blank piece of paper and a model that gives you unlimited resources — of money, material, and people. After you've assembled your dream team, begin paring it down. What can you do without? Who can be eliminated without degrading your team's performance?

Baseball teams have nine starters, and rosters that include roughly 25 members. For much of the first half of the twentieth century, a four-man team called The King and His Court barnstormed around the country, playing pickup games with local town teams. The team consisted of just one ace pitcher, a first baseman, an outfielder, and a catcher. The members of the team were astute students of the game, so they knew by a batter's stance where to position themselves. And they could shift positions — the catcher running to first base to make the putout on a ball thrown by the first baseman covering the shortstop position, for example. Mostly, The King and His Court won, using their skills to overcome their manpower deficit.

As a team leader, you should endeavor to do the same thing. You should always be looking to lighten your team, being consistent, of course, with the requirement that you neither overwork your teammates, nor put them in any danger. One of the benefits of team learning is that people can learn each other's tasks, so that if a team member drops out either temporarily or permanently, his knowledge is not lost to the rest of the team.

### *Who stays and who goes*

When you're putting a team together, the loss of a critical team member is the most worrisome thing, next to the failure to achieve your goal.

There's an old story about a computer company that was founded in the 1950s by three men who knew where everything was and had all the technology in their heads. Over a short 18-month span, this high-flying company fell apart when all three partners died in separate accidents. "The Three Wise Men," as they were called, had neglected to pass their knowledge on to others, so the company foundered.

How do you square the potential loss of a member with the need to make your team leaner? Assess exactly what it is that your team members do:

✔ Can any of their tasks be automated?

✔ Can any of them be outsourced at a cost that does not become a burden on the enterprise both in time and money?

✔ Is anyone not carrying his weight? If so, should he be let go?

✔ Do you have functions that will become redundant over time — such as public relations — after the introduction of a new product or service?

As a leader, you should be asking yourself these questions constantly. Managers juggle their lineups all the time, looking for the winning combination. Don't be afraid to do the same thing.

# *Making Time for Your Teams*

A successful team leader knows that he or she lives an in-between existence — in between responsibilities to the team and the team's goals, and the needs of people higher up in the chain of decision making.

Because it is normal for team leaders to live in between, team leaders must learn how to manage their time, so that they can give their teams all the direction they need and, at the same time, be responsive to the needs of decision makers higher up the chain of authority.

How do you live in both worlds at once? Through information, analysis, and involvement:

✔ **Information.** Teams operate on information. You need it from your team members, they need it from you, and your higher-ups need it as well. When you're asked to form a team, spend some time with the people to whom you report and go over their information needs. Do they want daily reports? Weekly? What form do they want reports to take? Is it a summary or a detailed analysis? Do they want the reports in writing or in person, or both? Make it your business to find out how your superior wants information, and how often, and then use that as your methodology in setting up your team. If your boss wants a written summary of the team's progress by close of business every Friday, then you should have your team members give you a written summary by close of business every Thursday.

You will also need more information than you're passing on. A general rule is that for each piece of information your superior wants, you will need two. For example, if your superior wants a chart showing week-to-week budget expenditures, you should also have your finance person do a 52-week moving average of expenses, and a projection of the following week's expenses, based upon that average. These more-detailed reports will help you spot problems before they crop up, so that making your reports will remain routine.

✔ **Analysis.** In order to make more time for your team, you have to become more analytical about the team's mission. You need to look for tools that enable you to know more quickly if the team is meandering off course. In business, there is almost always a "key number" that your team has to make in order to remain on target to reach its goals. In sports, it's usually a key play or plays, and in volunteer work, it's almost always the services of a key person. You should learn to analyze your own situation so that you know what you need to keep track of, and then make it your business to do so.

Before you can do analysis, you have to collect some baseline measurements for comparison. Much of that data is easy to come by within a company, but how do you establish the same kind of analytical framework when you've been put in charge of a team whose goal is increasing membership at your church or synagogue? You approach it the same way. You go to other congregations of your faith and get some numbers on congregation size, and congregation size as a percentage of total area population. You survey your own local population and determine how many people are nonaffiliated, and compare that number to the local or regional average. That is the base from which you're going to draw. Your subsequent actions will be based on becoming effective in delivering your membership message to that group.

✔ **Involvement.** Ironically, the best way to head off a higher-up from interfering with your team is to get that person actively involved in your team's project. You have to sell what your team is doing as the most compelling thing your superior can do with his or her free time, and you need to make a case for tapping in to your superior's wisdom and insights. Most managers don't want the boss looking over their shoulders, but you should learn how to operate out in the open, so that your superior can never say, "But I wasn't informed," or, "But I didn't have any input." You may think that having the boss around will retard your upward progress, but in fact, it will cement your relationship with higher-ups when things go well. Your boss may take part of the credit, but you'll get more than your share — and your boss will bring additional resources to your team if it's in trouble, to ensure that you don't fail.

In turn, you have to get more involved with your team. You have to use the time you've gained by not having to look nervously over your shoulder all the time to work in a hands-on manner with each member of your team. You will be fully aware of what everyone is doing all the time, not just when their weekly reports land in your inbox.

# Setting an Agenda

You're the team leader, so you must determine the agenda, which is the step-by-step process by which work will flow through your group. You have to decide what is important, where resources and effort must be concentrated, where the opportunities are, which ones are worth taking advantage of, and which are worth passing by. Your job is to bring discipline to the hydra-headed work group that is a team.

What does that mean?

✔ When you're the coach of a sports team, you write the lineup and decide who's going to start and who's going to sit on the bench, set the positions of your players in the field, call the plays, and make adjustments as plays are properly or poorly executed. That is agenda-setting at its most exquisite.

✔ When you're on a military mission, the flow of the team meeting is easy to follow. As commander, you speak first, because you know what your orders are, and you can apprise your troops of how well they are doing in executing them. Your quartermaster speaks next, because that person is in charge of resources, and, in effect, is the person who will tell you how far you can go on the supplies you have. The next person who speaks is your intelligence person, because he is the soldier who is in charge of knowing what may lie ahead. Only then will other team members bring the unit up-to-date on their status.

✔ When you're a team leader at work, or in a charitable organization, agenda setting is not so clear-cut. For one thing, there is no standard body of rules. For another, winning and losing is not as clearly defined, and often, the mission is one that changes as circumstances change. So you have to look for other ways to control the flow of play while keeping everyone informed.

## *Reviewing your agenda*

The best way to keep the team's agenda in front of everyone is with regular review meetings. Your meetings should follow a standard format every time the team comes together. You have two choices in how to run the meeting. You can run it in the manner of a Society of Friends meeting, where anyone who has something to say can get up and tell the team what is on his or her mind. Or, you can structure the meeting a bit more, with the leader speaking first, reviewing where the team is in achieving its mission. Either method can lead you to the same destination, which is enough information to be useful in planning what the team will do next.

## *Reviewing your goals and mission*

Agenda setting goes beyond controlling meetings. An agenda is also the combination of a mission and goals (see Chapter 6), as well as the day-to-day problems that beset your group, which you have to discuss with your group and then take action upon.

## *Reviewing your vision*

Setting an agenda also means bringing the team's behavior in line with its vision, as you can read in Part V. Because the purpose of the team is not simply to work but to achieve a higher purpose, you have to use your meetings to measure progress and to inspire your team members to move ahead when they may be content to continue in a comfortable, steady state.

# *Capturing Team Learning*

Just as regular formal reviews help you understand where the team is going, they can also help you ensure that everyone on the team learns from the experiences of everyone else.

Teams should make a record of what they've learned — not only their successes, but their failures as well — and keep that record up-to-date, as the team progresses. Just as leadership isn't permanent, team membership isn't permanent, and you will need to pass on what the team knows to each new member, or to the new team leader. You don't want your team members arguing with their new leader that they've already tried something and failed. You want to be able to show the person exactly what you did, and why it failed, or succeeded.

## Keeping a diary

As team leader, your task is to figure out the best way to capture the experiences of the team. Lewis and Clark kept a diary, and many researchers keep notebooks when they are working on a problem. A notebook that contains all the weekly reports, along with your analysis of a situation and your own observations of team behavior, discipline problems, morale problems, and your own responses, is probably the minimum record that you should keep. You should also keep any memos, internal correspondences, and hard copies of e-mails that have been generated about the solution of any problem that arises.

## Getting your team to share ideas

When a team member makes progress on a portion of a problem, you should expect that person to teach what he or she has learned to the entire group. Team skills need to be shared, so if someone learns a new way to solve a problem, that person needs to share the knowledge with his or her teammates. Teaching should be formal, which means that it should not just be reporting at a meeting. The person who has something to teach should take his or her new knowledge and put it within a context of methodology, so that other members of the team can quickly learn how to use it. For example, if you're working with a spreadsheet program and you develop a new macro that speeds analysis, you should be prepared to show it off in the context of the old method and what the old method produces. You also should show the instruction set for producing the new method, along with examples of what the new method produces.

## Embedding your best practices

Many teams run on what seems to be an *ad hoc* basis, making it up as they go along, so that when they do things right, they often can't repeat their good behavior. One of the hardest things for a team to do is to make their behavior routine. Part of what a team should do, therefore, is work toward a goal of embedding its best practices. For example, say you're running a quality control operation, and part of your team's work is to do telephone surveys. You find that by changing the survey technique and by changing the questions, your productivity rises, and what you can report back to the company improves greatly.

At this point, as the leader, you need to embed those new practices. You have to get new scripts produced for everyone and train them in the best techniques for using them. But you may also want to have the scripts put into the software so they automatically generate as prompts to previous questions.

Build the software that will not only measure the response, but compare it to a growing database of previous respondents, so that you will have a moving index of measurement.

Any enterprise can take its team's learning and turn it into an embedded practice. Each team should keep a manual of procedures and update it regularly as better practices supersede what came before. Your manual ought to include your analytical tools, your reporting requirements, and your methodologies for measuring your progress, as well as team expectations, so that new members — or a new leader — know exactly what to expect.

# Fixing the Problem, Not the Blame

As we explain in Chapter 21, one of the expectations of team membership is acceptance and another is forgiveness. As a team leader, keep your mind focused on moving ahead toward your goal and achieving your team's objectives and visions. Don't become overly concerned with fixing blame when things go wrong. Many teams work within continuous processes, so create the monitoring systems you need to monitor continually, or at least on a regular, ongoing basis. If you don't, and something goes wrong, it's your fault as the team leader. Your job is to find ways to anticipate problems and to correct them before they become critical. If you find yourself bringing work to a halt and screaming at someone, the failure is yours.

One of the best techniques for fixing problems instead of blame is to use the *loose constructionist method.* This term refers to an interpretation of the U.S. Constitution, and it says, "Anything that is not expressly forbidden is permitted." In a team situation, loose constructionism says that as long as people don't do something that is expressly forbidden, they are free to get their work done any way they want. If your team is in charge of building widgets, for example, the things that are forbidden may be introducing out-of-tolerance parts, and failing to adhere to the maintenance schedules for the machinery. How the team solves the problem of keeping the parts within tolerance is the team's problem, and it could range from setting up a measuring station to measure each part, to sitting down with the manufacturer of the part to work out a better way to produce it with greater consistency. By not tying your team's hands, you're encouraging them to come up with the best solution to the problems that they see as critical.

The opposite of loose constructionism is *strict constructionism,* and sometimes a dose of strict constructionism is what's needed to make a team work well. Strict constructionism is another constitutional law term. It states that "Only that which is expressly permitted can be done." Strict constructionism forces people to follow a format rigidly, and when your team's goals require tight adherence to tolerances, rules, and even to appearances, this is the way to go.

For example, most journalists are bound by informal work rules that govern who pays for lunch, and under what circumstances. Most publishers keep the rules loose, because they don't want ballooning expense accounts. When someone seems to have violated the rules, the managing editor needs to decide whether a rules violation has actually occurred, and what to do about it. That method is the loose constructionism method. If newspapers and magazines simply insisted that journalists pay for all meals, and that they never take any kind of gratuity, that would be a strict constructionist method. With strict constructionism, you'd never even have to ask yourself whether a story was influenced by a meal or other favor, but the paper would have to be willing to pay the cost of keeping its reporters unsullied.

# Allow Your Team to Find Its Own Path

One of the most satisfying aspects of being a leader is developing new leaders. The best way to do that is to, wherever possible, help your team find its own path. Where do they want to go? What do they think is a legitimate goal? How do they assess their own strengths and weaknesses? After you know something about your team, you should allow them increasing latitude in setting their goals and defining their mission. A leader with a team is much like a parent with teenagers. You know that you're not always going to be around to run their lives, so you are responsible for equipping them as much as possible with your values, testing them by giving them responsibility, and allowing them to test themselves by accepting that responsibility.

# Working with Other Teams

Your team does not stand alone. In sports, teams play within a league, which means that every team is dependent upon every other team for its very existence. In fact, every team is dependent upon the competitiveness of every other team for its vitality as well. If one team wins all the time, fans lose their reason to root, attendance falls, and the management begins to trade off all the expensive stars, quickly degrading the team's performance.

The same thing is true in business and in volunteer life. Your team will be one of many, competing for resources, but cooperating with other teams to get things done. Often, within a large company, several teams may be doing similar tasks. Make it your business to meet with other team leaders to share information and to share resources. Make it your business to develop an efficient but informal marketplace for knowledge, resources, and people, so that you can constantly jigger your team into a winning unit.

Even when you're locked in bitter competition with another team, find ways to cooperate. For more than 20 years, newspapers around the country have been doing exactly that. During the 1970s, as newspaper circulation began to dwindle, publishers launched expensive circulation wars to grab what remained of existing readership. The result was that papers lost even more money. The solution to their problems came with so-called Joint Operating Agreements, which said that different newspapers in the same town could share a single press and other operations, for cost-effectiveness, while they were trying to beat each other's brains out to gain circulation. A Joint Operating Agreement recognizes that, sometimes, a particular competitive environment is a zero-sum game with fixed costs, and that by sharing the costs, you keep everyone competitive and in the game to the benefit of all.

In professional football and basketball, this acknowledgment of common needs is done through competition committees and the reverse draft, whereby the worst team this year gets the rights to the best talent the following year, so that over time, most teams should be about equal as far as talent. In football, teams go even farther, forming scouting "combines" that look at players and share their results with all the combine members. All these situations are competitive ones in which teams acknowledge their interdependence upon each other, to their mutual benefit.

# Chapter 23

# Team Learning

*Live and learn. Live and learn. That's what Grammy Hall always says.*
—Woody Allen's *Annie Hall*

**I**n the previous chapter, we tell you about how important it is for teams to learn and to pass on their learning. In this chapter, we deal with how teams learn and how they pass on their knowledge.

If you have ever lived in a rural area, you know that the farmers have a kind of knowledge that does not depend upon scientific study or textbooks. A good farmer can sniff the air in the late winter and tell when it's time to plant or look at the spider webs and know when it's time to irrigate. This kind of knowledge — this *folk wisdom* — is the sort of hard-earned knowledge that groups pass down from one generation to the next. In this chapter, we talk about this kind of group learning.

Modern society has learned to take such folk wisdom seriously. More than half of all new medicines take their origins from folk remedies. Not only is the profession of *ethnobotany* (the study of plants in exotic locales) flourishing, but an entire company, Shaman Pharmaceuticals, is betting stockholder money that it can turn native remedies into powerful tools for healing. Shaman recognizes that learning lives in many places and that dismissing knowledge out of hand just because the source is not one with which you're familiar is unwise.

# Gathering Information

If the information your team needs for its decision making were all in one place, tied up in a neat little package, life would be easy. Unfortunately, life doesn't work that way. Your team needs all kinds of information, and that information resides in many different places. The following sections talk about some of the places in which you and your team can find the information you need.

As a leader, it is your responsibility to help your team learn. As the team goes about its business, making mistakes, correcting course, and pursuing its goals, the leader not only has to provide encouragement and resourceful help, but he or she also has to keep an ongoing account — written or mental — of what has been happening. When the team reaches a goal, the leader can either review what was learned with the team or move on and teach a new team how to achieve a similar goal more efficiently.

Where do you go to gather information? Most of what you need will come from the experiences of your team, but a lot of information will be "out there," waiting for you, as the leader, to bring it back to the team.

## The marketplace

A lot of the basic data you're going to need is competitive, demographic, or both. Whether you are starting a new business, organizing a charitable fundraiser, coaching a team, or managing a company division, most of the information that serves as the starting point for your decisions is going to come from outside your organization. You can get that information from government sources (such as the Statistical Abstract of the United States), from state and local sources, or from a United Nations Statistical Yearbook, if you are looking for international data. All of these are readily available in most public libraries. Make it your business to know who collects the data you need about your enterprise, and try to get the most up-to-date data you can.

When your sources are not government sources, they are often private sources. Foundations, private information collection agencies such as Nielsen, trade associations, and credit reporting agencies such as Equifax, contain mountains of information that can be valuable if you know what to ask for and how to analyze it.

## Your project

Your enterprise will generate its own information, which you have to place within a competitive framework. You will be generating financial information, performance data, production data, and other information that is relevant to your project. Your job is to decide what information is critical, and in what format it will be most useful. For example, you may be in the fast food business, collecting information on sales. You need to know not only what the sales volume consists of, but what its components are — how many burgers, how many combo meals, how many chicken sandwiches, and so on, you are selling. You also need to run a profitability analysis that compares individual meal sales to combo meal sales, and then measure that against marketing expenditures. You then need to put that into a comparative framework of other fast food outlets in your competitive area, and other outlets in areas with similar demographics and income.

Every project, every industry, every undertaking has at least one critical number by which everyone measures their progress. In retailing, it's sales per square foot. In mutual funds, it's net asset value. In insurance, it's premium income. In the airlines, it's load factors. As a team leader, you have to know what the critical number is, because that is what your team is going to be measured by. Everything you do, ultimately, will revolve around that number, until the time comes when you can prove that the number is wrong and that a different measuring tool will give you a more accurate result.

## Your people

Each member of your team not only has the knowledge of his or her work, but the members also possess their experience from prior assignments. Whether you choose a team or inherit one, your team members possess some experience, so learn to use it, and make sure that each person teaches what they know to other members of the team. If one of the people on your team is a production expert, have him teach the basics of production to everyone. If you are heading up a committee in charge of producing the food for a group dinner and one person has a number of killer recipes, have that person teach the recipes to everyone in the group. The next time you have to do the dinner, you'll be faster and more productive. If you have a player on your team who knows how to execute the double play, have her practice with everyone on the team until they can do it in their sleep. Your job as a leader is to ascertain the skills and experience of your team members and then help them disseminate that knowledge to the group as a whole.

## Your competitors

Learn to actively monitor your competition. By that we don't mean that you should be spying on them, but because you both do the same things, learn how the competitor does it. If the competition does it better, find out how they do it. In the automobile industry, a routine practice exists called *reverse engineering,* in which a company buys cars made by its competitors and disassembles them, piece by piece. They count the number of welds, count the number of pieces that go into a subassembly, and examine the metal that a part is made from. Because they know what it costs to make their own car, they can get a pretty good idea of what it costs a competitor to make *its* product. They can find out where they can cut costs without compromising quality, or they can gain a competitive marketing advantage when they learn that their competition is sacrificing quality for sales.

By monitoring your competitors, you also avoid being caught by surprise. New products, processes, and services are appearing every day, so you have to know when your competition is making a push. Keep an eye on the employment pages. Is your competition hiring and you aren't? That may mean a market expansion, a product expansion, a new product launch, or some other preparation for additional growth. (It may also mean that a lot of people have left, but you will probably already know if that's the case by the résumé flow to your own team.)

## The world at large

Learn by example. Your team is almost certainly not the first group to do whatever it is you're doing. Even if you're going off on an Antarctic expedition, you have the knowledge of hundreds of expeditions that preceded you. The same holds true with climbing Mt. Everest. Somebody beat you to it, so learn from their mistakes and emulate their successes.

The world at large includes the academic community, as well as the research community. Learn to keep up-to-date with what academia is doing in your area, by reading the research journals and by attending conferences.

The same is true of your competitors. Make it a practice to attend trade shows on a regular basis. Take your entire team and give them the assignment of collecting brochures, information sheets, and pamphlets, asking questions, and attending as many seminars as possible. Then return each night to your hotel room and pool your knowledge. As the leader, ask people to report on what they've learned. What did they hear that was interesting? What did they see? Whom did they meet? Did they come across someone who was doing something you're doing, but better? Did they find a potential recruit for your team? All these questions are part of covering the world at large.

The world also includes people and institutions that have absolutely nothing to do with your project. If your team needs finance help, the place to look may not be a competitor's finance person, but an accounting firm, for example. If your team needs production skills, you may find them in your industry, but a different industry may do things similarly, allowing you to learn from someone who is never going to be a competitor. The process of benchmarking is all about learning from the best, regardless of where they come from.

# Team Learning Comes from Experience

You may have heard the expression, "There's book smarts and then there's street smarts." Many people today are superbly trained in their fields at colleges and universities, and then perform miserably on the job because they don't have an ounce of street smarts.

*Street smarts* are made up of empirical observations that have been gained by people over many years. Often, the observations have been distilled into pithy sayings that are almost clichés. For example, there's this one about pilots: "There are old pilots and there are bold pilots, but there are no old and bold pilots." What does that mean? It means that a pilot who takes risks when he or she is young will, in all likelihood, have crashed before making it to old age.

Team learning often follows along the same lines as empirical wisdom. People accumulate knowledge as they do their jobs, and as much as you require them to formalize it by putting it into writing and putting together manuals of procedure, something is always missing. It's like following the recipes of a fabulous chef. No matter how good you are, your recipes never come out quite as good as the chef's. Why? Because he or she has left something out of the instructions. Not consciously, to be sure, but something nevertheless that has a profound impact on the way the final dish tastes.

Often, the chef doesn't know what's been left out, because he never thinks about it. It could be something like preheating the oven. He always preheats the oven for every pastry dish, so why would he tell you to do it for one particular dish? The same thing is true with team learning. People can be completely open about how they do things, and yet something inevitably will be missing.

## Learning prestidigitation

The hardest type of magic for a magician is so-called close-in-hand magic, or *prestidigitation*. You are within feet of the magician, and his hands are always right in front of you, and yet, he can pull cards and coins out of thin air. Try as you might, you can't tell how he does it. The empirical experience of team members is a lot like prestidigitation. You can follow along with a person while they are learning and still not learn everything, because you weren't there for the pre-preparation work. Steve Kindel once worked for about six months with a fellow who made cabinets. He learned everything he could about planing, sanding, joining, and finishing wood. When he made his first piece, it came out well in all respects except the finish, which looked blotchy no matter how many times he sanded it or how carefully he applied the shellac, he asked the cabinetmaker to watch him, and he told Steve he was doing everything right. So why was it wrong? The cabinetmaker smiled. "I warm my shellac slightly," he told Steve, sheepishly. "Not really hot, but just enough to change its flow characteristics off the brush." When Steve did the same thing, he got much better results.

As a team leader, you're going to confront this problem a lot. You can't spend all your time with each member of the team while they're doing their work, so you're always going to miss something that should be passed on.

Because most people don't know what they know, you have to coax it out of them gently. You can do that in a number of ways. The following sections show you how.

## Start a newsletter

Aside from contributing to team cohesiveness, team newsletters and bulletins can be used to serve another purpose. You can ask each member of the team to write down something useful that will help the team as a whole, and rotate the assignment throughout your team members, so nobody feels the burden too heavily. Say, for example, that your finance person uses a fairly sophisticated analytical tool. Ask her to explain it, and if an application is helpful in the outside world, make copies available to interested team members. For instance, many people maintain offices at home but don't know how to figure the depreciation on the office if it is a separate structure, nor do they know that they have to recapture a portion of the depreciation if they ever sell their property. If your finance person has been using a tool to do that on the property that is necessary to your work, she can explain it and modify the tool so that other members of the team can use it.

## Show and tell

Make your weekly meetings into "show and tell" sessions. Deputize one person for each meeting to explain in detail what they do and what their experiences have been in working through particular problems with this particular team. Most people will have encountered similar problems before, but the problems will often be slightly different because of circumstance, or because of the demands placed upon the team. Use this kind of discussion as a jumping-off point to figure out whether deficiencies are present in the makeup of the team, or whether a flaw exists in the mission.

## Master class

Most people are proud of what they do and of their ability to master a particular aspect of their work. As a team-building exercise, have each person on your team teach a "master class" in some methodology that has varied nuances. This exercise will force the person doing the teaching to think more about the "how" of their job, and less about the "what." It will also give people an opportunity to ask all sorts of questions, many of which may appear superficial, but all of which are useful. The questions will draw out your team of experts to explain what they do in lay terms, so that the other members of your team can benefit from their knowledge.

## Outside experience

Many people have outside experience that proves useful to the team, especially for team building and morale purposes. These experiences fall into the category of hobbies, skills, athletic skills, and so on, none of which may have anything to do with the task at hand, but all of which reveal something about the person doing it and their potential for doing something else. For example, someone who does model railroading or shipbuilding may be a person who is incredibly detail-oriented. When you need an extra hand to help on a spreadsheet project or to meticulously review the preprint advertising, that person may serve as your extra set of eyes and hands. You may have someone who climbs mountains or does a bit of white-water rafting on the weekends. That's the person whom you may want to stand up and do a presentation, because he is both self-confident enough to challenge himself physically, and careful enough to prepare well before each adventure.

As a team leader, your job is to discover the full range of each team member's skills and to use all of them to the maximum benefit of the team. Take it as a given that your team members are complex human beings whose skills and range of knowledge are rich and varied, and constantly press people to dig into their banks of experiences to bring more to the team.

# Chapter 24

# Spreading Team Knowledge Around

### In This Chapter
▶ Learning how to replicate teams
▶ Identifying and creating new leaders

*The final test of a leader is that he leaves behind him in other men the conviction and the will to carry on.*

—Walter Lippmann

The point in time will undoubtedly arrive when your team is running smoothly, your objective is in sight, and your mission is soon to be completed. You may have already received another assignment and are just waiting for things to come to an end so that you will be able to move on to something new.

Or maybe your team has managed to make a major change in the way things are done in your organization, and your superior has asked you to take what your team has learned and spread it throughout the enterprise.

In either case, you need to make some decisions about how you will pass on your team's hard-won knowledge to the people who will take your place. You can pass on what you have learned in a couple of ways, ensuring that your team's knowledge isn't lost and that your knowledge is spread throughout your organization.

# Replicating a Team

Perhaps you do volunteer work for an organization that builds playgrounds in your community, and it has won an award. Your organization asks you to help similar organizations in cities and villages around the country become more effective in building their own playgrounds. What do you do? You could try one of a couple of techniques for replicating teams, all of which work equally well.

## Each one teach one

This method is the most direct method of passing on team knowledge. An old saying tells us that what one person knows, another person can learn. If what you know is how to build playgrounds, you may want to have your organization send you volunteers from other cities to come and work with your team, so that they can observe and learn firsthand all the things that your group does so well. If you opt for the each-one-teach-one method, you will have to have systematized your knowledge — put it into a written, step-by-step format that can be duplicated and handed out. Otherwise, you will be gaining an additional pair of hands, but the person will not come away with the sense that she has gained much from the experience.

The following list includes the most important points in making the each-one-teach-one method work in distributing team knowledge:

- ✔ Pair up visiting people with members of your team, and have each team member teach the visitor with whom he or she is paired.

- ✔ Hold end-of-day review sessions during which newcomers can ask questions and exchange thoughts about what they have learned.

- ✔ Rotate assignments from day to day to allow for as much assimilation of knowledge as possible in the time available.

How organized should you be if you are taking large numbers of people into your group for a short time to teach them your team's methods? Be highly organized. Put your own team learning down on paper, and put together a manual of procedures that everyone can follow. This manual is the one you would have used in the past if new members were joining your team and needed to be brought up to speed. You should also have a number of team-building exercises, so that new people feel integrated into the team quickly.

These team-building exercises are part of the spirit and the doctrine of the team that you want a potential leader of another team to take back home. You are not only teaching what you do and how you do it, but why it is important and how to motivate other people to do it, too. In other words, when you do an each-one-teach-one drill, you are really training leaders for other groups. What they learn they will take back to their own groups and use to train their own teams.

## Boot camp

Boot camp is a technique for teaching a large number of people at the same time. If you are asked to run a boot camp, you are really being asked to train a large number of people in a very short time. You will have to be even more organized than if you are using the each-one-teach-one training method that we describe in the previous section. A boot camp is a highly structured operation that forces you to really know what you're talking about when you begin training.

1. **Create a complete manual of methods.**

   Ask yourself every conceivable question about how a playground gets built, because that is what you are going to teach. Your manual should start with site preparation. How do you select a site? How do you handle zoning and permissions? Move on to building materials and safety considerations, and so on, until you have constructed a complete how-to on playgrounds.

2. **Set out your theory and doctrine.**

   If your group is building playgrounds, then *why* is your group building playgrounds? What is the history of the group and how did it grow to its present strength? What makes your playground-building group so much better than other local efforts? You have to have well-thought-out rationales for these questions and need to communicate them succinctly to your new members.

3. **Communicate the process.**

   You have to explain what the steps of building a playground are. At this point, people will be working through their manuals, taking notes. (Make it a practice to put blank paper in each section of the methods manual you will have created so that people don't have to go looking for someplace to put their personal reactions.) In this section of learning, you may be talking about materials, labor, costs, and fund-raising techniques, as well as raising community awareness and publicity. You will probably have a number of breakout sessions that specialize in items such as zoning and permits, getting companies to donate equipment, building a playground on a shoestring budget, and other issues that you consider important.

4. **Go through case studies.**

   You have to walk your group through the process, step-by-step. Encourage each of the people on your team to speak about the problems they individually encountered, as well as problems that the team had to overcome. Have a variety of cases at your fingertips, so that you can show how to build playgrounds of varying cost, complexity, and environments.

5. **Provide actual experience.**

   Allow the group to build a playground by themselves, with your people acting as advisors. Encourage this group to become a team, even though they are going to go their separate ways after the boot camp is over. Get them to figure out how to solve problems as they arise. Make the problems the same as those they'll face when they go back home, so they know exactly what to expect.

# The assimilation technique

The assimilation technique is a way of passing on your team's knowledge that involves taking in a couple of new members, teaching them what you know, and then sending them out after a considerable period of time to form their own teams. In effect, you are assimilating them into the culture of your team and making these people your own — until they can function on their own.

If you have plenty of time, this technique is probably the best way to replicate team learning, because the person who is assimilated into the group learns without conscious effort. Their progress can be more closely monitored, and they can be given increased responsibility as they merit it. Missionaries have used this technique for centuries, bringing people into the fold, nurturing them, and then sending them back amongst their own people to spread the word.

# Pass it on

Still another way to pass on the collective knowledge of a team is to allow the team to temporarily grow in size, and then split the team in two. Appoint a new leader who will take half the members and who will grow her own team and split it in the same way. Your role as the leader is to pick the right person for the new leader's role. You will spend your time observing as your team members interact, looking for the person who not only embraces responsibility well and has the other leadership attributes — the ability to elicit cooperation from others, the ability to listen, and the ability to place others above herself — but you will also be looking for a person who is capable of working independently from you at some point in the near future.

Your choice will almost certainly be based upon which of your expanded-team members can master the most skills. When you are hiving off a "colony team," you should select a mixture of more- and less-experienced people, so that the team has adequate resources with which to solve its problems. When you are choosing a new leader, you are also choosing followers, so take care to make sure that the new group operates in a reasonably harmonious fashion.

## Outward bound

All the methods we have talked about so far have been based upon people coming into your group, learning from the team and the team's leader, and then taking their knowledge someplace else — usually to another team. But the other side of the learning coin is teaching, and all the methods we have just talked about can be applied equally well when you send people out from the group to teach what you have learned to other leaders or other teams. You should carefully prepare anyone whom you send out. They are going to become a de facto leader of a new team, at least for a while, until they have imparted what they have to teach, so they have to carry themselves with confidence and authority.

You should probably do the first outward bound mission yourself, and take along the person who is most likely to be able to replace you as the leader if you should move on. That person can observe while you do your teaching and can pick up valuable pointers. Thus, while you are teaching a new team, you are also grooming a successor to yourself for your own team.

After you've gone out with your successor, allow that person to go out on subsequent missions alone. This will be effective leadership training. Be certain to debrief your person each time he or she comes back from a training trip and then spend some time talking to the group that has been trained to find out exactly how it went. You need the new group's feedback if you are going to eventually trust this person with your own group.

# Identifying and Creating New Leaders

One of the first things we say in this book is, "All leadership is temporary." You are going to be the leader for a fixed period of time that is less than a lifetime appointment, unless you are a hereditary leader such as a king. And because that is unlikely, you have to begin thinking about who is going to replace you, how you're going to identify that person, and how you are going to train him or her.

If you believe, as we do, that leaders are made, not born, then your new leader could be almost anyone in your group, or perhaps someone from outside the group. No matter what, the new leader will be a person who can answer the following questions:

✔ **Do you understand the vision of the team?** Visions are supposed to be clear, easily articulated, and easy to communicate. In your conversations with potential successors, spend a lot of time talking about what President Bush used to call "the vision thing." Get people to tell you how they would extend your team's vision and where their ideas may carry them. Question them closely on the consequences of their ideas, and ask them to submit an informal plan that shows how the team can move in a new direction. A potential leader brings logic and clarity to his or her presentation and communicates a sense of excitement. If you get something you think is interesting, you may want to start the person off on her own mission while she is still a member of your team. That way, when it is time to make the transition, she will be pretty far along in the planning and development process.

✔ **Do you understand the mission of the team?** Being able to appreciate a lofty vision is one thing, but how is your potential leader on the day-to-day realities of running a team? Can the potential leader concentrate on the mission and sweat the details? Does he know what things are important and how to maintain control over those things that are critical to the success of the mission? Allow potential candidates a turn at being leader for a week or two if your project is one that stretches over months, or for longer periods if your project carries on over a year or more. Act as a coach and give advice where it is needed — you cannot, after all, allow things to go too far off track, or your own ability to lead will be called into question.

✔ **Do you understand the needs of the other members of the team?** How is your potential leader in dealing with other members of your team? Will her elevation create jealousy and resentment, or will it be applauded as a sound decision? Will people willingly accept your proposed new leader, or will shifts need to be made in the makeup of the team? It is up to you to be sensitive to the personality dynamics of your own team and to explain carefully to each member why you have chosen the way you have, after you've made your choice. If you are simply training a potential new leader, train several, and let all of them know that they have an equal chance of taking over your role. Almost everyone loves a challenge, and the people who do not want to lead will quickly tell you.

Sometimes, a person who tells you that he doesn't want to lead is really telling you that he lacks confidence rather than skills. This is especially true with women and minorities, who may not be afforded the same leadership opportunities in daily life as white males. If you're bringing along a person who is not confident in their right to lead, you have to explain to that person that he or she already has demonstrated leadership, or you wouldn't be considering him for the role. When kids have a tough time with a school problem and begin to think of themselves as stupid, for example, you should always stop and remind them of how much they already know and how much they've already learned. That reminder is the same kind you have to give someone who is unfamiliar with leadership.

# The leader's cookbook

Creating a leader is sort of like cooking. You can get something instantly, out of the box, or you can create a leader from scratch. The trick is in knowing when to do which.

## Out of the box

An out-of-the-box leader is one who comes to you with all the appropriate tickets punched. You take a look at his résumé and talk to him for a few minutes and realize that this person has been well trained and seasoned over many years by others. The out-of-the-box leader is prepared to learn quickly and will stand patiently at your side to absorb your style, as well as to absorb the flavor of the group. Such a person will usually be a master of group dynamics and will begin to take on team responsibilities almost immediately, so that before too long, he is doing exactly what you want him to do, and a lot more. These people are the kind we tend to call *natural leaders,* but they are not that at all. They are extremely well trained and have demonstrated their abilities repeatedly over time.

In emergencies, having one of these instant leaders on your team is great. If you have an instant leader, you can delegate a lot of the day-to-day management of the team to him, while you work on vision and long-range strategy. But you can also rely on such a person to take over if you should have to leave suddenly, or if you're called away for an emergency.

## Leaders from scratch

Alas, it is the rare group that has an instant leader on hand. You, as team leader, will probably struggle to find someone who can take over from you, for one of several reasons:

- **Nobody wants to stand apart as a strong leader.** You have a truly harmonious team, and everyone functions on approximately the same level. People naturally work together and seek consensus, and nobody moves too far or too fast to distance themselves from the group. In such a group, caution is the watchword. You have what we describe in Chapter 9 as a *jujitsu group,* one that pulls information and actions toward it, reactively, rather than being proactive.

✔ **People are too busy dealing with their own workload to worry about leading.** You have a group that is beset by its own internal problems, or one that operates within a difficult environment, so that the group feels that it needs to give all its attention to the daily problems of survival, rather than to its future. This group is one that does not want to deal with visions and would be horrified at the prospect that you are going to leave and that one of them is going to have to assume your role.

✔ **The task of the team is about to change.** This situation is not uncommon. Teams, after all, are generally brought together to solve specific problems, and when the problem is solved and the knowledge is embedded in the larger organization or passed along, the time has come for the team to change. The team may receive another assignment and may even become a kind of "Mission Impossible" squad, trusted by the organization with a succession of difficult endeavors. Under these circumstances, you'll need to figure out what kind of leader the team is going to need for the future, and keep in mind that the qualities that are successful in the present may not be those needed in the future.

You can probably envision other scenarios in which you can't automatically turn to someone, hand him or her the baton, and say, "Now it's your turn." What do you do in those cases? You create a leader from scratch.

You assess each person's basic leadership skills in the same manner that you assessed your own. You measure their abilities along the four critical skills — embracing responsibility, eliciting cooperation, listening, and placing others above themselves — and you come up with a number that represents each person's abilities. Then you analyze the problems they are likely to face, and attempt to figure out which combination of strengths is most suited to the new problems that will arise after you're gone. By this time, you should have two or three people who can fill the bill, even if no one person stands out. At this point, you should begin to increase their responsibilities, giving them new assignments and the leadership of small projects, until you are confident that they can lead the entire group. From this small group of potential leaders, an effective existing leader will be able to make the right choice.

The whole point of asking each person to articulate her understanding of the vision, her view of the mission, and her sense of the people with whom she works is to give you the chance to see whether she'd make a good leader for your team. Listen closely to how she responds, but don't tell her that you're considering her as your replacement. It could be that none of the people you select will be suitable, and you will either have to start all over again or begin to search outside the team for a successor.

But, assuming that you have one or two candidates, begin to force the issue. Give them additional responsibilities that tax their abilities. Ask them whether they are prepared to make a larger commitment to the group's success, with their own time and energy. Find out if they have issues at home that will impede their ability to grow, and either find a way to help them deal with those issues, or move on to the next candidate.

# Chapter 25

# When Followers Won't Follow

*When all your rights become only an accumulated wrong; where men must beg with bated breath for leave to subsist in their own land, to think their own thoughts, to sing their own songs, to garner the fruits of their labors . . . then surely it is braver, a saner and truer thing, to be a rebel in act and deed against such circumstances as these than tamely to accept it as the natural lot of men.*

—Sir Roger Casement

*I*n the old days, leaders had ways of dealing with recalcitrant followers. Ghengis Khan used to make small hillocks out of the heads of warriors who questioned his authority. Vlad the Impaler left people hanging from spears outside the wall of his castle. Tamberlaine the Great put an entire city to the sword when it refused to submit. So whenever things go wrong between leaders and followers, there's a natural tendency for the leader to want to wield the sword, even if only an imaginary one.

The propensity of leaders to want to have things too much their own way is one of the reasons why literature is filled with stories of rebellion. From *The Caine Mutiny Court Martial* to *Mutiny on the Bounty,* writers have tried to wrestle with the consequences of the failure of leadership. Much of what has been written on the subject, unfortunately, deals with breakdowns in command structures. We believe that, outside the military, the command method of leadership is dying anyway. We need a new way of looking at the dynamic of leaders and their followers and what can go awry between them.

# What Am I Doing Wrong?

Think of the relationship between leaders and followers as akin to the relationship between parents and children. We don't mean that leaders should take a paternalistic or maternalistic interest in their groups. Rather, we believe that good parents recognize, without even thinking about it, that they are responsible for nurturing their offspring. If children are misbehaving, then the fault lies with the parent who's failing to properly communicate his or her values and expectations to the child (absent, of course, some psychopathology in the child).

So the first questions a good parent asks is, "What am I doing wrong? Why don't my kids do what I want them to do? Have I properly explained the reasons why I want them to do this thing? Have I given them mixed signals, acting one way and telling them something else? Have I acted in an exemplary fashion, so that my kids want to emulate my behavior? Have I let them go too far or given them more latitude than they've earned? In short, have I been lax in determining their ability to make judgments?"

These are the questions any group leader needs to ask when things go wrong. But even before those questions get asked, leaders should ask themselves another, more important set of questions, which come under the heading of "What kind of failure is this?" As you'll see, a failure can come from several different directions. Knowing what kind of failure you're dealing with is critical if you're going to get your group back on the right path.

## Failures of vision

Visions must meet the test of being achievable within the context of the resources of the organization, the motivational skills of the leader, and the talents, capabilities and enthusiasm of the group. A failure of vision can come about for any of the following reasons:

- ✔ **The vision was too limited and was insufficient to motivate people to do great things.** If a vision is too narrowly conceived, groups lose their enthusiasm and motivation, and your most talented people will move on, looking for something bigger into which they can put their efforts.

- ✔ **The vision was superseded by a competitor's larger vision.** Even the best vision becomes worthless when someone else comes up with a better idea.

- ✔ **The vision was too grand and therefore unachievable.** If the vision is too grandiose, it discourages people and makes them believe that they are wasting their time building what the Italians call "cathedrals in the desert."

# Failures of mission

Failures of mission are failures of planning. A good leader is supposed to know where the group is supposed to end up and why. Often, leaders develop a sense of mission that blinds them to larger considerations, so that while they have taken the hill they've promised to take, they do so at a terrible cost to the group and then find out that the ebb and flow of events around them has made the taking of the hill unnecessary. Good leaders have to know why they're doing what they're doing and how it fits within a larger context so that they don't inadvertently squander resources and lose the trust and confidence of the group. Leaders thus have a responsibility to maintain good communication links with other groups and with the competitive marketplace at large, so that they can adjust their mission.

One of the ways to keep communication with other groups and with the market is with what Wall Street analyst Craig Gordon, president of Off-the-Record Research, calls *market checks*. If you agree that whether you're a leader in business or in a volunteer group, you compete within a marketplace, then you should have at least one person in your group constantly scouting the competition. What's the competition up to? What changes are they making? What do they perceive about the market that you may not? If you're constantly asking yourself these questions, you're much less likely to fail in your mission and therefore much more likely to maintain the confidence of your group.

# Failures of execution

Sometimes the vision is right and the mission is perfectly doable, but the group cracks up anyway. You send out your accident investigation team and find that failures of execution happened all over the place: People simply didn't do what they were supposed to do. Here are the questions you should ask:

✔ Was the work properly designed?

✔ Was the work beyond the skill and scope of the people doing it?

✔ Was the group properly trained in its tasks?

✔ Was the environment within which the group was working safe?

✔ Was there a change in the environment that may have been anticipated but wasn't?

✔ Did your group have the proper resources to get its job done?

Answer "no" to any of these questions and you have the makings for mistakes. More important, you have the makings for resistance. Nobody wants to go into a task knowing that they're going to fail. People don't like being told,

"Well, I know this isn't what we promised you in the way of resources, training, time, or safety, but try your best anyway. And, oh, by the way, if you screw up, it's your fault, not ours!"

When you encounter failures of execution, you have to look long and hard at the reasons. If you've been responsible about the way you set up your group and the leadership you've given it, then almost always, if a group member fails, the failure is at least partially yours.

## Failures of leadership

Failures of leadership covers everything in the previous sections plus a couple of additional sins. There is the sin of obtuseness, which is simply not recognizing when things have changed. Leadership is situational, and when situations change, the leader has to change and make those changes clear to the group. If a leader fails to do that, he is no longer leading, no matter what title he sports.

Think of leadership in a group as being like a school of fish swimming in the ocean. When the lead fish zigs, the school zigs. When the lead fish zags, the school zags. But sometimes, the lead fish stops paying attention to the environment and does neither. The lead fish swims right into the mouth of a larger fish, and the rest of the school has to zig and zag for its life, finally finding a new leader who knows how to zig and zag to safety. Good leaders have to be aware of their surroundings. Being obtuse leads the group into peril and costs the leader her mandate to lead.

Another sin is the sin of pride. Because leadership is about the willingness to embrace responsibility, then a leader has to act responsibly. You can't go around with your chest stuck out and your head full of yourself and your power, because there's always somebody around who is more than willing to challenge your authority, or worse, to undermine it. A good leader does not put much emphasis on the title, role, or trappings of leadership, but rather, concentrates on the responsibilities of leadership and keeping up good relations with the group.

# Did I Exercise Leadership?

When there is rebellion in the ranks, many leaders assume that the fault lies with their group, rather than with them. Making that assumption is the first step on the path to oblivion, because looking outward for someone to blame will simply create more animosity among your group.

Leadership is about the ability to listen, but listening requires that you be able to interpret what you hear. When your group tells you that things aren't going right, they're really asking you to exercise more leadership. When your group begins to question your authority, they're really telling you to accept the responsibilities that you've been given, beginning with rethinking your vision, goals, and mission. When a group openly challenges your authority, it's asking you to exercise leadership. The members want you to listen to them and to find a better way of eliciting their cooperation.

So you have to ask yourself, "Am I exercising leadership? Am I embracing responsibility? Am I eliciting the cooperation of my group, or am I just giving orders? Am I listening to their needs and asking the right questions? Am I placing the needs of the group above my own needs and my own ego?"

Exercise, as the word implies, involves work and the expenditure of energy. So part of the question of whether you're exercising leadership is whether you're working hard enough on your leadership skills. Embracing responsibility is one thing, but you may have set up some kind of invisible barrier in your mind that says, "I'll go this far and no farther. Beyond this mark, it's someone else's problem." If so, you're not making enough of an effort to embrace responsibility, and your group will know that you have set boundaries.

# Did I embrace responsibility?

One rationalization for not embracing complete responsibility is that you want your group to grow in its capabilities and that they have to learn how to embrace responsibility as well. Besides, you can't do everything. This sounds good, but a truly good leader shares responsibility with his or her group, rather than dividing it. Sharing responsibility means that, although they may have primary responsibility for a task, you're their backup, helping to guide them and keep them out of trouble. If your group feels that they're too much on their own, their next feeling is, "Why do we need you to tell us what to do?"

# Did I elicit cooperation?

Eliciting the cooperation of others takes a certain amount of work. Ignoring members of the group who seem less than enthusiastic about the group's latest mission or goal is all too easy in all the hullabaloo. Giving out menial tasks is an easier road than confronting the anxieties and problems of your recalcitrant followers. But eliciting cooperation means everyone's cooperation, not just the enthusiasm of a core few. The more people in your group whom you can bring around to your point of view, the greater your chances of succeeding, because your team members are going to reinforce each other's beliefs.

A lone malcontent, or someone left out of the flow is like attaching a lead anchor to your bright undertaking. Sooner or later, that person will attempt to drag you down. Even if he doesn't succeed, the time you spend repairing the damage he has caused will almost certainly force you to revise your goals or your timetable for reaching them, or both. You'll only be able to press on due to the additional sacrifices of the rest of the members of the group. Working at eliciting the cooperation of *all* group members is therefore like doing preventive maintenance.

## Did I listen and incorporate what I heard?

Learning to listen well is probably the hardest exercise of leadership there is. Leaders carry a lot of information around in their heads, as well as a lot of expectations. Because they have a plan and because they're expected to make decisions quickly, leaders are often guilty of what is known as pattern thinking. *Pattern thinking,* as the name implies, is viewing the world as a kind of mosaic. One of the most common mosaics is a plan, made up of many parts, and requiring proper execution by a lot of different people. When a leader hears new information, the first question asked is, "How does this fit against the pattern (the plan) I know?" Under the pressure of time, anything that does not fit the pattern is displaced or rejected.

You can easily spot quarterbacks who are too much the victim of pattern thinking on the football field. They have been told what to look for, how to "read" the defense, and how to find the right pattern against which to throw or run the ball. But sometimes the pattern doesn't fit, and when that happens, the quarterback is sacked, or he throws an interception to a defender who "wasn't supposed to be there." Did he misread the pattern, or was there new information that his mind simply rejected? It doesn't matter, because the outcome is the same.

In a competitive world, most of the innovation — and most of the success — comes from finding ways to defeat pattern thinkers. Listening, as we have said many times, is different from hearing because it requires analysis and interpretation. A good part of that analysis is figuring out how and why the information you've been given differs from the expected pattern, and then acting on it.

Groups don't like leaders who aren't good listeners, for the simple reason that the leader is very likely putting them at peril. Whether it's General Custer who didn't listen to his scouts about where the Sioux were located, or Bill Clinton who did not listen to Sidney Blumenthal when he was told that Monica Lewinsky had a "stalker's personality," the results are the same. Ultimately, if the leader doesn't listen to the group, the group won't listen to its leader.

## Did I put the needs of the group above my own needs?

Putting the needs of others above yourself is another difficult exercise. The failure of Communism was always less a failure of ideology than a failure of leadership. From the outset, Trotsky argued that the Bolsheviks couldn't lead unless they were the best-fed, best-clothed, best-armed group in society. Because Russia was slow to accept Bolshevik authority, Trotsky's decree created both militant resistance in a society whose resources were already depleted by the rigors of a war with Germany and endless confrontation between an increasingly elitist Communist Party and the people they purportedly led after the war.

By 1921, with the end of the world war and the end of a bitter civil war, the Communist Party had established itself as a permanent *kleptocracy* (government by theft), expropriating what it wanted from the people it claimed to represent. Because the Party always placed itself "in the vanguard" — a polite way of saying that it placed its own needs above those of the people — it never enjoyed popular support.

The collapse of Communism is an extreme example of what happens when leadership places its own needs above the needs of the team, but it's by no means the only example. Probably half the strikes and labor slowdowns in American history have come about because management has paid itself bonuses at the same time that it has laid off workers or cut their benefits or wages. Almost certainly, the revolution in leadership that has taken place in the United States over the past decade and a half owes its success to managers finally realizing that it truly is their workers who make or break them.

Herb Kelleher, the flamboyant CEO of Southwest Airlines, has repeatedly said that his employees are more important than his customers, because if his employees are happy, then they'll take proper care of his customers. Kelleher has been known to write nasty letters to complaining customers, telling them to take their business elsewhere, if he feels they are being abusive to his employees. That's what we mean when we say that you have to work at putting the needs of others above yourself.

# Was I Attentive?

How is paying attention different from listening? It's listening with alacrity, which the dictionary defines as "promptness in response." Nothing gets a group more frightened, and finally, more angry, than being left in the dark.

What used to be called the mushroom theory of management — feed your people a lot of manure and keep them in the dark — is a nasty joke that's all too common in practice, until it backfires on leaders who employ it. Team members have a right to be kept informed, and that right begins with timeliness of response.

Never leave people wondering. From the outset, establish a response policy for members of your group. That policy should take a certain form. For information that you want to convey, establish a regular meeting time, when you can tell the rest of the group whatever you need to tell them. For questions they have, you should have a policy in place that stipulates a time constraint for an answer, such as, "No more than 48 hours." If you can't get an answer within the allotted time, tell the person the reasons why and see if you can solicit additional information, which may help you get an answer more quickly. But in no case should you leave people hanging around, waiting. If the issue is one that affects the group as a whole, failure to listen with alacrity can slow the entire group down and severely erode your authority.

Promptness of response also means being quick to take action after you have an answer. There's no reason to delay a decision if you have the means with which to implement it. Decisions, unlike wine, do not age well, and like wine, decisions sour if left exposed to inaction for too long. Other circumstances will intervene, and all you'll be doing is breeding ill will among your group if one or more members know that you could have done something to help them and chose not to.

Promptness of response, finally, also means completeness of response. If you do a thing half-heartedly or halfway, the results are often worse than if you had done nothing at all. When you make decisions, you should be trying to close off debate, not raise a thousand new questions. So when you choose to take action, make sure that it's the action you want to take and that its purpose is to get the group back on the path of accomplishing its mission.

# Was I Open to the Outcome?

Being attentive has another meaning: being open to the outcome. Everything you do has consequences, like the rock thrown into the pond that causes an infinitude of ripples. If you don't want the ripples, you don't throw the rock.

Leaders have to realize that they are subject to Newton's Third Law of Emotion, which is that every action has an equal but opposite reaction. If you push your people, they push back, which leads to confrontation. If you pull away, they pull away, leaving a widening gap between you. A good leader expects the team to do what it's supposed to do, but is prepared to act when the team does something unexpected.

That includes team rebellions. No team is so harmonious that it doesn't sometimes question authority, except perhaps, ant colonies. Team leaders who expect to be loved and adored because they do everything right are often the most surprised when their fitness to lead is called into question. This is probably most manifest among so-called charismatic leaders, who thrive on the love of their followers and often resort to great cruelty when that love is withdrawn. (Think of Jim Jones or David Koresh.) Such leaders are totally closed off to the possibility that their judgment may ever be called into question, and they lash out at their group with a ferocity that makes the group flee in terror.

Leaders have to be open to the possibility that their judgment is flawed, and they have to be prepared to correct their mistakes swiftly. If not, they lose their mandate to lead and can be overthrown either from without or from within.

# Did I Tell the Truth?

Few people lie outright, but most people don't tell the truth, the whole truth, and nothing but the truth. We live in a society that places a value on evasion and partial information, where people are constantly taught about situations in which partial disclosure is preferable to full disclosure. Failure to make full disclosure and to live with the consequences is what brings people and businesses to the brink of scandal, and turns minor infractions into major embarrassments.

So what is it about lying and telling the truth? Are there such things as white lies — lies that are permissible? Most religions say that a lie is permissible if telling the truth to someone will cause them pain, as, for example, when you have to tell a loved one that they have an incurable disease and that they are going to die. But in our angst-ridden society, what one person can face causes another acute pain, and we often spare ourselves more than we spare others when we lie to them about things they may be able to face.

About a decade ago, a number of managers at a very large company actually committed suicide when faced with the prospect of having to lay off large numbers of people, because they had never had to do it and didn't know how. They hadn't prepared for the reality of sitting across the table from colleagues and firing them, and, rather than inflict pain on others, they inflicted it upon themselves. The company responded by hiring outplacement professionals, who had no emotional attachment to the people they were letting go, and by paying compensation to the families of the executives who killed themselves.

Telling the truth requires that a leader first be honest with himself or herself. What's the point that you're trying to get across? If you're merely conveying information, you should always convey accurate information, which is one kind of truth. But if you're attempting to convey an opinion, you have to remember that you're in the realm of the subjective, and that means you have to question your own motives before you speak.

For example, you may have a conflict with a certain team member. Do you tell that person straight out that he or she is unsuitable for your team? Do you find some ground upon which you can compromise? Or do you find the person another, less desirable assignment because you simply want to avoid confrontation? There's no easy answer to these questions, and effective leaders have dealt with the problem in each of the three ways. The main point is that you first confront yourself and tell yourself the truth, even if you are forced to be less than direct in the way you handle a team member.

# Chapter 26

# Can the Situation Be Saved?

### In This Chapter

▶ Knowing how not to get into the position where you wish you could start over

▶ Resolving problems with new information

▶ Knowing that leadership is temporary

*Keep strong, if possible. In any case, keep cool. Have unlimited patience. Never corner an opponent, and always assist him to save face. Put yourself in his shoes — so as to see things through his eyes. Avoid self-righteousness like the devil — nothing so self-blinding.*

—Basil Henry Liddell Hart

**I**n Kenny Rogers' song *The Gambler,* the final bit of advice is, "The best that you can hope for is to die in your sleep." Most leadership situations are not quite that dramatic. If you're doing everything that we outline in this book to the best of your ability, you're going to be a successful leader and continue to develop your skills throughout your life.

But life has a way of throwing up roadblocks, and sometimes — through your own failings, inadvertence, or the unyielding opposition of others — your leadership experience isn't everything you thought it could be. When that happens, you have to ask yourself three questions, which are the subject of this chapter.

## Can We Start Over?

The question of being able to start over is one we'd all like to answer in the affirmative. It's the answer that begins, "If only. . . ." If only I'd done things a little differently. If only I knew a bit more. If only I had more time. The plain fact is, if you are a situational leader — and most leadership roles are situational — you are not going to get many second chances. You have to make a flat-out effort from the beginning and treat every day as an opportunity to get it right.

We're not saying that you don't get any slack. Often, in the beginning of a new leadership assignment, you will have considerable latitude in finding your path: in describing your vision and giving it some detail, in the planning and execution of your mission, even in the definition of your goals. It is up to you to keep all those options within the realm of the sensible.

How do you do that? Four rules can help keep you from painting yourself into an irretrievable position. If you follow these four rules on a consistent basis, you won't have to worry about whether things have gone too far, because they should never get so bad that they are irretrievable. The following sections explain these rules.

## Never promise what you can't deliver

One of the nice features about being in charge is that you are the one who chooses the level of expectation that other people develop. No matter how confident you are of your abilities, no matter how well you seem to have matters in hand, allow for the unexpected. Remember Murphy's Law, which is that if something *can* go wrong, it will. Also remember that nothing is idiot-proof. One talent idiots have is that they can always find new ways to screw up. And though you have labored hard to put together a first-class team, somewhere out there you're going to encounter an idiot who is going to do his or her darnedest to make your life miserable. If you haven't allowed for that possibility, you're just asking for trouble.

The way you keep out of harm's way is to underpromise and allow for the possibility that you can overdeliver. If you have been handed a goal, for example, of raising bottom-line profits by 20 percent, and you know that the target is achievable, go into your management and fight as hard as you can to change the number to 15 percent. Lay out the worst-case scenario so that later, if things do go wrong, nobody is left with egg on his face. If you then come in at 20 or 25 percent, then everybody assumes that you and your team worked like the dickens to achieve the best possible outcome.

Likewise, never make promises or guarantees, period. Maybe Joe Namath could guarantee a Jet victory over the Baltimore Colts in Super Bowl III, but you're not a brash young quarterback with nothing to lose. You could take the advice that Gregory Peck gives to his fellow aviators in the film, *Twelve O'Clock High:* Think of yourself as already dead so that you have nothing to lose. You probably weren't raised with a nihilistic mindset, however, so you have to learn to exercise a reasonable amount of caution in the things you do. Making promises at the drop of the hat is careless. So unless you are absolutely certain that you can deliver on a promise, don't make it in the first place. Instead, use language like, "I think we may be able to do that," or, "There's a reasonable possibility we can do that, if . . ." and then lay out the conditions.

## Put it in writing

Hearing is not listening, and people listen and remember selectively. So learn to document everything. You may think that writing everything down is time-consuming and wasted work and that you could better use the time for more productive work. But we can assure you, based on long experience, that aside from helping you to cover your backside, writing things down is the best way in the world to clarify what you actually propose to do.

The exercise of writing requires you to focus your thoughts. Journalism teaches that writing is a mechanical process. The thinking is the hard part. If you're still thinking through a problem at the time you sit down to write, you haven't thought it through sufficiently. Put your pen down or get away from the keyboard; put more thought into what you're going to say and to whom. Think about content and style. What words are open to interpretation? Take them out and make your language as clear and as unambiguous as you can.

Practice writing in a structured, consistent style so that when you report, the same type of information appears in the same place all the time. For example, highlight the important points (good news and bad) up front. This approach makes it hard for the people who read your reports to say that they over-looked what you wrote. Anyone who says that he or she missed what you had to say is just trying to weasel out of a commitment.

Likewise, get everything in writing. Whenever you receive direction, make certain that you get it in clear language, with no ambiguity about deadlines and goals, and don't stop exchanging memos until you're satisfied. If clarify-ing issues means a face-to-face meeting with someone, then by all means have it, and *then* put together a final memo. This approach may sound unduly legalistic, but that's the kind of society we live in. Responsibility is diffused, so one of your jobs as a leader is to reconcentrate it.

## Never paint anyone into a corner

Your ability to lead depends on the willingness of others to follow, or at least to cooperate with you. If you give people ultimatums, you're simply setting them up for possible failure and taking your enterprise down with them. Don't get yourself into the position of creating confrontations that are going to come back to haunt you.

If you have to replace a person from your team, do so as quickly and as expeditiously as possible. Start by looking at replacements and adding them to the team as extra hands. After the extra help is integrated into the team, take whatever action you have to about replacing personnel. If you can't do that — if time or circumstance doesn't allow you a graceful transition — make your change quickly and muddle through. You do not serve yourself or the person you are dismissing by prolonging matters. Again, make sure that you have documented your complaints, both to the person and to higher-ups or personnel, and have the human resources people, if they exist, assist in the exit procedure.

Your obligations to your team include maintaining the harmony of the group; the best way to do that is to keep your group inclusive from the inside and from the outside. This *dual inclusivity* means that you should neither shut anyone out from your decision-making processes, nor bring them in so closely that they feel like they are being overwhelmed by responsibilities without authority. Strike a balance between the needs of the team and the needs of the mission, but the mission can't be executed properly without the team, so work on your people skills first.

## Always look for opportunities to say yes

People need encouragement in order to do their best work. If you can't give that, then at least avoid being discouraging. The old rule, "If you have nothing nice to say, say nothing at all," should be your motto for doing business both with your team and with the outside world.

We're not asking you to be a hypocrite — by being nice to people who are clearly making your life miserable — but you have to know how to encourage people to do things right. If someone does something wrong, show him how to do it right. If someone isn't achieving the results you expect, go back and look at the plan with that person and ask her to help you figure out why things aren't going as planned. If your group is straying from its mission, tell the group that you need their help to get back on course and listen to what they have to say. Maybe the original mission needs upgrading, or perhaps you missed something in your planning that's now becoming obvious.

If your team members ask you for a favor, such as a change in working conditions (or anything that doesn't imperil the mission, for that matter), try to say yes. Companies have policies, but try to treat your team as a group of privileged people. Run interference for them whenever you can, and as long as they don't abuse your good will, you should make life as satisfying for them as you can. If someone needs help with day care, don't just give the person the time off. Have an assistant dig into the day care issue so that you can provide your team member with some options. If someone needs personal time because of a family illness, figure out how you can help, and then do it. Your team members will show their gratitude by cooperating with you to accomplish your mission.

At Ryder Systems, Inc., whose yellow rental trucks are ubiquitous, Hurricane Andrew was an opportunity for the company to help the community in a big way. Chief executive officer M. Anthony Burns turned the company's headquarters into a giant relief center for all of south Florida. He insisted that his employees take the time not only to attend to their own needs in and around Homestead (the city devastated by the 1992 storm), but also to organize themselves to serve the community as well. Ryder has long been considered one of the best companies to work for in America, precisely because it puts its employees' needs first.

# Fighting for your life

What happens when you have to scramble to save your job? Perhaps a project has gone very wrong, and being given a second chance isn't a foregone conclusion.

You absolutely have to do a couple of things:

✔ **Always accept responsibility.** Your team may have screwed up, but the operative word is "your." Whatever goes wrong, it's on your shoulders, and the idea of embracing responsibility begins with understanding that, in bad times as well as good, the buck stops with you. Learn to not make excuses when things go wrong. Learn to not blame people. Even if someone on your team hides bad news from you, your reporting systems are supposed to cross-reference each other so that you can catch mistakes before they go too far. If they don't and something blows up in your face, it's your processes that have failed. Defense may indeed be a team activity, but when your team defense breaks down, you're the person in the goal who has to deflect the shot or take the blame when the ball goes in.

✔ **Never apologize.** One of the consequences of accepting responsibility is that you have

to let the chips fall where they may. If something has gone wrong on your watch as leader, you have to be prepared to accept the consequences, but it doesn't mean that you have to grovel. Take your medicine, resign if you must, and move on. Analyze what went wrong and make certain that it won't happen again. There's a world of difference between saying "I accept full responsibility for what happened" and saying "I apologize for what happened."

Accepting responsibility acknowledges that you are a leader and that you are willing to own up to those responsibilities. Apologizing is a form of begging. It is asking for forgiveness without actually accepting responsibility. "I'm sorry, and I won't allow that to happen again" means that you have no clue why it happened the first time, which makes you unfit to be a leader. "Whatever happened is my responsibility, and I won't let it happen again" says that you are going to make the effort to find out what went wrong.

# Do We Need New Information?

One of the ways you can retrieve a bad situation is to offer to go back to square one and revisit your vision, your plans, your mission, and your goals. You should have been doing that on an ongoing basis, but maybe you haven't been able to, and now your group has reached a crisis. Can you stop the world, get off for a couple days, and then get back on again, with the world spinning in a new direction? Sometimes you can.

If you're in one of those intermediate leadership situations that are increasingly common — you're only responsible for a portion of a problem, and you have upward and lateral reporting responsibilities as well as downward command — use that fact to your advantage. The people to whom you report are just as accountable as you for the failure of your plan — after all, they signed off on it. Don't be afraid to negotiate that point and ask them to sit down and review, in detail, what has gone wrong from a planning perspective. If you bring higher-up management into the picture at an early stage, you're sharing accountability. Doing so doesn't count against your leadership rating, but it does help to ensure that someone can help you if things don't go as planned.

After you gain permission to redo a plan, do two things:

- ✓ **Question every assumption.** Why did your plan go awry? All possible factors can fall into three groups: marketplace considerations, internal considerations, and people considerations. On 3-x-5 cards, record every possible system and process that is involved in your assignment. Pin the cards to a large board. Have one person per card explain the assumptions and deviations of each system. Write the accumulated deviations, including the dates, and put those on another board along a time line. After you finish that exercise, you should have a pretty clear picture of where things went wrong from an organizational perspective.

   Next, go through each point and attempt to figure out what intervention could have changed the situation. Who should have done what, and when? Who should have notified whom, and when? Tell your team that this exercise is not to fix blame, but to ascertain what the problems are. Stick to your commitment to avoid finger-pointing so that your team will speak freely. By the time you finish, you will know exactly what you did wrong, why, and, probably, what actions you have to take to get back on track.

- ✓ **Rethink everything.** Questioning what went wrong isn't enough. If you're in a situation where you're fighting for your professional life, you have to be brilliant, and that means that you have to rethink from the ground up. You may go through the exercise described above and come up with a simple answer, and that may be sufficient for you to regroup and go forward. But if you take the opportunity as one to question the very premises by which you've made your decision — your vision, your mission, even the makeup of your team — you may come up with an inspired idea that carries you off to a different and better direction.

# Do We Need New Leadership?

When all eyes are turned on you, and you are the one who has the final responsibility, sometimes you have to know when to say good-bye. To quote an old Noel Coward tune, "When you feel your song is orchestrated wrong, why should you stand idly by? When the love light has faded from your sweetheart's eyes, sail away." That's a very graceful way of saying that you should know when to throw in the towel and allow someone else to take up your burdens. Leadership is temporary, and you have to learn to know when your time is up. You don't want to end up like Mussolini, who was strung up by the heels by an angry mob, or like Mark Antony, who intentionally fell onto his sword after his failed attempt to defeat Octavian in battle.

Your responsibility as a leader is always to be able to step outside of yourself, to do a little self-monitoring of your situation. The reasons for self-monitoring are twofold: first, so that you can keep yourself on course; and second, to control your exit strategy, if you have to. And, as any military person can tell you, you have to have an exit strategy. What are the goals that you sought to achieve? Whether you achieve the goals or not, at some point, any additional commitment of resources — your team's or your own — is both foolish and ruinous.

Give sufficient thought at the beginning of your planning process to the end of the plan. What happens if you actually achieve your goal? Do you have something else to go on to, or are you just going to sit there celebrating or feeling depressed because your struggle is over? If you fail to achieve your goal, have you planned for that possibility as well? Someone once said that it is the responsibility of a captain to be the last person off a sinking ship. But it is your first responsibility to ensure that your ship has enough lifeboats, food, and water if its crew has to put to sea after a sudden sinking.

Planning your exit can occur in myriad forms, but you can employ a few techniques to improve your odds of coming out ahead if you have to relinquish leadership:

- **Keep your lines of communication to the outside world open.** Neither you nor your team should ever develop a *bunker mentality,* which is the misplaced idea that if you just keep your head down, bad things pass you by. They don't, but if you think that way, you'll withdraw into yourself and be unable to ask for help from the outside.

   Instead, you and your people should be keeping the lines of communication open and fresh. Scouting your competition to keep yourself out of trouble requires good communication lines anyway, but making contacts with the outside world allows you to ask someone out there for a lifeline if you have to leave. If you're doing good work, other people will know about it, and your name will stay in circulation.

✔ **Never alienate the people you leave behind.** When things go wrong, people have a tendency to lash out at others. Resist the temptation. People move around nowadays, and today's enemy may become tomorrow's ally if you leave on good terms. If people have the feeling that you made an honest effort and that your leadership failure was circumstantial, they may be able to open a door for you somewhere else down the road, but not if you've demonized them.

# Chapter 27

# Leading across Cultures

· · · · · · · · · · · · · · · · · · · · · · · · · · · · · · · · · · · · ·

· · · · · · · · · · · · · · · · · · · · · · · · · · · · · · · · · · · · ·

> *If we cannot end now our differences, at least we can make the world safe for diversity.*
>
> —John F. Kennedy

Do you remember the process of choosing up sides for a game when you were a kid? The "captains" of each team would start by choosing the best players and then their friends. Inevitably, toward the end of the choosing process, a couple of kids would be left over whom nobody really wanted: the overweight, unathletic, or unpopular kids. After a bit of discussion, to keep peace on the playground, a captain would grudgingly take them and put them somewhere in the field where they could do the least damage, or they'd wind up sitting on the bench.

Those days are, mercifully, long gone. One of the few benefits of the shift from playground games to organized sports for kids is that the adult coaches, the team leaders, and the organizations that support the teams, have made it a policy that "everyone plays." Volunteer organizations such as Special Olympics and AT&T's Telephone Pioneers have worked to include individuals with emotional, mental, and physical challenges in athletics and other activities. We can be generally proud of the efforts of these groups and others to include so many people.

Inclusion is a big part of what leadership has become and is about. A smart leader, just like the playground team captain, wants to put together the best possible team, but the definition of *best* has changed over the years. Winning is still the ultimate goal. However, smarter people have begun to question what the idea of winning really means. In this chapter, we look at ways to become a leader of a wider, more inclusive group of people.

# Leading in a Diverse World

Not by right, but by statistical preponderance, a leader is still more than likely a white male — and in many enterprises, a middle-aged white male who has spent a good portion of his career leading other white males. When women talk about "glass ceilings" and minorities talk about invisible barriers, at least part of what they're talking about is the fact that often, the biggest determinant in being given a leadership position is time in grade. People are promoted from below in most organizations, and women and minorities may not yet have large enough numbers in the white-collar work force to have become visible as leaders, although their numbers are rising as time goes on.

The need for organizations and groups to compete for resources in a free marketplace puts the heat on any leader to find ways to bring the best resources in the direction of his or her group. Women and minorities are important customers who spend real money and are quick to pick up on the hypocrisy of a leadership group wanting something and giving little in return.

The power of consumers — of goods, services, and volunteer activity — is probably one of the two or three factors most responsible for the profound shift in the way we perceive leaders and the demands we make on them. The power of consumers gives followers almost unlimited bargaining power, and thanks to the likes of people such as Martin Luther King and Jesse Jackson, what they have bargained for the most is a seat at the table of power.

The civil rights and women's rights struggles of the 1960s through the 1980s have given way to the struggle to become truly inclusive. No longer is it enough to take a token person from a minority group — like the schoolyard captain forced to take one or two unpopular players onto his team — and put that person in a place where she will be visible but have no real input. One of the great benefits of diversity when it is truly practiced is the way it enlarges the context in which you work. Other cultures, other points of view, other ways of doing things, can add immeasurably to a team's problem-solving skills and to its creativity.

For a typical white male organizational leader, the trick is to translate this knowledge into an active reality. How do you manage people who are different from you, without appearing patronizing or condescending? How do you communicate to people whose cultures and work habits may be substantially different from your own or what the team needs?

Likewise, if you are not a white male — if you are female, a member of a minority group, or both, you can't allow yourself to fall into the same sad ruts that older-style leaders have wandered. You cannot decide to favor your group just because you want to help people "make up for lost time" or because you have some notion of getting even. You still have to figure out how to build the best team, so that may mean including the best-experienced white males.

Start with the basics: Leadership is about eliciting cooperation from others, and listening to and putting the needs of others above your own needs. In order to lead in a diverse organization, you need to reverse the order of those three fundamentals.

Why reverse the order of the fundamentals? The more homogeneous and like-minded a group is, the easier it is to elicit cooperation. The more diverse a group is, the greater the number of variables, so this task is the most difficult and requires the most time and effort. The same thing goes for listening. If your group is a lot like you, you'll have a pretty good idea of what they are going to tell you, but if it's a diverse group, you're going to have to learn how to listen to different voices and actually hear them from their own viewpoint, not only your own. But putting others above yourself is the easiest thing to do when a group is diverse. Elevating the group is the most direct way for a leader to show that he or she is human and is willing to give encouragement and commitment at a human level to the group.

## Putting the diverse needs of your group first

The first and simplest question you have to ask yourself as a leader in a diverse world is, "If I am leading people who are different from me, what do they need in order to be able to work up to the level that I require?"

You may need to supply different tools, as the Volvo people found when they began hiring women to work in their car plants and discovered that conventional hand tools didn't fit a woman's hands. Or you may need to supply special equipment, ramps, and transportation, as a number of companies have found in bringing wheelchair-bound workers into their factories. You may need to expand medical benefits policies if you have workers who are HIV-positive. The point is, if you have workers who have special needs, they'll be more preoccupied with those needs than your needs or the team's needs until you can do something to improve their situations.

So begin from the perspective that it's your responsibility as a leader to help your team solve its problems. If you're about to hire a significant number of Hispanic workers, what do you need to know about their needs? Do they need bilingual training, or can your operating instructions be translated into Spanish? What are their social needs (such as dealing with a suspicious Immigration and Naturalization Service)? Do they need help finding affordable housing? The group may change, but the reality is the same: You must start by understanding what the group needs and then getting those needs fulfilled.

## Listening to voices very different from your own

Because you hired a group with an aim toward diversity, you want to profit from that diversity, which begins with listening. You know how you do things. But how do different members of the group solve similar problems? It may be that for each new method you have to teach, you'll learn one new thing, if you are open to that possibility. You should make it a practice to regularly review your business practices, with an eye on learning from your group.

Some people argue that the best way to deal with diversity is to create a "neutral" business world, a kind of artificial climate where everyone obeys an objective set of rules whatever their background while they are members of the team, and that at the end of the day, everyone goes their separate ways. The logic of this view sounds appealing, but it's based in fiction.

The fiction says that rules are objective. But rules by their nature are *subjective,* made for the convenience of smoothing transactions between and among individuals. In the ideal world, rules are based on conventions that have evolved through give and take, custom, and negotiation, and everyone agrees on the rules. But an ideal world doesn't exist and never did. We believe that there is no such thing as neutral business ground, only rules that one group can force another to accept. So accept the subjectivity of rules and conventions, and modify them to fit the needs of the group.

A good example of how subjectivity works in current practice is the ongoing struggle by large, Western-dominated organizations such as the International Monetary Fund and the World Bank to impose economic and business conduct rules on nations that come to both organizations in need of money. Governments are forced to accept a broad range of "reforms" which often serve to do little more than set in play extreme economic and cultural displacement across whole societies, all in the name of neutral business and lending rules.

A better way of dealing with the differences can be found in the Grameen Bank, a micro-lending organization founded in Bangladesh about two decades ago. The Grameen Bank makes tiny loans — usually around $100 — to Bengalis, often women, who want to start their own businesses. The borrowers have to be scrupulous about their repayments, and in fact, are. The loan loss rates for the bank are almost nil. The idea of the Grameen Bank has been successfully translated to the United States, where such neighborhood banks as the South Shore Bank in Chicago have begun their own community lending operations that are sensitive to the needs of individuals.

## Eliciting cooperation from a diverse group

Ever heard the Latin phrase *quid pro quo?* It means "this for that," and in a diverse world, the best way to elicit cooperation is to be able to trade. Because there's no such thing as a neutral business ground, you have to be willing to trade things that are non-critical to your team's ability to get a task accomplished for a diverse team's cooperation in and adherence to methods that will help it reach its goals.

Trading is more important in diverse groups than among homogeneous groups because, among people who are culturally similar, norms and behavior are usually accepted and agreed upon as a condition of existence. So, for example, until well into the 1960s, every white male who went to work in an office in the United States understood that he had to wear a white shirt, a suit, and a tie. But as the workplace became more diverse, new entries didn't have that knowledge. A conventional leader may impose the white shirt and suit culture on all new hires, "because that's the way it's always been done around here," but a better, more effective leader may learn to trade part of the dress code for a willingness of diverse members to take an additional training seminar on their own time.

As the leader, you have the final say on how your team is going to do its job, but that doesn't mean that you need to rigidly impose your ways upon the group when you can persuade it by trading favor for favor, and by using your abilities as a coach and mentor to bring the team around to your way of doing things.

Use your leadership position in a positive way. After all, you are the leader because you know what you are doing and have the vision. Solicit the views of team members, but persuade them that you have a lot to teach them and that if they are willing to learn from you, they are far more likely to achieve their goals.

# Emerging as a Leader from a Cultural Group

In a 1984 interview, the French feminist writer Simone de Beauvoir said, "The moment a woman gets power, she loses the solidarity she had with other women. She will want to be equal in a man's world and will become ambitious for her own sake." de Beauvoir perfectly encapsulates the problems of cultural diversity in that quote. If you are different, do you have to surrender that which is different in order to participate in a group larger than your own, and do you have to surrender your differences completely if you want to become a leader of a larger group than your own?

These questions are very powerful and important, because they go to the heart of what we expect of leaders. The basis upon which people give trust to a leader often begins and ends with familiarity. "He's one of us," or "she represents our values" are the kinds of sentiments you often hear when you question people about why they will choose one person over another as a leader in an open election. Those feelings put a burden on a would-be leader who is different to minimize their differences or erase them completely in order to be accepted and find a place within mainstream society.

With ethnic white males in the U.S., the subjugation of differences was relatively easy. Dropping the extra vowels from your last name, changing the way you dressed, getting some elocution lessons to eradicate a less-than-desirable accent, going to night school for more education were all sure-fire pathways to success for a generation of post-war Jews, Italians, Poles, and Greeks.

Women and non-white minorities, however much they may want to follow along the same path as ethnic whites, cannot. There exists, for want of better words, a visibility problem. A woman in a room full of men, even in a leadership position, is strikingly different in dress, appearance, and mannerisms than her male colleagues. A dark-skinned person amidst a sea of white faces stands out conspicuously, no matter how much everyone believes that race doesn't matter. Often, for a non-white, non-male person in a white-male dominated business world, moving up the organizational ladder evokes loneliness and separation from that individual's own group.

How does an organization deal with leadership issues when there are internal diversity problems? Perhaps the simplest way is for the topmost leader of an organization to mentor someone who is different from them all the way to the top. CEOs at both Time Warner and American Express have mentored blacks into senior executive roles, while other companies, such as Mattel and Columbia Pictures, have simply jumped women into senior executive positions and demanded that their male colleagues make the adjustment. This is using the power of leadership to impose diversity upon an organization.

A second, more practical way is to practice diversity from the ground up. Make it a policy to hire from a very wide pool of people. Many companies hire from the same couple of dozen schools all the time, because that's where their recruits have come from in the past. Make the effort to open up recruiting to other schools, even if it means that you have to forego a trip to your alma mater, or you have to turn down someone in the company who wants you to hire a relative.

# Strive to want more

Hiring from a wide pool immediately raises the question of quotas. Should you set aside a certain number of places for minorities? Should your hiring practices force you to hire in such a way that your workforce mirrors the population as a whole? The answer to both questions is emphatically "no." Hire whom you want, but learn to *want* more. Learn to *want* diversity. Learn to *want* other talents, other skills, and other points of view. Learn to appreciate the benefits of seeing your own group through the eyes of others. If women and minorities want to work for your organization or enterprise because they view it as a means to meet their own rising expectations, then you should learn to allow your own expectations to rise along with theirs.

# Toleration is a dirty word

One of the greatest stumbling blocks to creating a diverse workplace is *toleration*. The definition of the word is "the act of permitting that which is not established or accepted." Toleration at the very least is condescension. It implies that your way of doing things is better, but that for the sake of peace, you will allow another way to co-exist with your own. But your message of implied superiority is always going to grate upon those being tolerated, and it will degrade the cooperation they are likely to give.

Instead, as a leader, if you really want to promote diversity within your organization, you have to go systematically through all your organization's methods and procedures and either change them if they make no sense or explain them if they do. For example, say you operate a chemical plant, and a Hispanic male with a droopy mustache and a degree in chemical engineering comes to you for a position. If you tell him that it is a condition of his job that he has to shave off his mustache, without explaining that he cannot have any facial hair that may interfere with the safety respirator he may have to wear, then you have done him a disservice that he won't soon forget. You may even face a charge of discrimination and a lawsuit. But you have to enforce that rule with everyone. No long hair among your women employees, or anyone, for that matter. Everyone has to wear safety lenses of one sort or another. These are rules that make sense within the safety context of the job.

But if a rule exists because of tradition or someone's exaggerated sense of what a business place should look like, think seriously about scrapping those rules. Dress codes, for example, are one of the largest areas of contention among minority employees, as is hair length and hair style. People simply do not all have to look alike to be able to get their work done. Such rules are a vestige of the old-fashioned command economy and should be allowed to die the death they deserve.

# Leading across International Divides

Almost everything we've said above about how you lead when your group is internally diverse is even more critical when you are involved in international situations. To the normal cultural differences amongst your own group, you now have to add differences in language, customs, legal structures, standards, and other oddities, such as work rules and holidays. On the other hand, there are some really simple rules about working cross-culturally on an international basis. Because of all the biases we choose to ignore or refuse to acknowledge when we are dealing within our group, we freely admit to them when we are dealing with people who are obviously different.

## Commit your brightest and best

When you are putting together an international team, you want your smartest, most flexible people at hand. You want people who have the capacity to learn what the differences are that separate you from your foreign colleagues and who are able to accommodate themselves to those differences. The Romans once said that the definition of being civilized was the ability to live comfortably in another person's culture. So look for civilized people when you are forming your team.

Being civilized begins with *civility,* which is the granting of consideration to others. You will know by experience with your team who are the people who can quietly adjust to new situations, and who are the people who whine, complain, scream, or stamp their feet. Keep the first group and leave the rest home.

Sell participation in an international team as an adventure. Even the most civilized people are often reluctant to commit to something that takes them away from hearth and home, so an international team assignment has to be worth their while in some way that appeals to them. Find out what each person needs, and help him or her achieve it.

## Use the de minimus rule in making decisions

When you are working within a multinational or international context, you are going to find yourself up against different rules and regulations. In Germany, for example, boilerplate can be no less than a certain thickness. In England, it has to be at least a certain thickness, but one that is less than the German standard. Whose standard should prevail? If you use the de minimus rule — the minimum standard — you can't go wrong. Your German colleagues will continue to make their boilerplate thicker, because that's the way they do it, but they will not be violating the terms of your agreement by doing so. The added expense is entirely on their shoulders.

When you are sitting down with an international group to plan out a mission, getting such issues out in the open early is important. Language alone causes its share of misunderstandings.

## Understand that capital doesn't make right

There is a cynical version of the Golden Rule that states, "Whoever has the gold makes the rules." That version has undermined more international cooperation than probably any other idea, because people who have capital seem to believe that they have the right to set the rules for an enterprise. "I'm contributing most of the money, so we should do things my way" is the logic.

But there are assets beyond money. Markets are gold, and access to markets is worth at least as much as the investment required to open them up. People are assets, because they represent an opportunity for you to elicit their cooperation in the service of your cause. Knowledge of local customs is an asset, because these customs are integral to the fabric of the lives of the people you want to reach, so respecting local customs and assisting at the local level is imperative for international team success.

When you are deciding how to make your enterprise work internationally, discard the idea that only money counts. Money, although important, is only a small part of a larger equation.

## Leading in the Virtual Age

We could not end this book without acknowledging that a profound shift in the way we work is in the making. Increasingly, people do not come together in the physical sense to act as teams or to meet as groups. They network. They use the Internet, telephones, fax machines, and computers to cooperate with each other on projects they want to achieve in common. Leading in the Age of the Internet requires at the same time more skills and fewer skills, because certain things that conventional leaders struggle with are already givens.

Start with the need to communicate. Although we have said that smart leaders should communicate frequently and in writing, virtual leaders do that of necessity, because their communication is bound by a keyboard and by the structures of databases and spreadsheets. What you share via your Lotus Notes is there for all your team to see, so you have to learn how to write well, how to make your thoughts clear and concise, and how to set internal deadlines, so that people don't just stack your e-mail messages up in their in-boxes and then later throw them away. The Internet has the benefits of a formal logic structure, and virtual leaders take advantage of that structure.

The Internet also favors planners. Writing a business plan for a Net-based enterprise is easier than for many other types of business enterprise, because there are software limitations on presentation. Short of writing your own planning program, you are going to use an off-the-shelf program, so you are going to accept the conventions and limitations implicit in the program you choose.

Timeliness is also not a problem on the Net. Because virtual organizations operate in a 24/7 world — 24 hours a day, 7 days a week — when you communicate and share is less important than the fact that you do it. As a virtual leader, your major responsibility is sharing and managing the flow of information and then building validity checks into the information you receive, so that your plan does not go GIGO — garbage in, garbage out.

Diversity is also easier in a virtual enterprise. The person who is somehow unacceptable within the confines of an organization suddenly becomes wholly acceptable when he is working remotely. All you have to face is his structured written communication, and you judge him solely upon timeliness and results. There is no longer an arbitrary standard of whether he is "like the boss" in the sense of appearance or class or education, but simply whether he can meet a work standard.

On the down side, virtual corporations lack a certain human intimacy and camaraderie. Yes, people share jokes over the Internet all the time, and you can always pick up the telephone. But a joke is not the same when it appears with a routing list of over a hundred names as when someone puts his arm on your shoulder and pulls you close to him, to deliver the punch line.

Virtual leaders need to struggle with the problem of maintaining commitment when workers are remote and likely to be involved with their own local problems as much as the challenges with work. Ask anyone who telecommutes, and she will tell you the burden of maintaining concentration.

Virtual leaders thus have to focus even harder on listening (which in this case means learning to read between the lines) and communicating (which means picking up the phone and talking with people, or getting on a plane and visiting them) in order to maintain team rapport. Eliciting the cooperation of people who are working remotely is also more difficult, because measuring the impact of the incentives you are offering is more difficult.

# Part VII
# The Part of Tens

The 5th Wave    By Rich Tennant

"Remember when Bruce wanted to 'rally the troops', we all just got a memo in email?"

# In this part . . .

**R**eaders who are familiar with the ...*For Dummies* series know that near the end of every book, you'll find a bunch of top-ten lists on the subject. I have put together three good top-ten lists for you: a list of ten leadership mistakes to avoid, a list of ten characteristics of good leaders, and a list of ten activities that you can do now to brush up on your leadership skills.

# Chapter 28

# Ten Mistakes That Every Leader Makes

. . . . . . . . . . . . . . . . . . . . . . . . . . . . . . . . . . . . . . . .

. . . . . . . . . . . . . . . . . . . . . . . . . . . . . . . . . . . . . . . .

*T*here's no such person as a perfect or ideal leader. If there were, situational leaders would remain leaders for life. Even Moses, considered to be one of the best leaders who ever lived, made enough mistakes over the course of his life that he was ultimately denied entrance to his homeland and died with the object of his wanderings within sight. Every leader makes mistakes; the challenge is to know what the most common ones are, so you can be alert to them and try to avoid them before they do you in.

## Failing to Learn from Your Mistakes

There's no worse failing in a leader than refusing to acknowledge mistakes. Religious leaders may declare their infallibility, but that doesn't mean that they're right all the time. Dictators may create cults of personality that trumpet their perfection, but that only makes their downfall all the more sudden when it inevitably comes. But you don't have to be either a dictator or the head of a major religion to be guilty of the flaw of failing to learn from your own mistakes.

Most leaders like to believe that they got to the top by being smarter than the people around them and by being right more often. A wise leader recognizes that more than climbing to the top, he or she has *survived* to the top by over-coming hardship, missed opportunities, blown judgment calls, and poor human relations. But the leader who won't learn feels that none of that mat-ters — after all, they reason, everyone makes mistakes on the way up, and the fact that they made it to the top means that they've achieved a leadership Nirvana, a perfection that makes them infallible. We've known leaders who talk about being "inside the bubble," protected from the realities of the world by the trappings and power that come with leadership. Guess what? The bubble can burst.

Another instance of this problem occurs to people who are new to leader-ship, who feel that they have only one shot and so aren't allowed to fail, lest it reflect poorly on the people who chose them as leaders in the first place. This I-can't-disappoint-the-people-who-trusted-me syndrome puts almost unbearable pressure on leaders and blinds them to the possibility that things may go wrong on their watch. It causes them to retreat inward when things do go wrong, cutting them off from the people they are leading and creating a self-fulfilling prophesy.

# Failing to Be Flexible

Along with being willing to learn from your mistakes, a good leader has to be flexible. Situations change; the members of your team change; competitive pressures change; the marketplace changes; everything changes. If you can't accept change and the fact that much of your leadership energy will be devoted to helping your team adjust to those changes, you can never become an effective leader.

Indeed, your very position as a leader is based upon the fact that the people who have chosen you know that change is taking place, and they need some-one to guide them safely through the uncertainties that come with change. A vision gains its basis and authority from how accurately you foresee the out-come of the changes taking place around you. For example, you could be working in retailing when you draw up a plan for the company to expand into electronic commerce, which you then get to take the lead in implementing. Your selection as leader derives precisely from your vision of how comput-ers, telecommunications, and the Internet are going to create major shifts in the retail landscape. You are being asked to provide guidance and control the pace of change so that when your vision becomes reality, your firm will be in the vanguard.

But if you understand that change is normal, then you also have to learn to understand that the pace of change varies sharply. You may be able to predict the flow of events, but your timing may be off, unforeseen events may complicate or radically change the picture, a new paradigm may emerge, or the people you were counting on to help you may have moved on to other places. If you aren't flexible, then you will be left scrambling and playing catch-up. And that's when you make mistakes.

# Failing to Acknowledge Your Past

We've said it before and we'll say it again: There is no such thing as a natural leader. Leaders are made through training, mentoring, guidance, and circumstance, with the best leaders accumulating experience over the course of many assignments and jobs. Nobody wakes up under a cabbage leaf one day and appears at Camelot as the "perfect knight," prepared to lead troops into battle. And when people do come along seemingly from nowhere, their failures as leaders are out in the open and spectacular, such as Joan of Arc, a teenage girl who led an army that swept across France to put a young boy on the French throne. At the height of her success, seemingly invincible, she was captured and put to death, with none of her followers prepared to raise a hand in her defense.

Great leaders, like great rock 'n' rollers, return to their roots repeatedly in order to replenish themselves. They go back to the people from whom they've learned, and they learn some more. They allow for the fact that they don't know everything, and they get help from the people who have helped them in the past. Vain leaders and poor leaders make the assumption that appearing to lean on others is a sign of weakness, and so they refuse to acknowledge their past or even cover it up. Although you don't have to memorialize your past or to glorify it, you also don't have to eradicate it, because the past does point the way to the future.

# Commanding instead of Leading

In the military and in certain other situations, a leader needs unquestioned authority and instant obedience. But command is almost never an effective substitute for leading, and dictating behavior is never an acceptable substitute for eliciting the cooperation of your group. People are counting on you not only for guidance, but for motivation as well. They want you to articulate the reasons that they should make the sacrifices they know they should make, but need a reason or context for. If your answer is always, "Because I say so," or "Because that's what I'm telling you to do," or "Because I'm in charge," then you're leading the wrong way and breeding insubordination and anger in the ranks. You may enjoy watching a television series such as *Horatio Hornblower,* but the reality is that you cannot go around flogging people for their mistakes anymore, even in Her Majesty's Navy.

The idea that commanding is leading is an archaic idea, one not suited to a democratic society where government is by the consent of the governed. Instead of working on your commanding voice and presence, you should be working on your cooperation skills, perfecting your ability to get people to say yes to what you want them to do, learning how to explain things in a persuasive, clear, simple way that always shows people what cooperation offers them in benefits.

# Failing to Listen

A leader has to listen to many voices: the voices of the group, outside voices clamoring for a solution to a problem, the voices of the higher-ups in an organization who are judging your performance, the voice of the marketplace, and your own inner voice, which may be screaming out in panic and fear. All these voices not only have to be heard, but they also have to be listened to. You need to learn how to pay attention to the voices you hear and how to interpret properly what they are telling you.

Listening and interpreting effectively can be accomplished with reporting systems. The more confirmable information you can take in, the more reliable the voices are likely to be. It is a lack of knowledge that gets the voices clamoring for attention, so keep yourself well informed about every aspect of your leadership role.

Don't underestimate the importance of listening to your followers. Political pundits make unmerciful fun of presidential administrations that adhere to public opinion polls, but the writers are wrong. Although leadership is supposed to supply vision, it should also supply comfort and continuity, and one of the surest ways of doing that is to be constantly aware of the voices that keep your followers awake at night. If they're hearing different voices than you're hearing, you have to make it your business to listen to the voices that make your followers nervous. Those are the voices that represent the greatest challenges to your leadership. The most common complaint against leaders of all kinds who are turfed out is, "He or she wasn't listening to me."

# Thinking of Your Own Needs First

We see leadership as a set of responsibilities, but many leaders see it as a mantle of privilege — an entitlement to the perks that go along with being the top dog. The first thing you have to learn when you're a new leader is modesty. If you've been given a large office, turn it into a reception area and use another room as your office.

Senator Inouye, one of the most powerful leaders of the United States Senate, turned a large closet into his office, leaving the formal office as a kind of museum for his constituents visiting from Hawaii. By making the hometown voters feel comfortable when they came to visit him, Inouye ensured that they left with the feeling of being well taken care of. When his constituents saw the Senator's modest working quarters, they were convinced that he wasn't abusing his office, his power, or their trust. It's a lesson every leader should learn.

Unfortunately, leaders all too often make a fetish of the perks that come with power and look for new trappings to confirm their authority, from the ridiculous uniforms that Nixon outfitted the White House guards in, to the stripes that the Chief Justice put on his robe during the Clinton impeachment trial. All these trappings are for show, and all that show does is make people cynical about their leaders. Cultivate modesty whenever possible. It doesn't mean that you have to live like a monk, but it does mean that you should not glory in your office, lest you forget why you're actually there.

A good leader should take every opportunity to find ways of putting the needs of other people into the forefront. It is not enough to patronize a cause; as a leader, you should find ways to participate and promote those things in which you believe.

# Thinking Leadership Is Forever

An instructive TV commercial takes place inside a factory, where the workers are chanting, "We're Number 1. We're Number 1." Outside, as the camera pulls away, a sign on the factory which says, "We're Number 1" begins to vibrate, until finally, the letters *e* and *r* and the number *1* fall off, so the sign reads, "We're Numb." More good leaders have messed up their place in the history books by going from number 1 to numb than we care to recall. There seems to be an unshakable tendency among human beings not to know when to call it quits.

Good leaders know that times and circumstances change and that they have a limited window of opportunity in which to be effective. When the window is open, they have to do everything in their power to achieve their visions. But when the window starts to close, they also have to know how to plan for a graceful exit. Ordinarily, leaders tend to retire when they're older, so their influence fades from the scene as they do. But increasingly, our leaders are rising faster and leaving at younger ages, with lots of energy and time left to them.

The greatest leadership crisis of the twenty-first century is not going to be the shortage of leaders, but how to recycle effectively those young leaders who have completed their assigned task but still have a lot to offer. People like General Colin Powell, President Clinton, and a host of forty-ish CEOs are going to have to find effective ways to spend several decades in roles that go beyond occupying an honorary title on meaningless committees.

# Failing to Teach

Just as a leader needs constantly to learn, to upgrade skills, and to add to his or her knowledge base, a leader also has to be a constant teacher. Too many leaders make the assumption that there is an unbridgeable gulf between themselves and their followers, so they fail to impart what they've learned, allowing their followers to remain in the dark.

In a democratic society served by a competitive press, it's getting ever more difficult for political leaders to keep their followers in the dark. Outside the political realm, however, leaders all too often leave their followers in the lurch until trouble rears its head. The best course of action for a leader is to make every effort to keep followers informed and then to teach them new skills whenever possible so that the group can benefit as a whole. A good leader should also make it his or her business to have every member of the group be a teacher so that skills do not flow in one direction only. "Each one teach one" should be your guiding motto on the subject of learning. Your obligation is to teach someone, who can teach someone else, and so on.

Groups succeed because their knowledge and skill bases rise faster than those of competing groups, so it seems obvious that learning and teaching are integral to the success of leaders. Leaders who think that teaching is beneath them are leaders destined to fail.

# Failing to Have a Sense of Humor

John F. Kennedy was probably the first modern leader, someone who led by example rather than by command — a leader who made every effort to be inclusive. Whatever Kennedy's faults as a man, or even as a leader, the one thing that no one can assail was Kennedy's remarkable and often self-deprecating sense of humor. Kennedy's press conferences, where he actively jousted with the White House press corps, make memorable viewing to this day, and have set a standard for leaders that has yet to be matched.

Reuben Mark, the CEO of Colgate, is another leader who brings a refreshing sense of humor to his position. Colgate's annual meetings are akin to tent revival meetings, as endless numbers of small shareholders parade up to the stage to talk about their experiences as lifelong Colgate stockholders, all the while being subjected to Mark's good-natured jibes. Herb Kelleher, who runs Southwest Airlines, is another CEO who believes in a heavy dose of levity amidst the seriousness of business.

Unfortunately, too many leaders become pompous the minute they assume the mantle of leadership. The four words that annoy us most are "pillar of the community." Leadership is stewardship, which means that you are assuming a set of responsibilities, not getting your title carved in stone. The wise leader understands that being in the right place at the right time is every bit as important as anything that he or she brings to the job. If you can't laugh over the irony of your position and how you have become a target for every crackpot who thinks he or she can do your job better than you can, you don't deserve to be a leader.

# Seeing Things Only in Black and White

One of the fallacies of having a lot of information at your disposal is that you come to believe that decisions are either yes or no, up or down. You become guided by the data and the concrete "facts on the ground," as the military planners like to say, instead of recognizing that there are subtleties to every situation that often cannot be quantified.

One of the problems that comes with seeing things in black and white is seeing things in terms of moral absolutes. In your mistaken view, things are either right or wrong, good or evil. But life doesn't work that way. We suspect that one of the reasons that violence in schools has increased among teenagers is that they spend too much time in church hearing that their behavior is considered evil and aberrant. If you receive that message constantly, you come to believe that you are already damned, so what's the difference whether you live or die, whether you kill or allow yourself to be killed?

The world exists in myriad colors and subtle shades, and the leader who can learn to see the world in all its polychrome wonder and to make the fine distinctions in shadings that are required to solve problems without causing confrontations, is the leader who will ultimately succeed.

# Chapter 29

# Ten Characteristics of a True Leader

*T*hroughout this book, we talk at length about the characteristics and responsibilities of leadership as well as what leaders do and how they do it. So we guess it's time to put all of that together and distill a couple of characteristics so that you can know whether someone you meet has leadership potential. These are people you may want to get to know and may perhaps want to help on their way.

## Leaders Are Eager

We begin this book by telling you that leaders embrace responsibility. The word *embrace*, the dictionary says, means to take up readily or gladly. People who have the potential to be leaders do not shirk from accepting responsibility. They step forward to grab it, even when the responsibility is for an unpleasant task. Anyone can do the glamourous things, but the real potential leader is the person who volunteers for the tasks that no one else wants to do and then does them in such a way that everybody wants to help out.

Remember the story of Tom Sawyer and whitewashing the fence? That's a story about a leader in the making, not just a clever little boy who managed to get out of work.

If you want to become a leader, learn to look upon any situation as an opportunity to showcase your abilities. If your group is rebuilding a playground and no one wants the dirty work of clearing the site of garbage and debris, that's a key opportunity, because if the site doesn't get cleared, the playground doesn't get built. Turn the cleanup into a competition, awarding prizes for the most garbage, the most interesting piece of garbage, and anything else you can think of, and the work will go more quickly. Moreover, you will have shown people that you can take an unpleasant task and turn it into a joyful experience.

## Leaders Are Cheerful

You don't have to walk around like a grinning idiot, but maintaining a cheerful equilibrium in times of trouble helps everyone around you. A story about Sir Ernest Shackelford, who led an ill-fated expedition to the Antarctic, tells how he kept his men alive through the cruel winter by telling them jokes and droll stories. His men stayed alive in spite of having little to eat but blubber and the leather traces of their dogsleds.

Your role as a leader is to inspire the people you lead, and one of the best ways to inspire them is to help them face up to the realities of their situation — never lie to your people — and to make light of those realities, no matter how harsh they may be. A leader who is cheerful in the face of adversity disarms an opponent. Why is that person smiling? What does he or she know that I don't? These questions leave your foes guessing when you are able to maintain a bright outlook on the future.

## Leaders Are Honest

If you want to lead people, you have to communicate information directly and honestly. You cannot hem and haw or water down the truth. You have to keep your people — and the people to whom you report — grounded in the reality of your situation. Absolutely nothing is wrong with telling your superiors that your situation is hopeless if that's the case and if you have done the reporting and investigating that prove it to be true. Don't sugar-coat the truth, either. You don't have to be blunt, but when the news is bad, delivering it all in one piece and getting it out in the open is better than dribbling it out and leaving people waiting for the inevitable "other shoe" to fall.

Although most people believe that they are honest, few are direct. Women, especially, respect the social value of an indirect approach to problems, and that places them at a disadvantage in leadership situations. If you have trouble with the direct approach, put your points in writing and structure them so that when you go into a meeting, you can use your notes as an aid until you feel comfortable delivering verbal reports without them.

After you're comfortable being direct, practice your skills on your group in your daily or weekly reporting sessions. Keep a timer going and tell people that you'll cut them off if they take longer than, say, three minutes to deliver their reports. Keep discussions on track and remind people that your team exists to attain a goal, not to spend endless hours discussing it. Discussions are critical, but directness and honesty will keep your talks on track.

# Leaders Are Resourceful

A good leader makes use of the resources available, even if they are inadequate to the task. Your role as a leader is to get the resources that your team needs to attain its goals, but sometimes the money, the people, and the physical resources just aren't there. Do you give up? Of course you don't.

When resources aren't adequate, you, as a leader, should rework your plan in the context of what you can do with what you have. Maybe it means that everybody has to work longer hours. Put it to the group. If you can see a point where the effort will pay off, people will probably go along with you. Maybe it means that everybody has to take less money. Adjust pay scales from the top down. You can live on a lot less money, but the salaries of your lowest paid people should be left untouched, if possible, because the money is more critical to them. Maybe you have to change the location of where your enterprise is going to work, which imposes travel burdens. If the move helps you make your project a success and you believe it's worth doing, you may be able to persuade your people to go along with you.

# Leaders Are Persuasive

You're not going to get people to follow you if you can't persuade them that doing so is in their best interest. Either by words or by deeds, you have to make people want to go where you want to go and where you think they need to go. Not only do you have to have a vision, but you have to be able to articulate it in such a way that when people hear it they say, "Oh, yeah! Of course."

How do you become a persuasive figure? You start out by standing for something that everyone wants, but that no one thinks is attainable. At the turn of the century, John L. Lewis, then a young man who was the son of a mine foreman, began a campaign for mine safety after a number of disastrous cave-ins. The people who ran organized labor in those days were afraid of the mine operators and their hired thugs, but Lewis, who was tall and built like a modern football linebacker, used his physical size to intimidate people whenever he walked into a room. More importantly, though, he put endless practice into his speeches so that he knew exactly what he was going to say whenever he testified at a legislative hearing. He also researched his points thoroughly, so that no one could deny the validity of his arguments. Having carried the day for mine safety legislation, Lewis became a natural to head the nascent United Mine Workers in its struggle for better working conditions and higher wages.

You have to follow the lead of John L. Lewis. You may not be physically imposing, but you have to carry yourself as if you were. Walk straight and tall, with your shoulders rolled slightly forward, so that it looks as if you are leaning into people when you talk to them. There is a three-foot "social bubble" that Americans observe when they speak to one another face-to-face. If you lean into the bubble while maintaining your distance, you will "own" the physical space between people.

Use silence as a weapon. Do not immediately respond to what people say. If you think that they are giving you nonsense, don't argue back at them. Just cock your eyebrow and say, "Oh, really?" By making people defend themselves without asserting your own position, you cut the ground from under them.

Finally, when you do argue your position, don't be afraid to use phrases such as "Now I'm going to show you why you are wrong," or "Now we'll examine the truth." If you know your facts and can make a convincing case, don't be afraid to tell people that in advance. It will make what you have to say that much more effective in its presentation and make you a more persuasive speaker.

# Leaders Are Cooperative

Many people believe that an emotional or psychological distance divides leaders and followers or that leaders possess special knowledge and special burdens to which their followers will never be privy. A typical remark made by presidents to the ordinary people who criticize their policies is, "Well, if you knew what I know. . . ," as if by virtue of their office they have special insights. This is, for the most part, complete nonsense. A leader should have a clearer understanding of the big picture, but often, he or she is fuzzy on many of the details. Good leaders understand this, and they learn early on how to share information and how to cooperate with people who may have something they need.

In the old days, when a king or queen needed a bit of information, he or she could compel a subject to talk on pain of torture or death. But it just doesn't work that way anymore, thankfully. In a democratic, market-based society, people volunteer information when the inducements are right — and not before. So an effective leader has to learn how to coax rather than coerce, how to cooperate in an exchange rather than making transactions one-way.

Good leaders know that cooperation is actually easier than coercion. Because a leader always holds more cards than anyone else — that's what power is all about, after all — giving away something is easy. That something may be trivial to the leader, but it may have great meaning to someone else. The trick is to become aware of what you have to offer people, because those things become your bargaining chips. What you have to offer may belong to you, it may belong to the group, or it may even belong to someone else (think about soak-the-rich tax promises that populist politicians routinely make to their constituents).

Being cooperative rather than confrontational allows you to operate from a *position* of strength without having to exert strength. If you're willing to negotiate with people and willing to find small ways to make them happy, people will come to believe that you're a generous leader. Because most people believe that generosity comes only from strength, they'll also believe that you're strong.

# Leaders Are Altruistic

Altruism is a another way of saying that leaders place the needs of others above their own. But altruism is more than that: It's the willingness to sacrifice for a higher cause and to put aside your own needs for the needs of the group. Altruism invests vision with a higher purpose so that if your vision is strictly commercial, it adds something extra that is experiential. For example, when Walt Disney wrote his vision for Disneyland, a major component of his vision was the emotional experience he wanted people to come away with by going to his Magic Kingdom — a combination of wistful nostalgia for the America of yesterday and the excitement of the possibilities of the world of tomorrow. Disney didn't mention making a profit — he presumed that by appealing to people's better nature, profits would follow. And they certainly did!

Leaders need to remind themselves that altruism is important because, often, altruism is what lifts the mundane execution of a mission to a higher plane. For example, you may set as your goal an increase of 15 percent in division profits, and everybody will nod. But tell people that you want to raise the figure to 17 percent and use the extra two percentage points to fund a day-care center or to rebuild the playgrounds around your company, and people are suddenly willing to work a lot harder. That's why altruism is such a great motivator — it makes people feel better about the work they are being asked to do. A good leader learns how to build altruistic motives into every component of a plan.

# Leaders Are Courageous

You have to be brave to be a leader, and by this, we don't mean brave in the death-defying sense. As the person with the vision, you are going to take your group off into uncharted territory, and that's a scary thing. Leaders learn how to suck up their courage, trust their instincts, and move ahead into the unknown, even when they're just as scared as their followers.

Leaders use planning, experience, and resourcefulness to overcome their fears so that they can anticipate most of the likely hazards and roadblocks ahead. But every leader knows that no matter how well you plan, you may, at times, be faced with a completely unknown situation, or worse, a situation that makes you unpopular in your decisions. That's the point where you're going to have to be brave. You'll come under fire, and, of course, you'll make certain that you're not sticking to your guns out of stubbornness, but rather, out of a conviction that you're right, based on the information available to you. When that happens, you have to calmly explain to your people why you're continuing on your chosen path and why it's necessary for them to keep the faith.

Leaders who are wishy-washy or who are uncertain cause their followers to hold back support, and their lack of confidence can translate into outright mutiny and rebellion if the leader isn't strong enough or brave enough to make a decision stick. How do you become strong? By engaging in debate when it doesn't count. Use times when you're reviewing noncritical decisions to test your decision skills against those of your followers and your opponents. If you can prevail in those situations, then chances are good that in critical situations, people will be less likely to question your decisions.

# Leaders Are Supportive

The motto of every good leader should be, "He ain't heavy. He's my brother." As a leader, you're going to be expected to be a tower of strength and to lend support to people who are weaker than you. You can do this in one of several ways. You can literally carry people, in the sense of allowing them to draw emotional, intellectual, or physical support from you, or you can organize a carrying party, in which one of the purposes of the group is to provide support for all the members of the group. A good leader knows that his or her personal resources are finite, so they make their teams into support systems, where everyone lends a hand to everyone else, and where support responsibilities are delegated across the entire group.

Lending support also means stepping outside of the group to bolster good causes that the group may want to make their own. Lending support beyond the group is one of the best ways for you to extend your leadership skills and gain recognition as someone who can be counted on.

# Leaders Are Assertive

Whether you're a *karate* leader, who attacks problems head on, or a *jujitsu* leader who draws problems inward, you have to be assertive at the point of attack. When you decide that a problem is solvable, you gain nothing by delaying. If you have planned adequately, if your people are lined up and ready to go, and if you have the right resources in place, then what are you waiting for?

Perhaps one of the major criticisms of leadership in the modern era is that it is not sufficiently assertive to meet the challenges of a complex society. Leaders in democratic societies operate at a distinct disadvantage to dictators. They worry more about what their followers will think, and they worry about retaining their hold on leadership. So they are neither brave nor assertive. They allow their vision to be diffused by endless committee reviews, and they substitute caring for courage.

It's easier to send humanitarian aid to the survivors of the slaughter in Rwanda than to tell people that you need their support in preventing it, which is why we have the paradox of America and its Western allies simultaneously being the strongest powers on the planet and practically powerless to prevent human misery anywhere on the globe.

Good leaders need to work on their assertiveness skills. They need to work on their command voice and nail down their convictions, so that they are willing to stand up for them when the time comes.

# Chapter 30

# Ten Ways to Master Leadership Skills

*I*f you've read through *Leadership for Dummies,* you should be well on your way to mastering the skills you need to be a leader. But like the old joke about how you get to Carnegie Hall, you need to practice, practice, practice. Here are ten things you can work on to increase your mastery of leadership skills.

## Work on Your Preparation

You can't be too prepared. Leaders are constantly looking for new and better sources of information, better planning tools, and better methods of inspiring the people they lead. Make new discoveries from every situation and every person you come in contact with. Emulate the examples of great leaders around you, but find out what not to do from people who have tried and failed in their efforts to lead. They have just as much to teach you as the successful leaders.

# Choose a Cause and Make It Your Own

We believe that volunteering is a great training ground for developing your leadership skills, but a time will come when you'll want to actually exert leadership in a volunteer setting. That's the point where you have to commit yourself to a cause, embrace it, and develop your own vision for it. It doesn't matter too much what the cause is, as long as it improves people's lives or the world around you. Start at the local level, but expand your horizons as you become adept at dealing with your cause's issues and how people respond to them.

# Keep an Open Mind

Your vision is your own, but you should be open to the thoughts and dreams of others, who may have ideas similar to yours, only with slight differences. If you can see the benefits in someone else's ideas, your own ideas will become better, more dimensionalized. Along with being open goes the notion of embracing change. Learn not to be stiff or rigid about your decisions. After all, new information and new circumstances come along all the time, so if you're open to the possibility of change, then you won't be taken by surprise.

# Rehearse Your Speeches

An old Hollywood saying reminds us that if you can fake sincerity, you've got it made. Ronald Reagan was one of the greatest script readers of all time, and his blend of folksy manner and clear delivery turned someone who was probably a mediocre president at best into the Great Communicator. Reagan rehearsed his lines, practiced his delivery, and knew how to hit his marks, making the most of his training as an actor. You have to learn to do the same thing. Most people are relatively uncomfortable about speaking to groups — somewhere a survey put public speaking just above molar extractions as the most painful thing anyone has to endure — but being able to persuade people of the validity of your cause is necessary if you're going to be a leader.

Practice writing speeches that are to the point and that reflect your natural style. If your natural style is a little on the stiff side, work on relaxing. Tell stories about yourself, like the stupidest thing you ever did, if your speech is going to deal with mistakes of the team, or talk about the pride you felt in an individual accomplishment if you're about to make a speech about how the group needs to develop more esprit. The more you can link yourself to the group, the more effective a speaker you will become.

When you're rehearsing, have someone you trust, such as your spouse, critique your delivery. Work with a stopwatch so that you can trim your speech, but as you trim, keep slowing down the pace, until your delivered speech sounds like natural speech.

# Be Disciplined

Leadership is a set of disciplines involving the formulation of a vision, the development of plans, the execution of a mission, and the reaching of a goal. You have to learn to become proficient at each one of those skills and to be objective about your weaknesses and strengths. If your planning skills are weak but your vision and execution skills are strong, get someone to help you with planning. If you have any weaknesses, in fact, find the right person to bolster your skills. Watch what they do and how they do it and then emulate that person. You may not become much better — if you're weak in math, you're probably going to remain weak — but you'll develop a better idea of how people can help you.

Being disciplined also means being careful about how you form your teams. Don't allow sentimentality to cloud your judgment about a person whom you like but who consistently underperforms. If you want your teams to succeed, you have to strive constantly to find the best team members. Save your efforts for saving souls or saving the world for volunteer time.

# Master Deadlines

Most projects work better when everyone is under a deadline, and you have to be the person who sets and enforces the deadlines. Find out what it takes to get a particular bit of work done, and then look for ways to cut that time down. Find out how much time it takes for your entire team to get ready for a mission, and then make them put more effort into each time interval. But don't speed things up irrationally or create situations where one person on the team completes a portion of work and is then left with nothing to do but wait for the rest of the team to catch up.

# Maintain Contact with Your Group

The single biggest mistake that leaders make is allowing a distance to grow between themselves and their followers, so learn to keep that distance at a minimum. Ancient legends are filled with stories of kings who dress as beggars to go among their people to find out what they're thinking. You don't have to go to such extremes, but take advantage of lunches, breakfasts, after-work meetings, and anything else you can think of to keep yourself in close touch with your group.

Address your group's concerns swiftly. If someone has a problem, never say, "I'll get back to you on that." Stop what you're doing, listen to what the person has to say, and put the problem-solving wheels into motion. Ideally, this should be nothing more than pointing out how to do something and then giving the person a gentle nudge in the right direction, but if it's a serious problem, give it the time it deserves. Your group will learn not to bother you with trivial things, but it will trust your judgment on important issues.

Likewise, maintaining contact insures that your group doesn't leave you in the dark. By asking for and receiving and analyzing reports on a regular basis, you'll remain immersed in the activities of your group, and you'll be able to make the necessary shifts in policy or execution that guarantee your group's success.

# Remember to Listen

As the leader, you're supposed to be the authority figure of the group, but authority does not give you license to become a know-it-all. Develop your listening skills. Don't just hear what people have to say. Glean the nuances. There's an old joke that goes like this:

> It is the Second International, and Stalin is addressing the gathering of Communist leaders from around the world. Trotsky, his strongest opponent, is missing from the meeting and has been threatening to disrupt the fight for unified leadership under Stalin's direction. At the plenary session, Stalin addresses the audience and says, "I have here a telegram from Comrade Trotsky. It reads, 'You were right. I was wrong. I should apologize to you. Trotsky.'" There is thunderous applause from every part of the packed hall, except for one small man, who stands up, raises his hand, and says, "Excuse me, Comrade Stalin, but I think you have it wrong. Trotsky is a Jew, and he speaks with a rising inflection. The telegram should read, 'You were right? I was wrong? I should apologize to you? Trotsky.'"

If you can learn to notice the differences between the first and second readings of the telegram, you'll go a long way in developing your listening skills.

Listening also means getting to what it is that people are trying to tell you. Many people approach problems indirectly, and you have to get used to their signals. Someone may ask you if you're hungry, which means *they* are and they want you to join them for a meal. Someone may ask you if you need anything at the store, as a reason to go shopping. If you learn to listen, you will be able to translate the indirect into direct requests for action, and take appropriate behavior.

# Cooperate with the World around You

Modern leadership is built on teamwork, and teamwork is built on cooperation — with the people above you, with your team members, and with the outside world. Remember that today's opponent may become tomorrow's ally, and that you operate in a fluid, ever-changing world. Get people to cooperate with you for your mutual benefit so that you can deliver on your vision and they can achieve goals that they otherwise could not without your help. Learn to mediate disputes and to find a way for all parties to go home with a victory. Even if you are not entirely successful, people will remember your efforts.

# Always Put Others before Yourself

This is our last bit of advice. Some people are naturally altruistic and give to everyone, providing support for the world. Most people, though, have at least a small selfish streak in them, a desire to have it their own way. We live in a world that plays to that selfish streak and basically encourages you to take more than you need.

But as a watchword, you should get yourself a copy of an old Kingston Trio song, "The Ballad of Desert Pete." It tells the story of a person traveling through the desert, dying of thirst, who comes upon a well, a jug of water, and a note. The note says that there is just enough water in the jug to prime the pump, and that "you must have faith and believe" that if you pour the precious water down the pump head, you'll get more water than you need. The note concludes, "Drink all the water you can hold, wash your hands, cool your feet, leave the bottle full for others, thank you kindly, Desert Pete."

So when the selfish streak comes over you, learn to resist it. Learn to appreciate the needs of others, and when you can do a favor at little cost to yourself, do it. If you make a habit of helping others, when you become a leader it will be easier and easier to put the needs of others above your own needs.

# Index

**• W •**

**• X •**

**• Y •**

**• Z •**

# Notes

# Notes